A Catskill Catalog

A Catskill Catalog

Bill Birns

PURPLE MOUNTAIN PRESS
Fleischmanns, New York

A Catskill Catalog

First edition 2011

Published by Purple Mountain Press, Ltd.
1060 Main Street, P.O. Box 309
Fleischmanns, New York 12430-0309
845-254-4062, 845-254-4476 (fax), purple@catskill.net
http://www.catskill.net/purple

ISBN-13 978-0-916346-17-1
ISBN 0-916346-17-X

Library of Congress Control Number: 2011927390

Front cover illustration: Copyright @ by Pendor Natural Color
www.pendorcolor.com Used by permission.

Frontispiece: Kaaterskill Falls, a facsimile reprint
from Van Loan's *Catskill Mountain Guide*, 1789.

Illustrations from the collection of the author except:
pages 49 and 90 from the Town of Shandaken Bicentennial
Commemoration booklet; pages 79, 105, 113, 116, 125, 140, 147,
161, 169, and 178 from the Paul Dutcher collection.

Manufactured in the United States of America.
Printed on acid-free paper.

Contents

Acknowlegments 9

Seeking General Armstrong 11

A Visit to Cooperstown 13

The Whoop-de-doo is History 15

It Happened in Arkville 17

The Family Livingston 19

Alf, Doc Gallo, and the Village of Catskill 21

The Catskill Frontier 23

Music to Painting, Cole to Church 26

Patriot or Tory? 27

Governor George Clinton and
President Martin Van Buren 29

Our Friend, Johnny B. 31

A Drive to Vroman's Nose 34

Paleolithic Catskills 35

Ah, Fleischmanns! 37

Natives of the Place 40

Trout Fishing the Catskills 42

The Catskills in Congress Assembled 44

Baseball in Fleischmanns 46

Town Team Baseball 48

Catskill Mountain Bluestone 50

Mountain Theater 52

The Catskill Turnpike 54

Memorial Day in the Mountains 57

County Histories 58

New Kingston: The Chancellor's Gift 60

Camp Woodland 63

James Oliver and Marion Connell: Teachers 65

David Stradling's *Making Mountains* 67

An Old-fashioned Skimmelton 68

Rafting the Delaware 70

Simpler Times 72

Mountain Tanning 74

Manor Houses 76

The 3500 Club 78

Jay Gould of Roxbury 80

Dr. Orson M. Allaben 82

American Presidents Around the Catskills 84

Mountain Drovers 86

Slabsides and Woodchuck Lodge 90

Delhi and Tannersville: Candace Weaver 91

Anti-Rent War (#1) 93

Anti-Rent War (#2) 95

Anti-Rent War (#3) 97

Margaretville Memorial Hospital 100

Clarke Sanford 101

Poetry on a Rock: Dr. Gordon Maurer 103

Ivan Miller 106

SUNY Delhi's Outdoor Education Center 108

Catskill Mountain Books 109

Beach, Guyot, and Steuding 111

Night Before Christmas 114

Roads 116

Mountain Speech 118

Zena R. Travis 120

Election of '36 122

Mr. Fleischmann Comes to the Catskills 124

I See Ya, Joe DiMaggio 126

Jim Dutcher 128

Melvin Mayes' House 129

Jake Moon: Man and Restaurant 131

The Professor: Frank Russell 133

Reginald Bennett 135

Abe and Mia 137

Discovering the Common Schools 140

Corbett Acid Factory 142

Murder in Andes 144

Ethnic Catskills 146

Doug Faulkner: These Were Men! 148

Basil Todd, Short-form Memoirist 150

Poets in the Catskills 152

Catskill Mountain Quilters 154

Civil War! 156

Mountain Culture 158

Mountain Academies 160

Yoo-hoo, Gertrude Berg 162

Master of Mountain Writing 164

Yankees and Yorkers 166

Catskills on the Web 168

The First Fourth of July 171

Up From Revolutionary Ashes: NK, NY, USA 173

The Remarkable Scudder Family 175

Summer Camps 177

Catskill Mountain Cauliflower 179

A Tourist on the Home Turf 182

Index 185

For Rocco, Francesca & Rosella,
the rock outside my door.

Acknowledgements

ACH OF THESE ESSAYS has been published in the *Catskill Mountain News*. They have all been read. I give my thanks to those readers. You have been welcoming and encouraging. Publisher Dick Sanford has been an encouraging editor, as well as friend. My thanks go to Lisa Dutcher for generously sharing the impressive Catskill Mountain collection of her late husband, Paul. My wife, Gayla, has always been my first audience. Without her, what? I am grateful. Thank you to Alicia Curlew for reading—often hearing—each essay before publication as a column; to Paula Dutcher, first reader of this manuscript; to Quinn Ferris for her assistance preparing the manuscript for submission; and to Liz DeSiena for her work creating the index.

Seeking General Armstrong

"THE OLDEST BUILDING now standing is the General Armstrong house, on the hill east of the village." So reads Munsell's 1880 *History of Delaware County, N.Y.* in its description of Griffin's Corners, Fleischmanns before it became Fleischmanns. In 1996, I bought our house in Fleischmanns, up in Armstrong Park. (I think it was the only house that sold in Fleischmanns that year.) Armstrong Park? General Armstrong's house? What's the connection? Does General Armstrong's house still stand today? Who was General Armstrong, anyway? I began to nose around, try to solve the mystery.

When I first came to the mountains, the hill at the east end of Fleischmanns was home to several hotels: The Mathes, The Alpine, and The New Lorraine. Today, those three properties are all part of the summer Yeshiva that operates for eight or nine weeks each summer providing education and recreation for teen-age students from Borough Park and Williamsburg in Brooklyn. Back in '96, the New Lorraine was still operating, and Gerte, its proprietor, soon became a friend. If General Armstrong's house still exists, I'd find it somewhere on that hill.

I walked back along the road into the Yeshiva property. The first building was a big impressive house in the Adirondack architectural style that was popular for wealthy summer "cottages" in the post-Civil War period. That couldn't be the General Armstrong house. Too new. (This building has since been demolished.) The second building, the former Mathes Hotel, seemed to have the architectural structure of a converted barn. Didn't look like anyplace a general would live. The third building, a big old vacant house that was part of the New Lorraine but hadn't been used in years, looked old enough, but the building-block foundation seemed too twentieth century. The house was old, but that foundation? I walked around the porch. An opening in the cinderblock wall invited me to peer in. There it was. Laid up stone! The modern block foundation walls were a later addition that covered nineteenth century mortar-less laid-up fieldstone. This was it! I had found General Armstrong's house, the oldest house in Fleischmanns.

A little research brought General Armstrong to life and explained the history and importance of his house. Born in Carlyle, Pennsylvania, November 25, 1758, John Armstrong was the son of another John Armstrong who settled in Cumberland County, Pennsylvania from Ireland in the early 1700s. This first John Armstrong was a surveyor, who became a Captain and Colonel in the French and Indian War, and a friend and fellow officer of George Washington in the 1757 campaign in which the two men led an attack on the French garrison at Fort Duquesne, on the site of present-day Pittsburgh.

His son, our General Armstrong, attended Princeton briefly, but left college – he was seventeen when the Revolution broke out—to join the staff of General Mercer and, then, General Horatio Gates. Our General Armstrong fought at the Battle of Saratoga, the Patriots' biggest victory and the turning point of the Revolution. Later, he became Pennsylvania's Secretary of State, and in 1784 led that Commonwealth's troops in the Wyoming Valley military campaign. Our General Armstrong was a Revolutionary War hero!

General Armstrong's house looks west from its heights.

But it was his marriage that brought John Armstrong to us. In 1789, he married Alida Livingston. Born in 1761, Alida was the fourth of the five children of Judge Robert R. Livingston, whose own father, known as Robert of Clermont, had bought up nearly all of the Catskills, making the old Hardenbergh Patent Livingston land. Alida's father and grandfather both died the same year, 1775, and their heir, her brother, another Robert, known as The Chancellor, decided to divide his inheritance among his brothers and sisters. Alida and husband John got most of Great Lot 8, a narrow stretch of land drained by the Esopus Creek, containing much of today's Towns of Shandaken and Middletown, from present-day Arkville to Mount Tremper, or so.

John and Alida Armstrong's family estate was down on the Hudson. In their day it was called *La Bergerie*. Today, the estate is known as *Rokeby Farm* and is owned by members of the Astor branch of the Livingston family. The house in the Armstrong Tract—today's Fleischmanns—must have been intended as their August retreat, or, perhaps, their autumn hunting outpost. It was built, I found out, in 1842, but General Armstrong didn't get to enjoy it. After Independence, General Armstrong had had a distinguished political career. He served as U.S. Senator from New York and Minister to France. He was Secretary of War under President Madison during the War of 1812. Blamed for the burning of Washington by the British during that war, Armstrong was forced to resign, and he died, years later, in 1843, at Rokeby Farm. His house in the Catskills, the oldest house in Fleischmanns, was brand new at his death.

A Visit to Cooperstown

ON A BLUE-SKIED, clear and crisp early winter morning, I drove up Route 28 to Cooperstown, a beautiful and historic village a mere hour and a half north of the central Catskills. When my kids were young, a visit to the Baseball Hall of Fame was an annual event. But on this day, I was in search of one of Cooperstown's non-baseball wonders: The Fenimore Art Museum, located just north of the village on Route 80.

The Fenimore is a first-class museum operated by the New York State Historical Association, a membership organization "dedicated to collecting, preserving, and interpreting objects significant to New York history and American culture." The Association has a research library on the same campus as the museum, a sloping park on the shore of Otsego Lake on the site of an early farmstead home of the American novelist James Fenimore Cooper.

It is a fact of American history that great towns often result from the interest, investment, and philanthropy of wealthy families who reside there. Cooperstown has had two: the Coopers and the Clarks. Judge William Cooper founded the town that bears his name in 1786, when he laid out the village at the base of long, narrow, and glistening Otsego Lake. Cooper had gotten himself a huge land patent and sold over thirty-five thousand acres in just a few weeks at the end of the Revolutionary War. He wrote a guide to settlement in the wilderness and became a successful politician and entrepreneur. His son, James Fenimore Cooper, wrote a novel, on a dare, at age 40, and went on to practically invent American literature with his Leatherstocking Tales, peopling our upstate New York region with characters who still skulk about the woods on cool evenings: Natty Bumpo and Uncas and those last Mohicans.

The Clarks came later. Edward Cabot Clark was an early nineteenth-century Poughkeepsie lawyer who was the promoter and business brains behind the Singer Sewing machine, the one-in-every-home technological wonder of the hundred years or so between 1850 and 1950. His grandchildren, particularly grandson Stephen Clark, have been instrumental in the development of Cooperstown with business or philanthropic interests in the Otesaga Hotel, Mary Imogene Basset Hospital, the Baseball Hall of Fame, and the Fenimore Art Museum.

It was at Clark's invitation that the Historical Association opened the museum in 1945, and the collection has been enhanced by his family's artistic interests. I was particularly taken with the series of seventeen bronze busts, cast from lifemasks by a little-known early nineteenth century sculptor named J.H.I. Browere. Browere started his project by casting three of his neighbors in Tarrytown NY, old guys, by then, who had, as young men, captured the British spy Major Andre, the guy who bought the plans for the defense of West Point from Benedict Arnold. The sculptor would smooth succeeding layers of plaster on his subject's face, then crack it and remove the life mask, pour molten bronze into the mold, and make an exact replica of the subject's actual face. Pretty cool! He went on to do some pretty famous Americans. Thomas Jefferson was quite youthful and handsome, even at 82. John Adams was just old! His son, John Quincy Adams, had a clear, trustworthy face, while Martin Van Buren looked like he was up to something. Henry Clay appeared to me to be quite taken with himself. It was fun to meet those guys *in the bronze.*

The Main Gallery presents works from the permanent collection of Folk Art, the paintings, quilts, dollhouses, sculptures, and artifacts of wonderful artists who are self-taught, artists who were not specifically trained in the heritage and methods of the art world. Looking at a quilt recently donated by a local farm family, I thought to myself, "Homer Benedict's stuff should be here." As I was considering that idea, I turned. There was a showcase filled with Homer Benedict's whimsical woodcarvings, just as I remembered them from a day in South Kortright.

Homer Benedict was a local Delaware County guy, a farmer, and an artist of the first rank. He died recently, over ninety years old. I spent an hour with him a few years ago at his home in South Kortright. His house smelled of *old,* and the heat was pushed up too high. Homer was a gracious host. All the furniture, every bit of floor space was covered with his many carvings of horses and wagons, horses and carts, horses and sleds, each finely detailed with reins and leads and loads in the wagons, literally hundreds of wood carvings everywhere. Homer had grown up on a farm in Treadwell, and his art reflected his memories.

He carved horses in every kind of hitch, doing every kind of work. And now his work was exhibited in the Fenimore Art Museum just an hour's ride north of Homer Benedict's mountain home and mine.

The Whoop-de-doo is History

HISTORY is a funny thing. When we're young, history is the stories about what happened back then, in the day, before we were born. Growing up, I loved listening to my mother's stories about life on the home front, during the war. If you are of a certain age, the war is always WWII, the Big One, even if you just learned about it at school, or through listening to your parents' stories. Mother would tell me about ration stamps, and coupons for butter and eggs, and shortages of coffee and meat. She'd tell me about Uncle George working at a defense plant, and how Rosie the Riveter showed women how well they could do what had been men's jobs.

As we get older, history becomes a different matter entirely. History becomes the stories we tell about what we actually saw and did and lived through. I grew up with leftover World War II blackout shades on my boyhood bedroom windows. I remember going with my Civil-Defense-volunteer mother to the sixth floor rooftop of our local hospital to scan the skies for incoming Soviet planes, during the Cold War anxiety of the early fifties. That history is my witness rather than mere stories I heard. History becomes different as we grow older.

A few years ago, my wife and I drove to Cleveland. My mother was still alive then, and, when I told her where we would be, she replied like the true New Yorker she was, "Cleveland! What's in Cleveland?" Those of my generation know the answer to that question: The Rock 'n' Roll Hall of Fame.

I had an eerie experience at the Rock 'n' Roll Hall of Fame. For the first time in my life, I was looking at museum exhibits that memorialized events that I remember, events I participated in. I saw Otis Redding in concert wearing that red and black suit now on a mannequin in the showcase. The album covers behind the museum glass used to be littered across my college roommate's bed. I remember that poster. It was a strange kind of experience, like the first time you realize that the dentist is younger than you, or the Congresswoman.

I get that feeling a lot lately. I got it a couple of weeks ago when a museum case full of folk art was the woodcarvings of a guy I knew. I only met Homer Benedict once, spent about an hour with him, but honestly grieved when I heard he'd died, and felt like, at least a little bit, I knew him. He reminded me of so many of the wonderful, authentic, intelligent, and open-hearted mountain people I met when first arriving to live in the mountains, back in the early seventies. The Haps and Kennys and Sharkys and Dons, the Maybelles, and Ilas, and Elsas and Mildreds whose mountain way of life, country ways, and rural perspective so charged my suburban soul. There was something important here and I wanted to be part of it.

When you stay, you end up becoming part of the history, too. A few years ago, I attended a meeting in a church basement of the then-fledgling New Kingston Association. "We'd like to put together an oral history of the Whoop De Doo," one of the leaders said. "Anyone who remembers it, please let us know."

The Spirit of '76 animated the Whoop-de-doo in the bicentennial year.

Wow! The 1970s era New Kingston Whoop De Doo was a hugely successful community fundraiser and celebration. I was right smack-dab in the middle of it, and now it was history! Serious people wanted to research an event that had been part of my life. History had become different for me, once again.

The Whoop De Doo was the brainchild of the Reverend Bill Harter, the ebullient and highly effective co-pastor (with his wife, the late Linda Harter) of the Margaretville/New Kingston Presbyterian Church. The Whoop De Doo was a last weekend in August celebration of everything country. It began Friday night with an old-fashioned round-and-square dance, in the street, in front of the New Kingston Church. The celebrated Catskill mountain fiddler, Earl Pardini, led the band. Saturday was a riot of activities and attractions, including a greased-pole climbing contest and a greased-pig chasing contest. Literally thousands of people showed up to jam-pack little New Kingston.   Saturday night featured an original old-fashioned melodrama, directed by Bill Campbell, Delhi College drama professor, who went on to lead SUNY Delhi as a dean, and Delaware County as an elections commissioner. Sunday ended the Whoop De Doo with a bluegrass-style country music concert. Karen Beth was one of the outstanding artists who played little New Kingston.

The Whoop De Doo simply got too big. It ran for four or five years and, then, a retaining wall collapsed under the pressure of so many visitors' feet, and the crowds were just too big, and people started thinking about liability, and the Whoop De Doo became another part of our history.

It Happened in Arkville

WHEN BUS PECK was growing up in Arkville, Milton Berle used to spend summers there. Bus liked to talk about his childhood brush with fame back, in the early seventies, when he was working as a custodian at school, and I was a young teacher, new to the mountains.

Milton Berle was the first big star in television, his 1950s comedy show a must-see in the early days of TV. Bus used to talk about how he and his tough country-kid friends made life difficult for the summer-kid from the city, who later became so famous. Milton Berle's uncle, Bus explained to me, owned the hotel that sat on the hill at the corner of Route 28 and The Crossroad. Young Milton honed his earliest comedy routines in that hotel. Today the building houses the Catskill Center for Conservation And Development. As it turns out, it is also the building that gave Arkville its name.

Noah Dimmick was one of the earliest settlers in our area. He served as the

Supervisor of the Town of Middletown from 1819 to 1826. Around that time, Dimmick operated a hotel or tavern on that little hill that rises there. It was probably in a building that preceded the Catskill Center building that stands today, but one can see, even now, how that knoll makes that building the tallest spot in that area.

As we know too well, you don't have to spend too many years in the Catskills before you have to deal with flooding. In the early days of settlement, Arkville was known as Dean's Corners, because a Mr. Dean ran a sawmill there. Well, the Dry Brook and East Branch flooded, as they do, and all of the little hamlet was under water, except for that tavern on the hill, that seemed to rise out of the flood waters like an ark, an ark owned by a man named Noah. Thus, Arkville.

Interestingly, Dimmick is a name that resounds throughout the Delaware River Valley. Downstream from us, at the head of the Delaware Water Gap National Recreation Area, is Milford, Pennsylvania, home of a nineteenth-century tavern that is, today, a very good restaurant and steakhouse, still called *Dimmick's*.

The Catskill Center for Conservation and Development was a fledgling regional organization in the early 1970s when the old Dimmick Building was renovated and restored by the Arkville-Erpf Fund. Armand G. Erpf was a major player on Wall Street whose family estate is up Dry Brook. Mr. Erpf was an important benefactor to our area, helping to build Sacred Heart Church in Margaretville in the mid-fifties, donating to the church the large Georgia O'Keefe painting that hung over the alter there for thirty years, the important modern painting whose sale helped finance the church's Parish Center in the 1980s. Originally, Sacred Heart Church was located in Arkville, part of the big house, now a private home, known as The Maple House.

Mr. Erpf was committed to the Catskill region, and committed to Arkville. He instructed in his will that the old Dimmick Building be restored and used for the benefit of the community. But he didn't specify which community, or more particularly, how large a community he had in mind. The Reverend Bill Harter, then co-pastor of the Margaretville-New Kingston Presbyterian Churches, led a group of Town of Middletown locals whose vision was a local community center that would house Senior Meals, a youth center, a mountain crafts center, that kind of stuff.

The Catskill Center for Conservation and Development had more regional ideas, the use of the Arkville building as a center to seek improvement in the environmental, economic, and cultural life of the people of the entire Catskill Region, not just the people of the surrounding town.

The locals won the opportunity to give it a try, and the Erpf-Catskill Cultural Center was founded in 1974. The Center opened with a major Art Show, with rooms throughout the building set up as galleries. Rebecca Sloan, an artist who had recently moved to the mountains, arranged and hung a one-person show of one of her former teachers, Roger Van Damme, a Connecticut painter of some renown.

Van Damme had been a prisoner of war during the Second World War, and had spent time in a German Prisoner of War Camp. There, his only possession had been his cup. He ate out of his cup, drank from his cup, relied on his cup completely. That cup became his artistic subject for a number of years. The Arkville show was entirely paintings of that cup: large oils, small sketches, cups, cups, cups. It was pretty neat! Given Mr. Van Damme's experience in the war, it was also pretty moving.

The gallery was a success. The Erpf Center was able to set up some excellent cultural programs, but the senior meals went elsewhere, and the youth center didn't happen, and creating a local community center proved to be just too much. In 1980, the Catskill Center became a co-tenant in the building and, by 1993, the Erpf Gallery became a program of the Center that continues today.

The Family Livingston

ARMSTRONG PARK, Montgomery Hollow, Livingston Manor, even Margaretville are all local place names that trace their origins to the Livingston family of colonial New York. In fact, colonial American history in the Catskills really begins with the Livingstons.

We all learned in school that New York City began as Dutch New Amsterdam. The colony of New Netherlands stretched up the banks of the Hudson from the bay at the mouth of the river to Fort Orange, today's Albany. Unlike their fellow colonials in New England or Pennsylvania, the Dutch were not interested in establishing a New Jerusalem in the wilderness, or in converting the Indians. The Dutch were interested in profits!

At its height, the entire New Netherland colony was home to about 8000 settlers, 5400 of them Dutch, the others men and women of various ethnicities interested in making a buck. Eighteen different languages were spoken around Fort Amsterdam before the English gun ships arrived.

The English sent four war ships into New Amsterdam harbor in 1664, completely outgunning those settlers. Colonial governor Peter Stuyvesant led an eight-day resistance, but on August 26, surrendered. The English flag was hoisted over the colony, its name now New York, a reflection of the new proprietor, James, Duke of York, brother to the King. James took title to all unclaimed lands and recognized the titles granted to landowners by the Dutch colonial company.

Robert Livingston, the founder of the land-holding family line, arrived in New York from Scotland in 1674. Just twenty years old, Robert was a young man in a hurry, eager to rise in the new colonial society. He settled in Albany, got active in politics, and allied himself with the right people.

Livingston rose quickly, becoming county clerk, customs collector, member of the Colonial Assembly. In 1680, he sealed the deal by marrying Alida Schuyler Van Rensselear, widow of the Dutch Reformed Dominie, or minister, of Albany, daughter and sister-in-law of two of the richest and most powerful men in the colony.

Livingston used his contacts and social position to seek a land grant. In 1686, he got it, twenty miles of the eastern shore of the Hudson River, from present-day Hyde Park to Hudson. The grant wasn't specific on how far inland Livingston's new lands extended, so he took all of it, right up to the disputed Massachusetts border, 160,000 acres, pretty much the entirety of today's Columbia County.

Robert's new home faced a glorious mountain vista, the unclaimed Catskills. His son, Robert of Clermont, would make the Catskills part of the family conquest, as well.

In 1708, Queen Anne granted one point five million acres of Catskill Mountain land to eight men, led by Johannes Hardenbergh. Difficult terrain, lack of a survey, lawsuits, partners bickering, and bad business decisions all prevented the Hardenbergh patentees from making much of a go of their investment, opening the door for a shrewd operator like young Robert Livingston.

When his father, the Founder, died in 1728, Robert was forty. His older brother Phillip inherited the manor, but Robert got 13,000 acres carved out of the family lands. He built his house, Clermont, overlooking the river, and sought to extend his holdings.

In 1740, the first survey of the Hardenbergh Patent was begun, perhaps as an effort to buck up the sinking value of shares in the dormant investment. Livingston and his only son, Robert R., known today as "the Judge," explored the Catskills personally. Their guide was Henry Bush, a skilled woodsman who had settled near present-day Shokan.

The two Robert Livingstons followed the Esopus Creek to Pine Hill, then walked down Highmount to the East Branch of the Delaware to the flats that are today the site of Margaretville. This was in 1740! Shortly thereafter, Livingston began to buy up shares of the Patent until he had extended his holdings to one and a half million acres – nearly all the Catskills.

When that Robert, the Judge, died, in 1775, he followed the old aristocratic practice of leaving all his land to his oldest son, a practice known as *primogeniture*. That son was also Robert, Chancellor of the New York courts and a leader in the struggle for American independence.

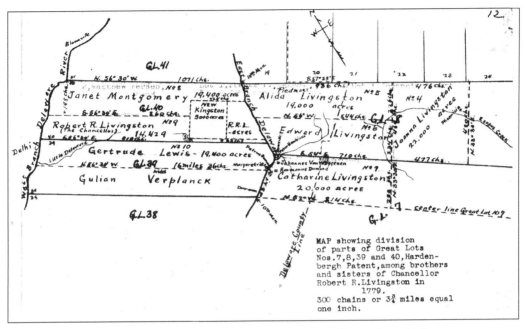

Map of the division of family lands by Chancellor Robert Livingston, heir to his father and grandfather.

Chancellor Livingston decided to do something unusual, an emerging American act perhaps, by dividing his land-inheritance among his brothers and sisters. His sister Janet Montgomery got a tract north of the East Branch, running east from present-day Margaretville toward Roxbury. Sister Gertrude, wife of Morgan Lewis, got lands west of present-day Margaretville, a village named after their daughter Margaret.

Edward Livingston received a tract north of the river, west of his sister Janet's. He lost his land in a card game, but that's another story. Sister Alida and her husband, John Armstrong, got lands running from around Arkville to Shandaken. Several other large parcels were given to in-laws.

The old Hardenbergh Patent had been divided, and the Livingstons were very much in control.

Alf, Doc Gallo, and the Village of Catskill

I ONCE LISTENED to a tape recording of the late Alf Evers, the great storytelling historian of the Catskills, whose book, *The Catskills: From Wilderness to*

Woodstock, is the gold-standard history of our region. Evers had been recorded as part of the Oral History Project that flourished in Arkville, in the seventies and eighties, under the auspices, first, of the Erpf-Catskill Cultural Center, and, then, The Catskill Center for Conservation and Development.

Born in New York City, Alf Evers lived in Woodstock for most of his lifetime, writing, along with his wife, children's books, and, later, on his own, histories of Woodstock and Kingston, as well as the 1972 Catskill Mountain book. On this tape recording, Evers spoke of a visit he had, years earlier, with Dr. William Gallo, the highly-respected physician who practiced medicine, for decades, in Roxbury.

Evers told the interviewer that he often ended his visits, with people in other parts of the Catskills, by asking them what they thought of Woodstock. Old Alf had both pride in his hometown and a sense of humor, knowing Woodstock's artist colony ways might elicit some interesting opinions. He was surprised, however, by Dr. Gallo's reply. The Roxbury physician allowed that he had never been to Woodstock, so he couldn't say anything about it.

Now, Alf Evers was one of the great promoters of the idea of the Catskills *as a region*, so he reacted strongly to Dr. Gallo's admission. "Here was an educated man, a physician," Evers explained to the interviewer on the tape I was listening to, "a man who had lived in the Catskills almost his entire life, and he had never even visited one of its most important towns, just forty-five minutes away!"

Evers was flabbergasted. So he asked Dr. Gallo, why? Why had the Roxbury physician never gone the short trip to the world famous artist colony?

On tape, Evers recalled Dr. Gallo's reply. The good doctor leaned back in his chair, rubbed his chin thoughtfully, gazed out the window, and said, "To tell you the truth, I have everything I need right here in my valley."

The Catskills tend to do that, nestle you in to the particular, hold you close to home. We come quickly to think of ourselves as from Halcott Center or the New Kingston Valley, or Broad Street Hollow. The larger Catskills seem, I don't know, distant, across the ridge, somebody else's valley.

But the Catskills are a region, made up of parts of four or five or six counties, depending on who's doing the defining. (Can you name them?) And in the Catskills, the old town of Catskill, NY, certainly has claim to being an important regional center. I say the old town, because, as long as I've lived in the mountains, Catskill has been down at heels, a bit dilapidated.

A few years back, my son managed a business over there, so I spent a little time in Catskill, and, to tell the truth, it wasn't pretty. Old, and historic, and interesting, maybe, but run-down and kind of depressed. Recently, a carpenter friend told me he was working over there, that some new investment was going on, and Catskill was changing. So, a couple of weeks ago, I drove up to Catskill, to see for myself.

One of the reasons for downtown Catskill's decades-long decline was the fact that, for twenty or thirty years, most of the retail expansion in town occurred in a kind of suburban sprawl on the Route 23 hill just above, and to the west, of the village center. How things have changed! The high ground shopping area is still very much thriving—Wal-Mart has opened a supercenter, and that appears to have actually spruced-up the Radio-Shack and Rent-a-Center and pizza place that were already there. But the downtown village center is hopping!

I parked my car on Main Street and got to choose among several trendy-looking cafes for lunch. Old buildings have been restored, and art galleries and antique and curio shops line the main street. A coffee house advertises a wireless internet connection. The movie theater, art and office supply store, and bank, that, just a few years ago, seemed lonely on Main Street, are surrounded now by new businesses and new investment. The building facades attract in brightly painted wood clapboard or sandblasted clean brick, giving an appearance of individual initiative rather than master-plan sameness. There are people on the street! Old Catskill is new.

Across the river, the City of Hudson, for twenty-five years, has been a great day-trip destination because of its funky cleaned-up main drag, Warren Street, lined with galleries and restaurants and antique shops and performance centers.

On our own side of the Hudson, our mountain-river town, Catskill, is undergoing its own *Hudsonization*, and makes a great little day-trip destination whenever you might feel the need to expand the Catskill Mountain experience beyond your own valley.

The Catskill Frontier

A S A CHILD, I was one of the first in my neighborhood to get a coonskin cap, the 1950s Walt Disney rage, symbolic of Davy Crockett, King of the Wild Frontier.

Popular culture in those days was suffused with the frontier, the Wild West, the lands just beyond the quiet settlements of eastern civilization. *Gunsmoke*, *Bonanza*, *Have Gun Will Travel*, television, and the movies all seemed to suggest that the lands on the edge of American settlement were the locale of romance and history and excitement. President Kennedy called his White House program "The New Frontier," and the space race with the Russians seemed to open a frontier-in-the-sky, ripe for exploration.

When I was in college, one of the exciting new ideas presented in my American History classes was the *Frontier Thesis* of historian Frederick Jackson Turner, the idea that the availability of open lands to the west was a crucial factor in the development of the American Character, and that the closing of the frontier in 1890 – the announcement by the Census Bureau that there was no more unclaimed, available, open land in the West—marked a profound change in the course of American history and in the development of the American culture, society, and economy.

Wilderness frontier: The Burroughs Range from Giant Ledge.

How exciting it is to realize that we Catskill Mountain folk live in what was America's first frontier. The earliest colonial settlements in the Northeast took place, of course, along the seacoast and in the major river valleys. Look at a map of the early American colonies. You'll see settlement patterns along the New England coast from coastal Maine north of Boston, down the coast to Cape Cod, Rhode Island, and along the Long Island Sound. Major thrusts of colonial settlement run north on both sides of the Connecticut River and the Hudson River. That's it. West of the Hudson, wilderness! West of the Hudson, our Catskills, the first American frontier.

The wilderness wasn't empty of human habitation, of course. The native peoples, Lenni Lanape, were here, and their troubled history, difficult to piece together, but vital to our historical understanding, must be an important story in our catalog. But, for European colonists, the Catskills of the eighteenth century were the very edge of settlement.

Rare was the adventurer who sallied beyond this frontier. In 1692, an Albany fur trader, Aernout Cornelis Veile, explored the Susquehanna, Alleghany, and Ohio River Valleys, west of us, but he sailed down the Hudson to begin his way west from New Jersey's Delaware River access, rather than take on the rugged mountain terrain of the Catskills. In 1735, amateur botanist John Bartram explored the mountains, but only to seek and collect balsam fir seeds, then highly prized by landscape gardeners. In 1740, two Robert Livingstons walked from the Hudson to the East Branch of the Delaware to survey a prospective purchase. The Catskills were not for the timid. This wilderness was rugged.

To this wilderness came a party of explorers, in the fall and winter of 1762, from Hurley, that early settlement on the big flats south of Kingston, whose Dutch-style stone houses today still speak to us of our colonial-era past. Hurley's residents had long sought woodlots in the lands to their west. In fact, old Johannes Hardenbergh himself had bested the Hurleyites, over fifty years earlier, in seeking a land grant for Catskill lands, the grant that became the one-and-a-half-million-acre Hardenbergh Patent. This time, the Hurley forces succeeded: four Hurley families made the move to the frontier, buying four farms from the Livingston-family, owners of Great Lot Number 7.

These settlers were of Walloon and Huguenot heritage, descended from Protestants who had fled Catholic Belgium and France to settle in the Dutch New World. Harmonus DuMond made a farm across the river from present-day Margaretville. His brother Peter DuMond settled on lands upriver from his brother. Near present-day Arkville, settled Peter Hendricks with his wife, the widow Kittle, and her sixteen-year-old son Frederick Kittle. Johannes Von Waggoner also settled on lands along the stream.

These first four families on the East Branch built shelter and cleared land, planted fields, and harvested a crop, that first spring, summer, and fall. They spent the winter of 1763-64 huddled against the mountain cold, out on the frontier, at the very edge of the new American society. I wonder if young Fred Kittle wore a coonskin cap!

The little frontier settlement grew. The Revolutionary War brought discord and strife, and when it was over, lands to the west of our mountains were opened for settlement, and used as compensation for military service. The frontier moved rapidly west, to the valleys of the Susquehanna, and the Genesee and the Alleghany Rivers, and our Catskills no longer were "out west." But, for a few years at the very beginning of our country, our mountains were the frontier, and the ground we walk on today was the Wild West.

Music to Painting, Cole to Church

A FRIEND OF MINE notes that, while there is not as much music in the mountains as there once was, art galleries, and the visual arts abound throughout our towns.

Back in the seventies, every bar and grill seemed to put on a band, and places like The Pine Hill Tavern and Mount Tremper's Whitewater Depot featured a musical act nearly every weekend. Bands like The Allen Harris Band, Pam Window and the Shades, Contraband, The Kryptonites, The Don Moore Band, Jasper, The Marc Black Band, and Tom Pacheco's Band played regularly around the mountains. Fans followed their favorites from venue to venue or sampled whatever music was available on any given weekend. Perhaps, this musical fest was a holdover from the Woodstock concert, or the result of a youthful population of the many young people drawn to the Catskills in the seventies. It was a happening time.

In the twenty-first century, things seem a bit more sedate. Weekend evenings regularly feature an art opening or two in one or the other of the many galleries in our area. Phoenicia and Margaretville both feature cooperative galleries operated by regional artists themselves. Painting, photography, and sculpture are in no short supply, and computerized video projection is a feature of at least one local nightspot. The arts are in!

Visual art and music are not mutually exclusive, of course, and there is still music to be heard in the Catskills, but I think my friend's observation is a valid one: the visual arts seem to be widely prevalent in the Catskills these days.

This is only fitting, I think. A good case can be made that American painting was born in the Catskills.

American painting was merely a derivative branch of British painting when twenty-four-year-old American painter, Thomas Cole, made his first trip up the Hudson River, to Catskill, NY, in 1825. Cole made several landscape paintings on that trip, romantic views of the American wilderness that accentuated the largeness of the outdoors, the dominance of trees, woods, mountains, and sky, and strong light luminous against clouds and hills. The next season, Cole exhibited in New York several paintings from that trip, including paintings of Kaaterskill Falls, South Lake, and Platte Clove, all locales easily visited today up State Route 23A, just east of Tannersville.

The exhibition was a sensation! Cole was hailed as the first great native-born American painter, and his style spawned America's first artistic movement: the Hudson River School—romantic landscape views in which nature looms so large as to dwarf humanity and light becomes the subject of art.

Cole soon moved to Catskill. His house, Cedar Grove, located on a bluff outside Catskill village, just above the Hudson, became a gathering spot for fellow landscape painters and students. Jasper Cropsey, Asher B. Durand, Samuel F. B. Morse and nearly one hundred other painters became associated with the Hudson River School, painting landscapes from around the world in the Hudson River style, emphasizing the sheer scale of nature, light, color, and perspective in literally thousands of paintings that today hang in museums throughout the world.

One of Cole's students was the son of a prosperous Hartford, Connecticut businessman, a talented and energetic youth named Frederic Church. Church spent two years in Catskill apprenticing with Cole. He made his big splash into the New York art world, at the age of 22, when he became the youngest member ever elected to the National Academy of Design, founded by Cole and Durand twenty years earlier.

In 1857, Church caused a sensation when he exhibited a monumental painting of Niagara Falls in New York, charged twenty-five cents a head to see it, and made a lot of money on the deal. A few years ago, one of the big corporations sponsored a latter-day showing of that painting in the lobby of its New York City office-building headquarters. I went to see it. It was amazing. The falls actually seem to move. One can only imagine how this huge, realistic close-up of the raging falls must have affected our great-great grandparents in that pre-moving-picture, pre- action-photography era. You can find an image of the painting on the internet. The light is remarkable.

Church traveled the world, producing large paintings in the Hudson River-style of landscapes in South America, Europe, and the Middle East. Middle eastern culture particularly impressed him. Between travels, Church bought a farm, just the other side of the Hudson from his Catskill mentor's home, and, with the help of one of the leading architects of his time, Calvert Vaux, built a magnificent, Persian-style house, which he called *Olana*.

Olana remained in the family after Frederic Church's 1900 death, and, when the house and its custom-made furnishings were in danger of being sold and dispersed, a group of local citizens formed Olana Preservation, and, with the support of art-loving Governor Nelson Rockefeller, Olana became a State Historic Site in 1967. It's located at the eastern end of the Rip Van Winkle Bridge. It's worth a visit.

Patriot or Tory?

HARMONUS DUMOND has his own website. At least, someone in the twenty-first century has maintained a website dedicated to the eighteenth-century Margaretville pioneer. DuMond headed one of the first four families to settle on the East Branch of the Upper Delaware, back in 1763.

Google *Harmonus DuMond*. You'll find a fascinating, but unsigned and unattributed, website that pursues a very cold case: the August 26, 1778, Arkville-area shooting of Harmonus DuMond. Was Margaretville's first settler killed because he was a loyalist to the king, or because he was a patriot in the cause of liberty?

From 1763 to 1778, nearly forty families from the Shandaken, Marbletown, and Kingston areas had joined the original four families from Hurley in the growing East Branch settlement then called Pakatakan. Frontier farms stretched along both sides of the Delaware River, from present-day Arkville, through present-day Margaretville, downstream to lands presently under Papacton Reservoir waters, as far down as present-day Downsville.

This frontier was Tory country, loyal to the King. Patriot General Nicholas Herkimer met with Iroquois warrior-chief Joseph Brant on June 27, 1777, to try to persuade the Six Nations of the Iroquois to join the American cause. "You are too late," the well-educated Brant told Herkimer, "I am already engaged to serve the King." The forces of the Six Nations would dominate the frontier for the next couple of years.

Now, western New York's greatest landowner, up to that time, was Sir William Johnson, who had made a fortune trading with the Iroquois. His heirs and dependents sided with their Six Nation friends, and remained loyal to the king. One, John Butler and his son, Walter, formed an irregular loyalist-militia that, allied with Brant's native warriors, began an escalating series of raids on frontier farms and settlements in the winter of 1777 and 78. Their goal was to buy, steal, or confiscate food, fuel, and fodder from the farms and, equally importantly, to keep those coveted supplies out of the hands of the patriots.

How about the locals? Which side were they on? Catskill mountaineers, Henry Bush and Nathanial Park, were reportedly seen raiding along with the Iroquois, downriver from Pakatakan settlement, in April 1778. In July, literally hundreds of supposed Tories were seen on the road between Catskill and Batavia, today's Windham. Rumor had it that a great Loyalist rendezvous was planned for the big flat at the bend of the East Branch of the Delaware– Pakatakan. Further rumor suggested this encampment would include upwards of five hundred British soldiers who had escaped, or deserted from, the major patriot victory at Saratoga, the previous October. From the East Branch, rumor had it, this enlarged loyalist army would move to Catskill to reinforce English General Howe on the Hudson. In wartime, rumor creates suspicion creates havoc.

Add to this web of rumor, Butler's Rangers, the Tory raiders who were actually reported to be raiding farms downriver from the Pakatakan settlement. A story goes that Pakatakan's settlers were forewarned of a raid by a friendly Indian—Tunis. Legend has it Tunis warned the sleepy pioneers that Iroquois raiders were coming. The settlers were able to escape, up over Pine Hill, to Shandaken. In that story, Harmonus Dumond and James Burrows decided to stick around. The truth, it appears, may be a less romantic story, in a logical chain of events.

That summer of 1778, the frontier was in turmoil, and the East Branch of the Delaware River was right at the heart of the trouble. On August 19, New York Governor Clinton wrote to Colonel Cantine, commander of the Ulster Patriot Militia: "It will be best to remove, if possible, the grain and all kind of provision from the settlements on the Delaware…and if it cannot be effected I think it would be better even to destroy it than to let it remain there and fall in the hands of the enemy."

In response, Colonel Cantine ordered Patriot troops from Fort Shandaken to march up the valley of the Esopus to Pakatakan, to evacuate the valley, and to bring to Shandaken all the settlers and as many of their goods as possible. This was done. Immediately upon arrival at Shandaken, Harmonus DuMond and John Burrows headed back over Pine Hill to fetch more of their stuff.

Meanwhile, Colonel Vroman of Schoharie decided that it was *his* responsibility to calm the frontier. He ordered a unit of the Schoharie Guards "to scour the headwaters of the Delaware" to "arrest certain disaffected persons" and "destroy supposed Indian settlements."

When Harmonus DuMond and James Burrows made their way back down the Bushkill to the East Branch, back from their brief evacuation to Shandaken, on August 26, 1778, the Schoharie Guards were mopping up their operation, and heading back to Schoharie. The Guard ordered the two men to halt! Witnesses tell us they turned to flee. The Schoharie Guards fired. Burrows got away. But Harmonus DuMond was mortally wounded. They took him to a nearby house. The soldiers who fired apologized to the dying man. He died.

Now, did Harmonus DuMond run because he was a Tory, and this was a Patriot militia patrol? Or did DuMond, the Patriot, mistake these Schoharie irregulars for Butler's irregulars, the Tory raiders whose expected arrival led to that morning's evacuation of Pakatakan to Shandaken in the first place?

Patriot or Tory?

Governor George Clinton and President Martin Van Buren

THE FIRST GOVERNOR OF NEW YORK was from Kingston, and he would have been president if it weren't for a guy from Virginia named Madison, who beat him out.

George Clinton was elected Governor in 1777, just after New York created a state constitution, and established the office. He served until 1795, both when New York was part of a loose and ineffective confederation of states, and when New York was more closely united with the other states under the US Constitution. In fact, the early part of New York State history is often referred to as the Age of Clinton. Pretty good for a farmer's kid from Ulster County.

You might remember from high school history that Thomas Jefferson teamed up with New York's Aaron Burr, in 1800, to form what, today, is the Democratic Party, then called the Democratic-Republicans. Jefferson represented the southern land-owning planter class, and Burr, a lawyer by trade, represented the city artisans, and independent farmers, of New York. Both were united against the strong-central government Federalists of New England.

The shame, of course, was that this union gave a northern endorsement to the slavery practiced widely by southern planters. Slavery existed in the north; it was less profitable than in the south, and had less popular support. In the 1780s there were 19,000 slaves in the state. New York outlawed slavery in 1799, when it passed a gradual emancipation law, that did not actually end slavery, outright, until 1827. Sadly, Ulster County was one of the last areas of the state to abandon the practice entirely.

George Clinton, like other concerned New Yorkers, joined the Manumission Society to urge farmers to free any slaves still in bondage, but his passion was what they used-to-call *Artisan Republicanism*—a politics aimed at benefiting the economically independent artisans, craftsmen, and farmers, who owned small plots of land, were far from wealthy, and probably in debt.

Perhaps you remember that Aaron Burr turned out to be something of a cad, that he tried to steal the election for president from Jefferson, who was supposed to be his running mate. They had to change the Constitution to prevent anyone from trying Burr's trick again! Then, he went and killed Alexander Hamilton in a duel at Weehawken, New Jersey, and rumor always dogged him that Hamilton shot in the air above Burr's head to fulfill their stupid code of eighteenth century honor, and Burr then shot Hamilton right in the heart. Later, Aaron Burr was charged with treason, when he supposedly tried to set himself up as Emperor of Mexico or Louisiana or some empire of his own delusion, out in the new West.

Anyway, Thomas Jefferson needed a new running mate, when he ran for re-election in 1804, and George Clinton, of Ulster County, New York, was just the right guy, the logical successor to Burr to continue the union between Virginia planters and New York artisans and farmers. Jefferson won re-election with Clinton as vice-president.

So when it came time to choose the Democratic-Republican candidate for President in 1808, Clinton assumed it was his turn. After all, Vice-President John

Adams had succeeded President Washington, and Vice-President Jefferson succeeded President Adams, so shouldn't Vice-President Clinton come next? His nephew, DeWitt Clinton, was Mayor of New York, and a strong supporter of his uncle.

But James Madison was Jefferson's choice to succeed him. George Clinton had opposed the ratification of the Constitution that Madison had largely written. The party caucus went for Madison. George Clinton of Kingston was nominated for another term as VP, and he served until he died in 1812. He is buried at Kingston's Old Dutch Church.

The next time our region would be home to a Vice-President, he did become President. Martin Van Buren was born and raised in Kinderhook, across the river from the Catskills, in Columbia County. The son of a tavern-keeper, Van Buren grew up around the family hostelry's overnight guests, traveling the old Post Road from New York City to Albany. These included both Burr and Hamilton.

Young Martin became a lawyer, and dove into politics full-time. He was, perhaps, the first *professional politician* to become president.

As leader of the state's first political machine, known as *The Albany Regency* by its enemies, Van Buren strengthened partisan power by putting control of all job appointments in the hands of the governor, rather than in an independent commission, thus creating political patronage. The machine further established a party platform, an ideology that all party members were to espouse, under fear of discipline, if they dared be mavericks. And, Van Buren's political operation had its own media outlet, the *Albany Argus*, a newspaper read statewide.

Van Buren was a logical choice to team up with another southern planter, Andrew Jackson, whom he served, as secretary of state, minister to England, and vice president. In 1836, Van Buren was elected president to succeed Jackson. An economic panic marred his term, and "The Magician," as he was called, was defeated for re-election. He bought an estate, Lindenwold, just outside Kinderhook. There, as ex-president, he entertained prominent guests and kept his hand in politics, running, once again, for President, in 1848, as the Free Soil Party candidate, opposed to the extension of slavery where it wasn't already legal.

Lindenwald, on present day Route 9H, operates, these days, as an historic site, run by the National Park Service, and is open for visitors, during the warmer months.

Our Friend Johnny B.

SOONER OR LATER, the newcomer to our part of the Catskills discovers John Burroughs. If that newcomer is fascinated by nature and the outdoors,

Walt Whitman, who revolutionized American poetry and motivated John Burroughs to write out of his passion for the outdoors.

by literature, writing or philosophic reflection, that discovery often becomes a revelation. The ghost of Washington Irving, author of "Rip Van Winkle," might animate the steep mountain escarpment of the Catskills that rises over the Hudson. The spirit of James Fenimore Cooper may hover over the region just to the north of our mountains, an area that today bears the name of his *Leatherstocking Tales*. But here on the west slope, where Delaware waters gather for the long winding journey to the sea, the spirit of John Burroughs resides.

In the early years of the twentieth century, John Burroughs rivaled Mark Twain as the most widely read and well-known writer in America. He was a naturalist who wrote nature essays that appeared regularly in America's top magazines, a poet and literary critic who drew his readers toward a worldview that valued simplicity in living in harmony with nature. His essays appeared in a widely used school reader, so Burroughs was as familiar to one generation of school children as Dick and Jane would be to another.

John Burroughs was born on a West Settlement farm just above Roxbury in 1837. From childhood, John was uninterested in the farm chores that were the daily regimen of his hard-working, uneducated parents and eight brothers and sisters. John liked to read and to write, was interested in books and poetry and the natural world around him. He took to his studies eagerly at the local one-room schoolhouses near his home, one of which still stands up Hardscrabble Road in Roxbury.

When John was twelve, a new teacher came to Roxbury, James Oliver, newly graduated from the State Normal School in Albany. John's schoolmate was Jay Gould, who went on to become a controversial and powerful financier, reputed to be the richest man in America in the late nineteenth-century gilded age. Both boys were profoundly influenced by Oliver, who, with intelligence and enthusiasm, opened the larger world of ideas to the two mountain farm boys.

Ralph Waldo Emerson, of Concord, Massachusetts, was the most celebrated literary figure in America, at that time. Emerson was a poet, essayist, and lecturer who was seen as America's first native-born philosopher, and the *Transcendentalism* that emerged from his writings was powerfully attractive to the minds of sensitive and thoughtful young people coming of age at the time.

Emerson's system of thought put nature at the center of our experience, celebrating the natural world as the window into the deeper meaning of life and the true nature of the universe.

Perhaps, Mr. Oliver introduced young John to Emerson's thinking. Or maybe the young scholar became an Emersonian when studying at the Harpersfield Seminary, or Ashland Collegiate Institute, or Cooperstown Seminary, all secondary schools that John attended, paying the tuition himself. However it happened, the young writer's first published essays and poems were closely derivative of Emerson's style. Interestingly, his first publications were in the *Bloomville Mirror*, a Delaware County weekly newspaper.

John taught a few terms in Tongore, now Olivebridge, in Ulster County. The one-room schoolhouse where he taught still stands. In Tongore, he married Ursula North, with whom he later had one child, a son named Julian.

In the early 1860s, John and Ursula left the Catskills, both to find steady work in the bursting bureaucracy of Civil War Washington, and to meet Walt Whitman. Burroughs had read Whitman's *Leaves of Grass*, the book that created a new American poetry, unlike anything the Old World had imagined. Burroughs mind was energized by Whitman's seemingly free expression of self, and, ambitious to succeed as a poet himself, he very much wanted to meet this new American bard.

He did. Burroughs and Whitman became fast friends. John's first book was a study of Whitman. Frustrated with his lack of success as a poet, John asked his mentor for advice. "Publish your personality," Whitman told him. It was then that Burroughs' writing turned to the subject he knew best and loved most: nature and the experience of the outdoors. He never looked back.

Today, many look on John Burroughs as a mentor across the gap of time, since his death in 1921 on a train traveling back to Roxbury, where his summer home, Woodchuck Lodge, still stands.

Burroughs still has disciples. SUNY Cobleskill's Lynn C. Spangler created an educational video about Burroughs, designed to introduce him to another generation of kids. The video, underwritten by the Catskill Watershed Corporation, was introduced to Burroughs home town, at a public library screening, by long-time Burroughs enthusiast Joe Farleigh, who taught physics and other science – and a little bit of Burroughs—to a couple generations of Catskill Mountain kids, mostly at Gilboa, but also at Downsville and Windham.

A Drive to Vroman's Nose

THE WINTERS are long in the mountains. About February and March, a day of blue sky and sunshine seems as necessary and valuable as nourishment. So, on a beautiful, clear, cold Saturday afternoon, a pair of friends and I took a ride up Route 30 to explore Vroman's Nose.

Vroman's Nose has been described as the perfect place to hike for those who want the maximum payoff in "wow-factor," and in views, with the minimum investment of time and energy. It is a six-hundred-foot- high rock formation that rises sharply from the Route 30 roadway just outside Middleburgh, in the heart of the Schoharie Valley.

When I first came to the mountains, Route 30 seemed to be a more prominent entrance roadway to the central Catskills than Route 28 was. At that time, our region had yet to be discovered by many in the New York metropolitan area, and connections to Albany, and points north, seemed to carry more traffic than those to New York and the south. Even so, Route 30 could be a hair-raising adventure, as late as the early seventies. I remember well driving too fast—I was young—to negotiate comfortably the big sweeping-turn bridge that carried the road over the railroad tracks at Hubbell Corners, at the entrance to Roxbury, a turning roller-coaster rise in the road that could take the unsuspecting motorist by surprise. My heart may still be in my throat!

Farther up that state road, near Bouck's Island at the entrance to Fultonham, the old road used to follow an ancient native trail that hugged the side of the mountain on a steep cliff, the precipice on the side of the road a sheer drop of fifty or so feet. For a kid from the suburbs of New York, my first ride to Margaretville on that cliff-side pathway was a clear indication, to me, that I was entering a rural world, outside of my previous experience. To tell you the truth, part of me was a little disappointed when the state rerouted the road to safer, saner low ground across Bouck's Island. I liked the adventure of that old trail.

Bouck's Island was the home of the "Dutch Governor," William C. Bouck, a farmer and a Jacksonian Democrat, who was the fifteenth governor of New York, serving in 1843-44. Bouck, it is said, spoke with a distinct German accent, although he was born right in the valley, a valley that was settled in the early 1700s by Palatine Germans, refugees from the Thirty Years War-ravaged Rhine River valley. Americans from the very beginning of our nation, many continued to speak German as their first language well into the nineteenth century. We've always been a land of many languages.

A ride up Route 30, to the lush and fertile Schoharie Valley, provides a number of pleasant diversions and attractions. The road climbs out of Grand Gorge, leading the day-tripper to all this and more: the Gilboa fossils; Minekill Falls;

the power-pump storage electrical generating plant; Minekill State Park; Lansing Manor; the Blenhiem covered bridge; some of the most beautiful agricultural fields in the state; the Revolutionary War Middle Fort; Middleburgh, the oldest settlement in the Schoharie Valley; the architecturally significant village of Schoharie; and Vroman's Nose.

Called Onistagrawa, or Corn Mountain, by the native peoples, Vroman's Nose was formed by the melting of the ice cap and northward retreat of the glacier that covered virtually all of our state, 20,000 years ago. Once an island in the huge post-glacial Lake Schoharie, Vroman's Nose today rises above the flat and broad valley floor. That valley was formed when a break in the natural dam that held the lake led to a powerful rush of water that broke through the rock to form the Grand Gorge and the Delaware River valley that begins in that rift.

The easiest climb up the nose begins in a parking area on its northern, or back, side. You'll recognize the nose-shaped promontory, on the left side of the road as you approach it, driving toward Middleburgh. Just past Bohlinger's Fruit Farm, take the first left onto Middleburgh Road. The parking area is a half-mile up.

The trail leads up across a knoll, turns right to follow an old wagon road up the shoulder of the mountain, then turns left again to lead the hiker to the summit. It is a four-fifths of a mile walk, moderately steep. The summit makes any momentary huffing and puffing worth it.

At the top, the views are spectacular. The carefully laid out farm fields and orchards are beautifully arrayed before you. The meandering Schoharie Creek glimmers ribbon-like below. The farms below look like a kid's toy model from this eagle's-eye view. The summit itself is a flat, plateau-like dance floor of rock.

No guardrail or fence separates that nearly ten-acre table from the sheer drop six hundred feet to the valley floor. You might get a touch of vertigo. While snow cover prevented my friends and I from any close inspection of the rock floor at the summit, I'm told that scrape-marks in the surface of the rock show the direction of glacial retreat, marked by gravel and stone dragged over its surface, 12,000 years ago.

Looking to get outdoors for a bit? Try Vroman's Nose. The payoff is in the view.

Paleolithic Catskills

A Catskill Catalog: history, geography, day-trips, arts and culture, in and around our Catskill Mountains. Pretty comprehensive. Covers about everything I might be interested in writing about, or so I thought, until I visited my old friend Joe Hewitt.

Joe is a retired state trooper, *a legend*, as we used to say in college about graduates who cast a big shadow, years after they'd left school. He's the former New York State bee inspector, an outdoorsman, and the possessor of a wonderful collection of Native American artifacts he has found in our region. Who better, I thought, to fill me in on the history of the native peoples who inhabited our mountains?

The problem, I realized, as Joe began to show me his collection and explain the meaning of each artifact, is that these stone tools are not a part of history. History is the story of the past pieced together through an interpretation of the documents of the past. History requires a written record; it depends upon language. Joe's artifacts presented me with something I wasn't ready for. I spent thirty-six years teaching English. My head is swarming with language. It's how I make sense of the world. These artifacts left by native peoples are beyond language. They do not tell; they just are. I was entering a new world, an archeological world, with a new way of thinking.

What I came looking for was words, and names, to explain our pre-European past, words like *Iroquois* and *Mohican* and *Lanni-Lanape*. Let's save those words for a future essay, one about history. Joe was introducing me to pre-history.

If you are like me, the word *prehistoric* conjures visions of Tyrannosaurus Rex, cave paintings somewhere in France, and ancient skeletons found in East Africa.

Thinking of the past of our own area in prehistoric terms was, frankly, a bit of a jolt. Perhaps, it shouldn't have been, but it was.

I held in my hand a chipped stone javelin point with fluted sides. "That's paleo," Joe explained. Wait a minute! Paleo? Archeologists date the Paleolithic era around 8000 BC. The Clovis point I held in my hand was 10,000 years old! And it was found in our region! In fact, the eastern edge of the Catskills, just overlooking the Hudson River, is home to two significant Paleolithic sites: West Athens Hills and Kings Road. There, archeologists have uncovered numerous stone tools used for cutting, scraping, and boring holes, as well as for hunting.

The archeological record suggests that our mountains were part of the migratory range of early men and women who moved extensively around the Northeast in search of food. They seemed to travel in bands of twenty or so individuals, related by blood or mating, who wandered freely over a scantily populated, vast wilderness, following migratory game animals. Numerous Mastodon skeletons have been found in Orange County, just to the south of the Catskills. These extinct beasts, reminiscent of the elephant, were a major source of food, and many of the fluted flint javelin points were designed for hunting these large mammals.

Stone tools found from this period indicate a people who were skilled in working with wood, leather, and bone, and the Pennsylvania jasper and Normanskill flint that these people napped to create their tools indicates the vast distances they traveled.

Those travels brought these early people to our valley. Right in our backyard, Joe found Paleolithic artifacts in Dunraven, at the upper end of the Pepacton Reservoir. Just north of Roxbury on Tyler Flats, Ralph Ives excavated a Paleolithic site, years ago. Ancient peoples lived 10,000 years ago where we live today. I find that exciting.

The archeological record continues, of course, to trace the inhabitants of our area through time. Smaller notched points, beveled adzes, and fishhooks are representative of the Archaic Period from 4500 BC to 1300 BC. These people were less dependent on large game and developed a hunting, fishing, and gathering culture that is often called *Lamoka*, after the Lamoka Lake archeological site out in the western part of our state. The fishhooks these Lamoka people fashioned out of flint and bone would still catch fish today, and sinker stones and net-sinkers attest to these people's skill as fishermen.

The next stage of culture was marked by the development of ceramics, and the transition from a hunting, fishing, and gathering economy to an agricultural one. This is called the Woodland Stage, running from around 1000 BC to European contact. Numerous local sites have produced artifacts from this period of development, including a cache of hunting points uncovered years ago at Big Rocks, just north of Margaretville along Route 30. Clay pipes and ceramic shards point to a more settled village life.

That settled agricultural village life was the Woodland Culture that entered the written record, in 1609, when one of Henry Hudson's sailors described the natives he encountered sailing up the big river. It was with that writing, four hundred years ago, that history began in our region, and the pre-historic phase of our human development came to an abrupt close.

Ah, Fleischmanns!

ONE SUMMER, in the mid seventies, I had a job teaching English to Japanese kids at Camp Furusato, in Fleischmanns. In the seventies, the Japanese economy was cooking, globalism was in its infancy, and many Japanese people were living and working in the New York metropolitan area. The Japanese educational system is rigorous, so many of the children of these international executives, skilled artisans, and entrepreneurs attended special Saturday sessions in Japanese, during the regular school year, and educational sleep-away camps, like Camp Furusato, in the summer. The camp was run by Dr. and Mrs. Lynch at the old Breezy Hill Hotel, about a mile up Breezy Hill Road, above the old Fleischmanns fire hall.

English classes were in the morning, so my day ended a little before noon, and I would drive home, through Fleischmanns, to New Kingston, where I lived at the time. I remember distinctly creeping down Fleischmanns' Main Street in my '65 Plymouth Valiant at about five miles per hour because the street was full of, literally, hundreds of people. Even so, the town elders were saying, then, that Fleischmanns was dying.

That's because they remembered when those hundreds were thousands. Take a drive through Fleischmanns, my home village now for the past sixteen years.

You'll notice, tucked away behind many houses and commercial buildings, a little bungalow or cottage or converted garage that once was rented-out to summer guests, when space to stay was at a premium, and local folks could supplement their income by taking in boarders.

Of course, for many people in our region, providing hospitality to summer visitors *was* their income. Hotels thrived in the mountains from the time the railroad made transportation from New York City to the mountains affordable, until the time air-conditioning and cheap airfares made the trip unnecessary.

Fleischmanns, particularly, was "one of the major summer resort centers of the Catskill region," to quote from the 1940 travel guide to New York State,

Main Street Fleischmanns, early 20th century.

compiled by the Writers' Program of the Works Project Administration. The WPA was a New Deal program of President Franklin Roosevelt, and its Writers Program was designed, as much to put writers back to work, as it was to put together what is probably the greatest series of travel guides published in America, one for each state. The WPA also financed the construction of many of our local schools, including the old Fleischmanns High School, Margaretville Central, Downsville Central, and many others.

My late Aunt Lillian, recalled, when I moved to Fleischmanns, a childhood visit years before. Lots of people had such memories. With fewer than five hundred full-time residents, Fleischmanns' population swelled every summer to approximately ten thousand. Tell somebody, today, that little old Fleischmanns once boasted a summer population of ten thousand and they'll tell you, "Yeah, sure, right." So, that number really needs to be footnoted, don't you think?

The newspaper of record, *The New York Times*, in 1976, sent reporter, Richard Severo, to Fleischmanns to investigate a rash of fires which had destroyed a significant number of unoccupied hotels, camps, private homes, and boarding houses in the preceding five years. "Thirty years ago," Severo wrote, "this community had a population of under 500, that rose to 10,000 from the Fourth of July to Labor Day."

The reporter called Fleischmanns schnitzel-belt, not borscht-belt, because its mostly Jewish clientele was from Germany, Austria, and Hungary, and, at the time of his visit, "one can still hear German and Hungarian spoken on Main Street," although, "the tourists are old and there probably aren't more than 1000 of them."

When those older guests died, their adult children found affordable vacation opportunities in Europe and the Caribbean. Besides, the rationale for summering in the mountains had always been the sweltering heat and humidity of city summers, a problem nicely corrected by air conditioning. Fleischmanns fell into decline. At one point in the late eighties or early nineties, *The Catskill Mountain News* published a story on the closing of what was, then, the last store in Fleischmanns. As I recall, the headline was something like "You Can't Buy a Loaf of Bread in Fleischmanns Anymore".

You can today. The little village boasts a terrific Mexican restaurant; two groceries, one specializing in Mexican products; a convenience mart/gas station; two taverns; a couple of art galleries; a publishing house; a bank; a mini-fitness center; several motels; a vintage baseball team; and a pizzeria.

Of course, Fleischmanns' modest gains of the past decade are a long way from its heady heyday. Back in '76, local resident, John Hoeko, cataloged for reporter Severo what Fleischmanns had had back in the fifties and sixties: "Four butchers, three barber shops, a bowling alley, three produce markets, three bakeries, an A&P, three doctors, and as many dentists."

Fleischmanns, then, was glitteringly alive! A good friend of mine, who grew up in Margaretville, recalls fondly how he used to accompany his father when he had business in Fleischmanns. How they loved to watch together the parade of elegantly dressed visitors down Main Street. Fleischmanns was, then, a great attraction.

Natives of the Place

I've wanted, for a while, to write about the native people who inhabited our mountains four hundred years ago, when Henry Hudson's *Half Moon* first opened our region to European ways. The problem is that the very idea of "The Native People of the Catskill Mountains" is framed in a particularly non-native way of thinking.

Living in the mountains is a comparatively recent thing. For Americans, mountain living was romanticized in the nature-centered artistic and literary consciousness of the 1800s. Before that, people just took it for granted that the best places to live were in lowlands, near water, and flat fertile fields. It's tough to make warm secure shelter in the mountains, the ground is rocky, and the growing season short. Mountaineers must sacrifice easy communion with people, at great distances, because travel in the mountains is difficult. Most people would rather live in the valley.

That was true of the native people of our region, as well. When we were in school, we learned about the early river valley civilizations along the Tigris and Euphrates in Mesopotamia, or along the Nile in Egypt. Civilization developed the same way here – in the valleys, along the streams and rivers. That's where native people lived.

The Lenni Lenape were called the Delaware Indians by European settlers, after the bay and river along whose shores they lived, a bay and river named in honor of Lord De La Warre, Thomas West, third colonial governor of Virginia. Lenni Lenape means something like *Common People* in the Algonquin language, spoken in three different dialects along the river. The northernmost dialect was called Minsi or Munsee, and the people who lived upriver were often referred to as Munsee Indians.

Sane people seek lower ground when the winter wind blows heavy mountain snows our way. The Munsee Lenape were exceedingly sane. They came up river as far as the flats where Arkville now stands and camped for the warm weeks, when berries and nuts abound, the trout run, and game is plentiful. Summer and fall have always attracted people to this place. When they broke camp and left, they traveled downriver toward present-day Pennsylvania and New Jersey, for the cold months.

I'm told that representatives of the Delaware Tribe, headquartered today in Oklahoma, visited Arkville some years ago, and authenticated some cave drawings and inscriptions, located somewhere on a side hill. The guy who told me was told by a guy who told him. I believe both of them. Old maps and other documents point to an Indian camp—a kind of movable village—called something that sounded like Pakatakan—on the East Branch, often called, back then, the Pepacton.

The winding river flat behind the Delaware & Ulster Rail Ride grounds would be a logical spot for that camp, as would the big field stretching from Route 30 to the river, called, since I've been around, Howdy Davis's Flat.

A more permanent Indian castle, or village, was situated on the Esopus Creek, down at the Hurley Flats, near present-day Kingston. These Esopus Indians were also Algonquin-speaking Munsees, of the Lenape People. They controlled, and were nourished by, the rich valley of the Esopus, from where it empties into the big river at Saugerties, to its sources in Shandaken, up the Woodland and Oliverea Valleys.

The Lenape's major enemy was the Iroquoian-speaking Mohawks, who controlled all the lands of the river named for them, and all the streams draining into that river. The Schoharie Creek runs northward into the Mohawk. Hence, lands in the Schoharie Creek's watershed were Mohawk lands, fiercely protected by the aggressive and powerful Keepers of the Iroquois Confederation's Eastern Door.

A couple of major Iroquois meeting sites are up on the Schoharie, just outside the present-day villages of Midldleburgh and Schoharie, in big cornfields along modern Route 30.

The boundary between the Algonquin Munsee and the Iroquoian Mohawk is right here in the Catskills. It was the east-west ridgeline that runs north of present-day Route 28, a ridgeline that stretches from Plateau Mountain, in the east, through West Kill and North Dome Mountains, to Halcott Mountain, then pivots, northward, at the head of the Halcott, Red Kill, Denver-Vega, and Roxbury Valleys, then west, along the southerly side of present-day Route 23, all the way to Mount Utsayantha at Stamford.

To the south of that ridge: Munsee lands: Lenape. To the north, Mohawk: Iroquois. That made our mountains an important border, between two significant, and unfriendly, nations.

I've often wondered about the Tuscarora, the sixth tribe adopted into the Iroquois Confederation. These people moved from what is now North Carolina to an area around the Unadilla River, to our west. But evidence seems to point to some Tuscarora activity, or settlement, nearer to the Delaware. The venerable private fishing club in Millbrook is called The Tuscarora Club, and some sources claim a Tuscarora camp or settlement on the East Branch.

With Mohawks to the right of them, and Tuscarora to the left, the Munsee speaking Common People of the Delaware River Valley must have felt a bit pinched, up here at the headwaters.

Trout Fishing the Catskills

TO TROUT FISHERS, the Catskills are the home country, the old sod, the reverently referred-to birthplace. Words like *Beaverkill*, *Willowemac*, *Esopus*, and *East Branch* are uttered almost like prayers, the names of the steams where trout and fly first made their American acquaintance, at the beginning of our national life.

In his 1856 *History of Delaware County*, Roxbury native Jay Gould tells of "a regular disciple of Isaac Walton," who fished the West Branch of the Delaware, as far back as the late 1780s. Isaak Walton—the *k* is the correct spelling—was the seventeenth-century English author of *The Compleat Angler*, the original bible of fishing lore. Walton spent forty years fishing, and writing about the recreation (or is it a spiritual pursuit?) that was central to his life.

Fishing and writing have gone together ever since. Judy Van Put, who writes for several Catskill Mountain papers, has been fishing and writing for decades. On a Saturday in March, twenty or thirty local folks eager for opening day, gathered at Margaretville's Fairview Library to see and hear the world premiere of Judy's excellent power-point presentation on the "History of Trout Fishing in the Upper Delaware Valley."

While never much of a fisherman, I learned in my first months in the mountains to adopt a certain reverence for the native trout—Brookies! My first Spring here, the late Dan Morse got me out, fishing with worms up the small streams, seeking the small, lively, colorfully-spotted brook trout that were, even then, getting scarce, but were highly prized by even the most casual fisher. Dan, who taught history to high school kids in Margaretville for thirty years, was a mentor to so many of his young teaching colleagues, as well as to his students, and learning to fish was high on his list of required country skills.

Those native brook trout were once amazingly abundant in the cold, clear, highly oxygenated fast-running streams that feed the East Branch. With no creel limits, nineteenth-century fishers would take upwards of a hundred fish in an afternoon's fishing. Judy told the story of a single fisherman, in the late 1800s, who caught 384 trout in a single day's angling, feeding all hundred guests at the hotel where he stayed, with fish leftover (there was no report of how many loaves were consumed along side). On July 9, 1884, three thousand trout were taken out of the Millbrook.

That venerable stream was the site of an important moment in trout fishing history. On the Millbrook, sometime in the 1840s, Judge Fitz-James Fitch tied an imitation fly he inexplicably named the Beaverkill, one of the first artificial trout flies tied in America. Fitch was born in Delhi in 1817, moved to Catskill when he was 38 years old. He did well there, becoming Greene County Judge. This pioneer of fly-fishing also invented the creel harness, and was an early proponent of catch-and-release, the now-environmentally sensitive preference of many of today's trout fishers.

In Roxbury, the first hotel in town, the 1798 structure, now gone, that became the Hendrick Hudson House, was known as the "Fly Fishermen's' Hotel." Arkville and Margaretville, Cold Spring, and Shandaken were all important destinations for serious nineteenth-century anglers. Hudson River School painters Worthington Whittredge, Sanford Gifford, and Jervis McEntee were frequent visitors to the Arkville area, sketching mountain landscapes while fishing for mountain trout.

Judy Van Put is a well-known and accomplished fly-fisher herself, as is her husband Ed, whose 2007 book, *Trout Fishing in the Catskills*, belongs on the shelf right next to the 1983 *Catskill Rivers: Birthplace of American Fly Fishing* by Austin M. Francis. Both tell the

Legendary fly-fisher and fly-tier Theodore Gordon on the stream.

stories of some remarkable people, regular folks who worked regular jobs, but made their lives remarkable through the tying of feathers, and the study of trout. One was Niles Fairbairn, born in Seager, in 1886, whose skill and intelligence led to a varied career as Outdoor Camp Director, State Fox Trapper, and Animal Advisor to Walt Disney Pictures.

It's said that Niles Fairbairn did his most successful fishing on moonless nights. Reminds me of my old neighbor, Bob Russell, who seemed to knock on my door at the end of every rainy day to show me an old enamel pan filled with five or six fat trout he'd just taken out of the Plattekill. Interestingly, Niles Fairbairn taught Helen Keller to fish in 1935, while she and her family stayed in Dry Brook.

The neat thing about the history of trout fishing in the Catskills is that a new chapter is written every April first with the opening of each new fishing season. Great fishers—an inclusive term that sounds more natural with continued use— still populate our mountains. One of them, the accomplished Lenny Millen, was on hand that March Saturday to demonstrate the flourishing Catskill Mountain arts of fly-tying and fly-casting. Our history is alive.

The Catskills in Congress Assembled

THE CONGRESSIONAL DISTRICT on the Upper East Side of Manhattan is known as the Silk Stocking District. Now, clearly, that nickname reflects the wealth of the people of that neighborhood, but it also suggests a Congressional District that has a history and an identity beyond the identity of the particular person holding office, a district that exists to be represented by a series of elected representatives over time. Kind of like basic democracy: the district exists before the representative.

The Catskills, unfortunately, have never been recognized as a distinct and integral region whose people share a mutual identity and community that deserves to be represented in Congress. To be fair, even the most generous geographic definition of the Catskills can only yield a population that is a couple hundred thousand short of the required population of a Congressional District.

So the Catskills have always been a part of a larger district, or, more accurately, parts of the Catskills are added to a number of Congressional Districts whose real population centers are somewhere else.

In the nearly 40 years I've lived within the boundaries of the same town, in the same county, my Congressional District has been changed, something like, four times. I think we've been part of the 27th, 28th, 25th, and 20th Congressional Districts.

A few years ago, the Towns of Shandaken, Middletown, and Halcott, contiguous on the map and homogenous in culture, were represented by three different Members of Congress!

Right now, the Catskill region is divided among three Congressional Districts. Most of the Ulster and Sullivan County Catskills are presently within the 22cd Congressional District, a district that stretches across the state from Poughkeepsie and Kingston, on the Hudson, to Binghamton and Ithaca, in the Southern Tier. Presently represented by Maurice Hinchey of Saugerties, the district seems to be have been created to contain several communities of urban Democratic voters within a single district.

The 20th Congressional District runs from Essex, Warren, and Washington Counties in the eastern Adirondacks, through Saratoga, Rensselaer, and Columbia Counties, on the other side of the Hudson, before jutting suddenly west across the river to take in the Greene and Delaware County Catskills. It seems designed to bring together rural Republican voters from a variety of geographic locations, making particularly surprising the victory of Democrat Kirsten Gillibrand, in a brutal contest with incumbent John Sweeney in 2006.

All of Schoharie County is tacked onto the Albany-Schenectady-Troy-Amsterdam-based 21st Congressional District, held now by Paul Tonko.

This cutting and pasting of Congressional District lines, helter-skelter, through the Catskills, has been a constant since the beginning of our national life. I've been trying to research the history of our representation in Congress. (Who else would do this for you?) It is confusing because the Congressional Districts, and their identifying numbers, change with the new census, every ten years.

In the first Congress of the United States, 1789-1791, John Hathorn, of Orange County, represented New York District 4, the lands west of the Hudson below Albany. Hathorn was succeeded by Cornelius Schoonmaker, and then by Peter Van Gaasbeck, of Ulster County, before being elected once again in 1795.

Serving a term, and then letting the other guy serve, was common in the first decades of American political life. Artisan Republicanism was the prevailing political spirit of the day, and it called for each citizen to take his turn serving in the government, each white male Protestant citizen, that is.

As the state's population grew, new Congressional Districts were created every ten years. In 1802, much of the western slope of the Catskills was in the new District 14, and Erastus Root of Delhi was elected to Congress for the first of his four terms. Root was a migrant from Connecticut to what was then, in 1796, Ulster County's backcountry. Called "General Root" by his neighbors, he pushed for, and helped preside over, the 1797 creation of Delaware County.

But Congressman Root's four terms were spread over four decades, as others took their turn. For a while, civic leaders from Delhi and Cooperstown passed the Congressional seat back and forth. Later, as the Congressional District lines were redrawn once again, Delhi and Catskill seemed to take turns sending a Congressman to Washington. Woodland Cemetery in Delhi is the present home of at least five Congressmen, and the separate Delhi Cemetery boasts one other.

The last Delhi-based Congressional Representative was Marian Williams Clarke who served out the term of her late husband, from 1933 to 1935. John D. Clarke was killed in a fiery automobile crash near Delhi, the Sunday before Election Day, 1933. He had already served two terms in Congress when, in 1924, he lost a new-fangled primary to a Binghamton candidate. By then, willingly taking turns was so previous century! Clarke won his seat back two years later, won three more times, and was a vigorous sixty when he was killed. He and his wife are buried in Hobart.

Baseball in Fleischmanns

JACKIE ROBINSON DAY is an every April 15th celebration of the man who broke the color barrier in baseball. It was 1947, that first season in Brooklyn, when Jackie, stoically, took the curses, slurs, and verbal brickbats hurled at him by opposing players and fans alike. The story of Kentucky-bred shortstop, Pee Wee Reese, putting his arm around Jackie's shoulder in full view of a howling stadium, signifying to all "hey, this is my teammate," has always struck me as inspirational.

Baseball adopted Jim Crow segregation in the late nineteenth- century. As a response, African-Americans established baseball teams and leagues that became institutions in the black community, and vitally important to the development of baseball. The history of black baseball is well documented, and justly honored, at the National Baseball Hall of Fame in nearby Cooperstown.

The first black ball club was organized by Frank P. Thompson, headwaiter at the Argyle Hotel, in Babylon, Long Island. The Cuban Giants—race prejudice was such that Mr. Thompson figured calling his players "Cuban" would make them more acceptable to the hotel's wealthy clientele—quickly became a baseball power, playing and beating teams of any and all colors. They pioneered winter baseball, playing in Florida during the cold months, based at a hotel in St. Augustine. The Cuban Giants were so good, an entire display case is devoted to them at the Hall of Fame.

I mention them because I've held in my hand, at the Fleischmanns Museum of Memories, a scorecard that records a game, played at the turn of the century, between these Cuban Giants and the local Mountain Athletic Club. The Mountain Athletic Club beat them! That's how good the local team was.

The Mountain Athletic Club was established by Julius and Max Fleischmann, playboy sons of multi-millionaire Ohio yeast magnate Charles Fleischmann, who, in 1883, founded, for his family and friends, the summer resort that today bears his name. The elder Fleischmann, one of the richest men in America, was kind of the Bill Gates of his day – yeast was the everybody-needs-it software in a culture of daily bread baking.

In the summer of 1877, wealthy New York banker, Joseph Seligman, had been turned away from the Grand Union Hotel in Saratoga, a hotel he and his family had stayed at for many summers before. An ugly wave of anti-Semitism swept through society. Mr. Fleischmann would establish a pleasure ground where such insults would be unthinkable. His sons brought in the baseball.

By 1900, 29-year-old Julius was the boy Mayor of Cincinnati, and he and his ball-playing older brother, Max, owned what the Cincinnati Enquirer called, on September 12, 1900, "The strongest independent team in America." The Mountain Athletic Club played in front of large crowds of summer vacationers at the grandstand-enclosed diamond the Fleischmann brothers built on the flat below the family home. They also toured, playing New York State League teams in Albany and elsewhere, traveling to Ohio for a much anticipated match-up with the National League Reds.

That game never came off, but one of the largest crowds ever to watch a game in Cincinnati's League Park watched the "Mountain Tourists" play the Shamrocks, a Cincinnati group that may have been the Reds playing under assumed names.

The Catskill Mountain team won, twice.

As well they might. Julius Fleischmann's Mountain Athletic Club had a future Hall of Famer, the five-foot-six-inch fireplug Miller Huggins, at second base. A law school graduate, Huggins went on to manage the Yankees of the 1920s. He was Babe Ruth's manager. Scrappy Charley "Red" Dooin was the catcher. He went on to play for, and manage, the Philadelphia Phillies. Dooin still holds the Phillie franchise record for games caught.

Third baseman George "Whitey" Rohe broke into the fledgling American League the following year, playing for the Baltimore Orioles and Chicago White Sox. Pitcher Fred Mitchell began, in 1901, a twelve-year major league career with Boston and New York in the American League, Philadelphia and Brooklyn in the National. Fellow right-hander Barney McFadden, fresh from college ball at Villanova, later pitched for the Reds. The Mountain Athletic Club's best pitcher was a left-hander named Harris—which may have been a pseudonym for a college pitcher from Georgetown named Harry White, who went on to pitch for the Phillies and White Sox. Max Fleischmann played right field. You don't have to be Babe Ruth if you own the team.

In 1902, the owner of the Cincinnati Reds was threatening to move his team, so city political boss, George B. Cox, put together a group to buy the team and keep it in Cincinnati. The Fleischmann brothers provided the money, and Julius and Max became major league owners. With a big league team back home, their interest in Catskill Mountain baseball faded. Baseball, however, continued to be an important part of mountain culture, with teams popping up in nearly every town.

Town Team Baseball

OFTEN, when I would run into the late Kenny Miller, I'd ask him for the Satchel Paige story. Kenny was the longtime proprietor of Bussy's Store, on the main corner in Margaretville, who served several terms as Mayor of that village. He was also a baseball player. As a young man, right after the war, Kenny was a minor league catcher in the Brooklyn Dodger organization. Working out with the big club during spring training one year, Kenny played in an exhibition game against the Cleveland Indians. Fireballer Satchel Paige was pitching.

Satchel Paige was the seemingly ageless pitching wonder who broke into the big leagues in 1948, two days after his 42nd birthday. Satch had been, for years, the hardest throwing pitcher in the old Negro Leagues, and was well beyond his best by the time he got a chance to play in the majors. Like Yogi Berra, Satchel Paige was famous not only for his skill on the diamond, but also for his witticisms, like his classic advice on staying youthful that I can't keep myself from quoting below.

"How To Keep Young by Satchel Paige: #1. If your stomach disputes you, lie down and pacify it with cool thoughts. #2. Keep the juices flowing by jangling around gently as you move. #3. Go very light on the vices, such as carrying on in society. The social ramble ain't restful. #4. Avoid running at all times, and #5. Don't look back. Something might be gaining on you."

When I would run into Kenny, I'd ask him to look back on that long ago spring day he faced Satchel Paige. "I got up to the plate and I heard three pitches," Kenny would say. "Then I sat down."

Kenny Miller was just one of the remarkable baseball players who populated the mountains a generation or two ago. Baseball truly was the national pastime, and nearly every Catskill Mountain village had its own Town Team. The National Semi-Pro Baseball Congress was founded in 1935 to bring some degree of organization to the myriad industrial, service, and town teams and leagues playing on sandlots around the country. Each year it published a directory.

The 1939 *Semi-Pro Congress Directory* lists a number of Catskill Mountain teams. The Naponach Chevvies represented Ellenville. Hunter had a village-sponsored team called the Indians. The Phoenicia Town Team was listed, as were two teams from Rosendale, seven from Kingston, and the Woodstock AC.

Catskill Mountain locals like Bob Reed, Chan DeSilva, Bill Lutz and Dutch Merritt built substantial regional reputations as ballplayers. Min Pultz, a stand-out pitcher for both Margaretville and Fleischmanns Town Teams, went on to play second base in Triple A minor league ball, down in Pennsylvania.

Roxbury, Downsville, Delhi, and Andes all had teams, and clubs from Kingston and Oneonta would compete with the mountain boys both home and away. Each village had a ball field, in a park, or out behind the village some-where. The wonderful little baseball diamond just behind the village of Hamden, on Route 10 between Walton and Delhi, is a lasting reminder of those days, when baseball belonged to the whole town together.

In the early 1900s, every mountain village and hamlet seemed to have a ball team.

The town team tradition got a renewed shot in the arm in the late forties, when scores of veterans returned from Europe and the Pacific, eager to start families and have a little fun. Sunday baseball thrived. It continued through the fifties and sixties. In 1972, I watched the Downsville Town Team play at the Fireman's Park diamond in that village, but town team baseball was dying by then. Perhaps, regular TV broadcasts of major league games made local baseball seem quaint, or perhaps the rise in popularity of other sports—football, basketball, soccer, golf—hastened the demise.

An interesting theory is posed by Tim Wiles, librarian at the A. Bartlett Giamatti Baseball Research Center and Library, at the Hall of Fame in Cooperstown. Tim thinks insurance killed Town Team baseball. Municipalities worried about the liability costs of playing hardball on public lands. Softball seemed a solution. Softball leagues grew, baseball faded. The present Vintage baseball revival brings back a slower, less dangerous game.

But there's something nostalgic and romantic about the days when each of our little mountain towns fielded a team, and a good ballplayer could forge a degree of regional fame on the diamond. Most of the old-timers, from this side of the mountains, agreed that the best player in these parts was New Kingston's Ruthvan "Robbie" Robertson. Born in the 1890s, Robbie made his living driving a truck and manufacturing cauliflower crates, but he made his name playing baseball. He was a pitcher and a hitter, and those who saw him play say he could have been a major leaguer.

I knew Robbie. He was a quiet man, but if you sat with him awhile and didn't ask questions, just sat on the post Office porch at noontime and waited, he'd give you a story. In his grand gravelly voice, he'd tell you about a ball game in the past, or share his views on the game itself. Robbie always said Henry Aaron was the best hitter he ever saw, long before Hammerin' Hank broke the career home-run record. "It's all in his wrists," he'd tell me.

Robbie stopped playing ball at age 54. He hung up his glove, despite the pleading of the manager of the local Town Team, begging him to play one more year. Like Satchel Paige, Robbie was ageless.

Catskill Mountain Bluestone

THE FIRST SETTLERS in the Ulster County Catskills discovered, on their properties, outcroppings and ledges of a hard bluish-gray stone they soon found could be mined and cut and put to a variety of uses around the farm. Catskill Mountain Bluestone began as a domestic product: a carriage stone here, a pickle-crock cover there, a walkway around back, a flat piece of bluestone on the chimney top, propped with stones to create a downdraft-reducing chimney cover.

In the early 1800s, domestic use gave way to commercial trade, as local artisans developed a bluestone craft, creating durable, practical, and beautiful bluestone livestock troughs, chicken feeders, hitching posts, and other implements of rural life. By the 1830s and 40s, the inland trade spurred by the Eire Canal brought new importance and prosperity to the port cities of New York and Albany. That urban growth led to a desire for improvements, like paved sidewalks. "North River Bluestone" was the perfect paving material, and a quarry industry developed.

A quarry in the Catskills soon became something like a gold mine, as, first, Albany and, then, New York City, went on mid-nineteenth century sidewalk-building binges. Quarries abounded throughout Ulster County, giving the Saugerties hamlet of Quarryville its name, dotting the banks of the Sawkill Creek, the Hurley Woods, the local hillsides. Bluestone is highly desirable for sidewalks because it is very hard and durable, dries quickly after a rain, and doesn't wear to a slippery sheen with constant use, as many other stones do.

In the years before the Civil War, bluestone from the Catskills was dragged out of the mountains to Hudson River sloops, which took the stone to pave sidewalks in cities as distant as Milwaukee, St. Louis, San Francisco, and even Havana, Cuba. When the Ulster & Delaware Railroad opened in 1871, new quarries opened along the railroad line for ease of transport. Mines were established in Phoenicia, Margaretville, Roxbury and throughout Delaware County.

Catskill Mountain Bluestone is a kind of layered sandstone that was formed by the action of a great inland sea which, when it withdrew and dried up millions of years ago, left compressions of sand become stone: bluestone. It is made of feldspar, mica, and sand, and largely free of organic elements. It may appear blue or gray or even a bit pinkish-brown, its name derived from the color of the stone first dug and cut in eastern Ulster County.

Today's bluestone industry has migrated to the west of our mountains. We have largely exhausted the rich line of bluestone deposits that stretched from Albany south, through the eastern Catskills, down to Pike County, Pennsylvania, around Milford and Matamoras. Pennsylvania Bluestone – today's preferred name—is quarried out of over 150 mines in western Delaware County, south-central New York, and north-central Pennsylvania. Montrose, Pennsylvania is today's unofficial bluestone industry center, an industry that produces about $100,000,000 of bluestone a year.

On the last weekend in March 2008, the center of the bluestone world was the Veterans' Arena in Binghamton, as the New York and Pennsylvania Bluestone Associations jointly sponsored *Bluestone Expo*, a trade show. Made curious by the poster in my bank's window, I went. I found an arena floor filled with 66 booths representing the varied businesses that serve, and prosper from, the quarrymen who dig out the rock. Banks and insurance companies, energy suppliers and engineers, dealers in tires and forklifts and lubricants and lumber, all were there to do business.

Everywhere were the myriad tool companies who manufacture, or import, and sell the diamond bluestone blades, carbide chisels, rock drills, and other tools that are essential to the quarryman. Central to the Expo were the guys who dig rock every day: two separate truck raffles were open only to New York or Pennsylvania quarrymen who had paid-up their dues. I spoke to one who works a mine in Trout Creek. He's been quarrying thirty years. "It's mind over matter," he told me when I suggested quarrying must be hard work. "It don't matter if you don't mind."

The states of Pennsylvania and New York were on hand, our state represented by a couple of mining and reclamation specialists with the state Department of Environmental Conservation. As you might expect, quarrying today is a highly regulated activity. To start, one needs a Bluestone Exploration Authorization through an application process with the DEC. If the quarrying exceeds certain limits—in amount of material extracted or size of mine—one needs to get a Land Reclamation Permit. Today's quarry needs to be cleaned-up when the mining is done.

The New York State Re-vegetation Procedures Manual lays out the requirements to grade and reduce the slope of former surface mines, rebuild the layer of topsoil, and plant appropriate grasses, legumes, trees and shrubs, returning the quarry site to something like its pre-mine state. Today's quarry, tomorrow's grassy slope.

Mountain Theater

COMMUNITY THEATER thrives in the Catskills these days. Margaretville's Open Eye Theater auditions for productions in their new theater building, a converted church, first converted, years back, into a thermometer factory. For a couple of decades, the Shandaken Theatrical Society has provided an active theater program at their wonderful little Phoenicia Theater. Seems odd that 30 years ago, we went to the movies in that same building.

Where once the movies flourished, live theater now is found. Not too many years ago, Margaretville, Fleischmanns, Phoenicia, Walton all had movie theaters, and up near Maplecrest, between Hunter and Windham, was a drive-in. I saw *The Exorcist* there. Last time I've been to a drive-in, I think.

Woodstock's Tinker Street Theater survives, and The Catskill Mountain Foundation underwrites the movies in Hunter, but generally we must drive to the Multiplex at the Mall, or the art house on the river, to see a movie, while we can fill our summer dance card with local theatrical productions at a variety of venues – not just theaters, but barns, community centers, and church halls. I've seen Shakespeare come alive as local actors played against the Tudor architectural lines of Lake Delaware's St. James Church parish house, and Thornton Wilder's Our Town become ours in the Dry Brook Community Hall.

In the decades after World War II, live theater was pretty much found only on Broadway, or downtown off-Broadway, but within a pretty limited geographic area called New York City. Sometime in the sixties, resident professional theaters arose in the provinces: the Guthrie Theater in Minneapolis, Hartford Stage and The Long Wharf Theatre in Connecticut, Indiana Repertory. In Manhattan, the Roundabout Theatre Company—which flourishes in the former Studio 54 as a Broadway house today—was established in an vacant supermarket.

(Okay, here's the spelling lesson: "t-h-e-a-t-e-r" is the general American spelling of the word. The British spell it "t-h-e-a-t-r-e." That's the way I spell it when I want to put on the dog, you know, appear, I don't know, sophisticated. Notice how different theaters use one or the other spelling. Draw your own conclusions.)

These regional theaters are professional companies, not local community groups, and their productions are directed and choreographed, designed, lit, and acted by professionals under collective bargaining contracts negotiated, with Actors Equity and other unions, by the League of Resident Theatres, or LORT, the professional association of resident theater companies.

The closest LORT professional theater to the Catskills is Capital Repertory in Albany, a organization celebrating nearly 30 years as the resident professional theater of the state capital, and one with decidedly Catskill Mountain roots.

In the seventies, the best theater in the country was produced, each summer, in Lexington, New York. The Lexington Conservatory Theater was the brainchild of a group of young, professionally trained actors and directors – trained in places like the Yale Drama School and the American Conservatory Theater in San Francisco. They pooled their money and leased an abandoned resort in Lexington, a collection of ramshackle buildings on Route 42 that had previously served as a kids' theater camp. It's right where the road crosses the Schoharie Creek. Later an organization called Art Awareness operated there.

The central figure in the group was a young playwright and director named Oakley Hall III, son of the author of the novel *Downhill Racer*, a child prodigy who started college at 16, after not fitting-in at Andover, the California wild-child in a nest of New England conformity. Young Oakley graduated from the Theater Department at the University of California at Irvine, did graduate work in Creative Writing at Boston University, under John Cheever, master of the post-war short story. Called a genius by many, and described by a colleague as "the most magnetic person you ever met," Oakley Hall III teamed up with Michael Van Landingham and Bruce Bouchard and an incredibly talented bunch of young, hip people to turn the property into a complex of two theaters and a café, with a leaning old hotel as actors' dorm.

Opening night 1976 is legendary. Oakley Hall had adapted Mary Shelley's *Frankenstein* into a particularly gory and eerie production. The coincidental timing of an old-fashioned Catskill Mountain lightening storm with the planned pyrotechnics of Hall's production led to such frightening realism that children ran in fright from the theater. I wish I could say I was there.

I was there for the magnificent production of Oakley Hall's play *Grinder's Stand*, a play written in Shakespearean blank verse about the latter days of explorer Meriwether Lewis. Albany critic Dan DiNicola called it "A richly significant piece of American drama," and it was. I also saw the best production I've ever seen of Tennessee Williams' *Streetcar Named Desire*, set on an abandoned New Orleans houseboat, on a stage open to the Schoharie Creek.

A tragic accident incapacitated Oakley Hall and led to the end of the Lexington Conservatory Theater's run in the Catskills. After five years here, they pulled up stakes and moved to Albany where they became Capital Rep, right on Pearl Street, our nearest professional resident theater, 75 miles and 30 years from Lexington.

The Catskill Turnpike

I discovered the Catskill Turnpike quite by accident. I had passed it countless times on the way to Oneonta, making a straight crossroad junction with Route 28, about eight miles north of Delhi, at the top of Meredith Hill. For years, of course, there were no road signs, so when that seemingly anonymous crossroad finally did get identified with a green sign, and it turned out to be named "Catskill Turnpike," it took a while for it to register. "Catskill Turnpike," I remember thinking, when I finally did notice. "That can't possibly go all the way to Catskill."

It can. And does, and goes all the way past Franklin in the other direction, and it turns out The Catskill Turnpike has quite a history. Called the Susquehanna Turnpike at the other end, the road was built by a private company in 1800, and for the first 25 years of the nineteenth- century was the major way west for New Englanders seeking land in central New York, western Pennsylvania, and the Ohio Valley.

Turn right at Meredith off Route 28 onto the old turnpike and be transported

The Catskill Turnpike: straightest road in the mountains.

to an earlier day. The first thing you notice is how remarkably straight the road is, more like a road in Indiana or Iowa, rolling up and down with the contour of the land while traveling dead-ahead straight from point A to point B. The mountains don't allow for such precise direction for more than a half-mile or so, before a turn is required, but the old road is remarkably straight for those of us used to driving curving mountain roads.

Early road building in the new American republic was heavily influenced by the Roman system of road construction. Americans looked to the historical Roman Republic as the model for the new American republic to emulate, and road building was one of the great accomplishments of Ancient Rome. Roman roads are still in use, I'm told, and the Roman way was as-the-crow-flies, straight ahead, fit-road-to-terrain not a consideration.

The New York stockholders of the 1800 Susquehanna Turnpike Corporation wanted their road built quickly, taking the most direct route to the Susquehanna River. Think of early roads in America as long portage routes between rivers, the major avenues of travel through the wilderness. Wattles Ferry, in present-day Unadilla, was the port on the Susquehanna, from which travelers could either cross to the lands of central New York, or float down into Pennsylvania, perhaps to another portage to the Alleghany River, to float into Ohio.

From Meredith, the road travels east through some beautiful farmland, with farms still in production, as well as time-capsule ruins of farms, prosperous a century or two ago on a major through-route. The road passes in front of the West Kortright Center, the country church turned Performing Arts Center whose middle-of-nowhere location now makes sense to me on the old turnpike. Turnpike road soon merges for a bit with Elk Creek Road, separates, then merges with County Route 33, the Bloomville-West Harpersfield Road, before it joins State Route 23 at Harpersfield, following the state road through Stamford.

The Catskill Turnpike served nineteenth-century Catskill Mountain farmers as a major thoroughfare for the transport of their goods to market. The corporation that built and operated the turnpike charged tolls for "every score of sheep, or, hogs, cattle, horses, or mules" in the early years. Farmers would use it to drive livestock to the Hudson and to cart butter, grain, and other produce. The New York market was merely a river sloop journey from Catskill.

Dorothy Kubik has written a comprehensive history of the turnpike, *West Through the Catskills: The Story of the Susquehanna Turnpike* (Purple Mountain Press, 2001). In it, she quotes from the diary of New Kingston farmer James Thompson, who wrote of his 1839 selling trip to New York City, a twice-yearly event in the lives of many early Catskill Mountain farmers. The entire trip took ten days. Thompson might have traveled over Bovina and Warren Mountains to pick up the turnpike at Stamford.

From Stamford, the old turnpike leaves State Route 23, bearing left onto South Gilboa Road, County Route 14. You'll climb the ridge north of 23, and once again find yourself traveling at an elevation, rather than along the river valleys—the easier, more favored, routes for road building once the state got into the act. You'll gradually come down off the hill to Route 30, the other side of Grand Gorge, up toward Minekill Falls.

There, the Turnpike once went straight, but now is cut off by the Schoharie Reservoir. Turn left onto Route 30, right onto State Route 990V, drive by the Gilboa school and Gilboa dam, through West Conesville and Conesville to Manorkill, where you take a right onto Durham Road which takes you over Durham Mountain to State Route 145.

Route 145 is a straight shot along the old turnpike route. Then, take a left onto the modern four-lane highway, that is Route 23, approaching Catskill. Bear left onto 23B, and follow that through South Cairo, and Leeds, into Catskill village. If you keep yourself on the old road, snug along the Catskill Creek, you'll reach the restored nineteenth-century freight terminal on the Hudson that was the beginning of the Susquehanna Turnpike, and the end of the Catskill Turnpike that I first came upon sixty-something miles away up in Meredith.

Memorial Day in the Mountains

WHEN I WAS GROWING UP IN SUBURBIA, Memorial Day was the first day of summer, the day the local pools opened, the day my job at the beach club started. Oh, we watched the President at the Tomb of the Unknown Soldier on TV, but mostly Memorial Day was the season's first hot dogs and hamburgers, outside.

Moving to the mountains introduced me to Memorial Day. Here, the holiday was crepe-poppies in lapels, folks putting-out little flags on the graves of veterans, an entire community coming together for a parade and a speech in front of the Legion Hall, followed by free ice cream and busy taverns. Memorial Day mattered.

In the early seventies people on both sides of the national debate over the Vietnam War listened intently to the Memorial Day speaker—generally a clergyperson—for hints to his or her true attitude toward the war. No one that I remember ever got too political, but some fairly intense political debates could arise out of somebody's interpretation of what the Reverend seemed to say.

Memorial Day has small town roots. In 1966, President Lyndon Baines Johnson declared Waterloo, New York, "The Birthplace of Memorial Day," ending a longtime contest for the title among competing claimants. That Finger Lakes village was home to Henry Welles, a small-town pharmacist, who suggested, at a social gathering, that the decoration of graves would be a good way to honor the many young men of the village killed in the Civil War. The idea took off, and Decoration Day, as it was then known, began to spread as a springtime ritual.

It was set on May 30 in 1868 by order of John A. Logan, first national commander of the Grand Army of the Republic, the brotherhood of Union Veterans that was a powerful force in American life for half a century. In 1873, New York became the first state to make Decoration Day an official state holiday, one that was only observed in the north. After World War I, Memorial Day was extended to honor Americans who died in every war, not just the Civil War, and in 1971 was moved to the last Monday in May to insure a three day weekend.

A few Memorial Days back, Irwin Kasanof, of Halcott Center, was honored as the last World War I veteran in our area. He was, I believe, a hundred years old at the time. I hate to think of the Memorial Day to come, when our towns will honor their last World War II vet.

That group is famously tight-lipped about their experiences in the war. Growing up, there were, around us, a lot of war veterans and few war stories. It seemed they wanted to forget. As one recently told me, his eyes glistening, "Those guys went through so much." My informant spent the war sweeping for mines in Europe himself, but his near-tears are for "those guys, who had it a lot worse than me." Typically, my WW II veteran friend does not want his name used.

"This place lost so many for such a little town," he told me, referring to the handful of villages and hamlets at the head of the East Branch that mean home to him. "At least eight guys died."

Imagine. We are all pained when we read of the death in Iraq of a kid from Highland, or from across the river. Imagine eight dead soldiers, sailors, airmen, and marines from among the kids who were just in your high school, and the high schools you play in sports.

When you get a chance, visit the Margaretville American Legion Hall to see the wonderful wall of photographs of the men and women of World War II. Play bingo one night just to get in. The wall is worth a visit.

Marian Connell had been teaching math, general science, chemistry, and biology at Margaretville High School for seven years, or so, when the Japanese bombed Pearl Harbor. A photography enthusiast, she resolved to photograph every local man and woman who went off to war. The results are staggering. The photographs extend down the entire side wall of the Legion Hall – so many pictures! One truly understands the scope of the mobilization for war that was World War II when one sees just how many young people went off to war. A whole generation!

When I taught European history to tenth graders, a few years, I had the kids do a project called "Margaretville in World War II." Each student would find a person to interview who lived through the war: might be a vet, or somebody on the home front. It was fascinating to learn that Fleischmanns High School cancelled the Prom for the duration. The problem: no boys.

Miss Connell was a legendary teacher when I was her colleague. She taught 42 years. My World War II veteran friend graduated high school in the late thirties, but he still gets excited when describing her classroom. "Miss Connell made you feel like you were part of something!" he exclaimed. About the best compliment a teacher can get.

County Histories

A COUNTY is an administrative subdivision of a sovereign jurisdiction. The theoretically sovereign state of New York has 62 of them. Six can lay claim to parts of the Catskills: Ulster, Greene, Delaware, Sullivan, Schoharie, Albany.

Give or take Albany.

The English divided the newly established Province of New York into 12 counties on November 1, 1683, almost 20 years after their nearly bloodless conquest of the former Dutch territory of New Netherland. It was early in the learning curve for English colonial administration.

Albany County comprised most of western and northern New York. The east side of the Hudson was organized into Westchester and Duchess Counties; the west side of the river into Orange and Ulster. Living in an overseas outpost, the great majority of New Yorkers resided within ten miles of tidal waters – sea, sound, bay, or the tidal estuary that is the Hudson.

A couple of large tracts of land were outside the county sub-divisions. All of present-day Columbia County were the Manor lands of Robert Livingston, and today's Rensselaer County contains much of the old Patroonship of that family name.

In the years just after the settlement of the independence question, New York enjoyed a land boom that propelled the rapid growth of the state population and economy. By 1830, the Empire State led the nation in population, domestic production, transportation, manufacturing, banking, and commerce. The state population grew from 340,000 in the first national census, 1790, to almost two million in 1830.

Cheap, abundant land was the early American equivalent to the cheap, abundant oil of more recent days. It was the readily available energy that activated all economic activity. Settle a family on a piece of land and you've got a customer for tools, seed, milling, and finance, a producer who will invariably create something of value with which to pay. It was the sale that kept on selling.

In May 1786, William Cooper put up for sale 40,000 acres west of the Catskills in the upper Susquehanna valley. He sold out in 16 days! In Cooper's own words, the buyers were of "the poorest order of men." He got rich providing them with mills and stores, a bank and provisions. His son, James Fenimore Cooper, wrote the books that gave their Leather-stocking District its name.

Of course, new counties were established, as new lands were settled and new landholders found their mutual interest. These community activists would petition the State Legislature to form a new county. It only took five years for Cooper's "poorest order" to successfully petition the formation of their own county: Otsego.

Settlers on the upper Delaware were next. In 1797, Ulster County state Assemblyman Ebenezer Foote, of Delhi, and Otsego County Assemblyman John Burr, of Harpersfield, led the fight to establish Delaware County from parts of their two counties. The petitioners to the state included many with longtime mountain family names like Griffin, Beardsley, Harper, Parsons, Fuller, and Ingalls. A similar petition process led to the formation of Greene County three years later.

Tim Duerden of Franklin has written a narrative *History of Delaware County, New York: A Catskill Land and Its People 1797-2007*, published by Purple Mountain Press of Fleischmanns. Tim is Director of the Delaware County Historical Association in Delhi. The DCHA operates the Frisbee House Museum in the tavern house where the first county business was conducted.

Tim looks at the history of Delaware County through the prism of today's concern with land use, natural resources, and conflict among those with competing land use visions. The book is a general history, an overview, lavishly illustrated in the high quality, visually pleasing manner that has become the hallmark of Purple Mountain Press.

The publisher touts the history as "the first comprehensive history of Delaware County since 1949." That was the year of publication of John D. Monroe's *Chapters in the History of Delaware County*, an increasingly difficult book to find. If you have one, keep it.

I am not sure I have ever even seen an 1898 *Delaware County New York* by David Murray. They seem very rare. Not to mention an 1856 Jay Gould *History of Delaware County and Border Wars of New York*. You need to go to a fancy auction house for one of those, although reprints are available.

Years ago, happily, I bought a 1976 reprint of W. W. Munsell's 1880 *History of Delaware County*. It's a great source. In 1987, Purple Mountain Press published *Two Stones for Every Dirt: The Story of Delaware County, New York*, also a collaboration with the County Historical Association. The publisher does not qualify that one as a comprehensive history, because it is organized thematically rather than chronologically.

Separated by 20 years, but united in subject, the "Story" and the "History" make a nice, two-volume companion set on Delaware County, from a Delaware County publisher who has set the standard for quality New York State Regional Books for over 35 years.

New Kingston: The Chancellor's Gift

I confess to a weak spot for the Livingstons. Perhaps it's my fondness for New Kingston, the historic little village on the upper Plattekill founded on land that Chancellor Robert Livingston donated to the victims of the British burning of Kingston in the Revolutionary War. It's a great story.

In October 1777, British forces under General John Vaughn sailed up the Hudson from New York in a flotilla of flatboats, carrying over 1100 British and Hessian soldiers. The British aimed to take control of the strategic Hudson Val-

This beautiful valley was the Chancellor's gift.

ley. Knowing the force was coming, the people of Kingston had plenty of time to prepare, retreating to the safety of higher ground, taking with them their live-stock, and most treasured possessions.

The Kingston colonials could not take their houses, of course, and when the British landed at Kingston Point on October 16, the village was theirs for the sacking. Colonial newspapers reported the British burned some 326 houses, and the barns on the grounds of each of them. Grain, gunpowder, and supplies, including 12,000 barrels of flour, were destroyed. The settlement was burned to the ground.

The fourth Robert Livingston had recently inherited the lands of his grand-father, lands that included nearly all the old Hardenbergh Patent, the Catskills from about Woodstock to the West Branch of the Delaware: 2,000,000 acres of Livingston land. Robert was a New York delegate to the Continental Congress, and a member of the committee appointed to draft the Declaration of Independence, along with John Adams, Benjamin Franklin, and Thomas Jefferson. Livingston, later, became the chancellor of New York State's new judicial system, and administered the first presidential oath of office to George Washington, in New York City, in 1788. A regular founding father, he was.

He was also, I think, a generous guy. After the British attack, the Chancellor offered the burned-out residents of Kingston any 5000 acres of unsettled land in his vast domain, west of the Hudson, on which to establish a new community. The war, and instability on the frontier, kept the Kingstonians from acting on his offer right away. In 1784, Revolutionary War veteran, Jacob Van Benschoten, and a surveyor named Cockburn, made their way up the Esopus Valley, over Highmount, to the East Branch, then followed the quick running Plattekill up to the point where its source-streams merge. There, they laid out 100 fifty acre lots. Some of the original stone wall lot-boundaries are still there.

Those lots were then distributed, free of charge, minus the cost of the survey, to 100 residents of Kingston who were burned out. Many held on to their titles to the land, only to sell them, but some migrated to the mountains to establish New Kingston, a hamlet now over 200 years old, which has recently gained Historic District recognition. Some descendents of original settlers still reside there, including direct descendents of that first explorer, Jacob Van Benschoten.

Chancellor Livingston was the son of Judge Robert R. Livingston and his remarkable wife, Margaret Beekman, a woman of Abigail Adams-type strength and resiliency, whose own house was burned to the ground by the British. Besides the Chancellor, her 10 children included her eldest, Janet, the widow of General Richard Montgomery, hero of the Siege of Quebec, killed on the last night of 1775, leading the patriot attack on that British fortress city. Her son, Edward, was a founder of Louisiana, congressman, and minister to France. Her daughter, Alida's, husband was a secretary of war, and her daughter, Gertrude's, husband a governor of New York. All this success and power in one generation was in addition to that of the Chancellor.

Now, it turns out, historians are increasingly turning their attention to an historically overlooked member of that remarkable generation of Livingstons. Catherine Livingston was forty-one years old when she was finally able to overcome family opposition to marry Freeborn Garretson, a brilliant, but socially unacceptable, anti-slavery Methodist, circuit-riding preacher who was, decidedly, not the kind of man Livingston woman generally married. Catherine had earlier undergone a spiritual awakening, through the Methodist approach to Christianity, an approach that stressed personal sanctification and growth toward Christian perfection, beyond sin. Her conversion was not unusual for the time, but it was strikingly unusual for an aristocratic, high-church Episcopalian Livingston. Her family did not approve!

Rachel Cope, when a graduate student at Syracuse University, presented a paper, "Conversion as Process: Catherine Livingston Garretson's Search for Sanctification" at the 29th Conference on New York State History, held in Saratoga Springs. It seems Catherine Garretson kept a Spiritual Journal that can be compared to the mystical writings of Teresa of Avila and John of the Cross, a

2000 page compendium of spiritual searching, dreams, visions, memoir, prayer, evangelization, and reflections that follows the classical pattern of the mystical tradition: purgation, illumination, the dark night of the soul, and mystical union with the divine. This spiritual journal is gaining a lot of academic interest. A Drew University doctoral dissertation is in the works.

I do have a weak spot for the Livingstons. Imagine, a genuine American mystic in our own historic back yard.

Camp Woodland

A FRIEND OF MINE, native to the mountains, will, as we tour the hills together, frequently point to some stray roadside basketball court, one that's weed-infested, seen-better-days, and say: "Played a lot of basketball there when we were kids."

Seems that the mountains were home to a number of summer camps, and local kids provided the camp basketball teams with spirited, and talented, competition.

I was one of the few kids in my class, at suburban Theodore Roosevelt Elementary School, who didn't go to camp. In the fifties and sixties, most of the kids at my school went to sleep-away camp, and, evidently, a lot of those camps were here in the Catskills. There are still a few here, of course. Timber Lake Camp in Shandaken is a world-class facility. Check out the video on their website sometime to see an enticing array of facilities and programs for children and teens. Frost Valley YMCA camp is also state-of-the-art, and its programs and facilities are available, year round, to locals, young and old.

I remember Camp Ta-Ri-Go on Red Kill, above Fleischmanns, and Camp Oquago on Perch Lake, in Andes. The latter operated on that crystal lake from 1930 to 1993. Their campers would overrun the local bowling alley on a rainy summer day. The students at Fleischmanns' summer yeshiva, Moshe Y'oel, think of themselves as being at camp, although they do a lot more studying than my elementary school classmates did at summer camp, back in the day.

Phoenicia's Woodland Valley has a summer camp history that can, I think, rival that of any place in the country. One of the first campgrounds for children was established there, in 1903, when the headmaster of a private school in the city brought his students to camp on the property of Roxmor, an inn and vacation community founded by New York City amateur photographer and entrepreneur, Edward Miller, six years earlier. They called their temporary camp on the inn grounds "Camp Burroughs," after one of the Roxmor Inn's more celebrated guests, the great writer and naturalist John Burroughs.

Mr. Miller found the idea of a sleep-away camp for boys both worthwhile and profitable, as he sought to develop his hostelry, so he hired a teacher, Harry W. Little, a recent graduate of Connecticut's Wesleyan College, to establish and run a permanent summer camp. Camp Wake Robin was born in 1904, named for one of Burroughs' well-loved book titles.

Mr. Little operated Camp Wake Robin for 25 years, retiring, on doctor's orders, in 1928. The Roxmor had grown by that time into a full-scale vacation community, a colony of leased lots where the tent platforms and cottages of summer residents shared the 70 acre hillside with the camp and the inn, which soon went the way of Camp Wake Robin, closing in 1930. The Roxmor community is still there.

Perhaps the competition from a second Woodland Valley camp contributed to Mr. Miller's decision to close Camp Wake Robin upon Mr. Little's retirement. In 1913, Erwin S. Spink established a boarding school for boys on a 300-acre farm, at the head of the Pantherkill, on the western ridge over Woodland Valley. He called his school "The Woodland School," built a home school and a dormitory, high on the hill, and set up a curriculum rich in outdoor activity and farm chores, as well as in academics. In the summer, he operated a camp which attracted local children as well as those from far away. I've talked to one former camper, now in his nineties.

Camp Woodland, located on Irondale Road, was surely the most famous camp of all the Woodland Valley operations. It was founded in 1939 by Norman Studer, a teacher and Director of New York City's Downtown Community School, who had been a student of the educational philosopher, John Dewey, at Columbia. Camp Woodland was a workshop for the ideas of progressive, child-centered education, as taught by Dewey. The camp was ethnically integrated, unusual for the time. At its peak, 200 campers attended, boys and girls, ages 8 to 16.

The essence of the Camp Woodland philosophy was the importance of children knowing their roots and understanding democracy, through an investigation of the traditions and backgrounds of the American people. Thus, campers at Camp Woodland were consistently exposed to "culture bearers," singers, dancers, fiddlers, and story-tellers: mountain men and women who shared with the young the traditions of rural life. Locals would come to the camp to demonstrate such country crafts as bark-stripping, blacksmithing, water-witching, shingle-splitting, and square dance calling.

Music and folklore were central to the Camp Woodland program. Music Directors Norman Cazden and Herbert Haufrecht were composers, as well as teachers. They and their campers collected Catskill Mountain folk songs, a camp activity that later led to the publication of *A Catskill Songbook*, in 1958, and the two-volume *Folk Songs of the Catskills*, in 1982. Every August, the camp held a Catskill Folk Festival, open to all.

Camp Woodland's progressive, integrated, and democratic approach became a victim of the paranoia of the McCarthy witch-hunt of the fifties. Studer was called before the state legislature's Un-American Activities Committee, and Cazden was blacklisted, unable to find academic work for 16 years. The trustees withdrew support, and Camp Woodland closed in 1962. Its legacy lives on, in the music and folklore its campers collected.

James Oliver and Marian Connell: Teachers

I'VE only recently discovered James Oliver, but I like him. He's the graduate of the State Normal School at Albany who came to teach in Roxbury in 1849, when both John Burroughs and Jay Gould were about 12. Think of the future naturalist and the future capitalist as seventh graders: little Johnny the reluctant, uninterested, underachiever; little Jay the brightest kid in the class. Mr. Oliver had a profound effect on both of them, drawing-out young Burroughs' natural curiosity, and directing young Gould's restless energy.

Perhaps, James Oliver can be the patron of Catskill Mountain schoolteachers, a fellowship I proudly claim. When I joined the faculty of the Central School, several of my colleagues had begun their teaching careers in one-room schoolhouses. Dot Lunn, school secretary, still answered the phone, "Central School!", as if centralization, even then 20 some-odd years old, was still something of a novelty. I was the guest of the American Legion, a couple of times, at their "Delaware County Schoolmaster's Dinner." Seemed Ichabod Crane-like quaint even then.

My point is, I guess, that we are not all that distant from the days of the one-room schoolhouse, where one teacher organized the lessons for every age, big kids taught little kids, and all the children of a particular valley went to school together from age six to fourteen. You can see nicely preserved one-room schoolhouses in Margaretville, on Route 28—The Old Stone Schoolhouse—and in Bovina up at the head of the Little Delaware River.

Often, the teacher would be only a few years older than the students. When John Burroughs graduated from Mr. Oliver's eighth grade, he spent a few months reading borrowed books, then got a job teaching a one-room school in Tongore, now Olivebridge. That was in 1854. The schoolhouse is still there, identified in front by a blue sign historical marker.

There were over 400 one-room school districts in Delaware County alone by the late 1800s; 26 in the Town of Middletown, 23 in Andes, 20 in Roxbury, each district covering maybe three or four square miles. The curriculum was based on recitation and rote: reading, writing, and arithmetic, with an emphasis on memorization and outward correctness. Reading lessons emphasized reading aloud with correct pronunciation. Comprehension was secondary. Writing often meant exact copying of model texts, with an emphasis on penmanship.

I do not mean to suggest that quality education was lacking. Merely that the curriculum was often dry and repetitive. A teacher like Mr. Oliver would be a revelation to his young scholars, with his emphasis on poetry and self-expression, nature study and history and curiosity about the wider world. He instilled in his students the excitement of learning.

Opportunities in the mountains for a secondary education were scarce right up through the nineteenth-century. Burroughs used his teaching salary to pay for a semester at the Ashland Collegiate Institute in Greene County. Later, he studied at Cooperstown Seminary. Both were secondary schools.

Closer to home, Delaware Academy in Delhi can trace its history to 1820, and the Delaware Literary Institute in Franklin, founded in 1835, was the precursor of that town's public high school. Farm kids who wanted a high school education would often board in town, renting a room Monday through Thursday night in towns like Andes or Fleischmanns or Margaretville to attend the high schools that were, later, established there.

Modern high school education came to this side of the mountains when Marian Connell came to Margaretville in 1932, having just completed a Masters Degree in physics from Syracuse University. Marian taught modern science and math, one of the first women in New York State certified to teach the hard sciences – biology, chemistry, and physics. In the crimped and narrow depression days of the thirties, science seemed, even more so than today, the door to, not just progress, but the wonders of the universe. Miss Connell opened the doors to the universe for a couple generations of Catskill Mountain kids.

A ninety-year old friend, Margaretville High School Class of '37, told me "She wasn't like those teachers who put you down. Miss Connell made you feel like you were part of something!" A fifty year old lawyer, Class of '76, said the same thing. Miss Connell demanded rigor and attention. She was a formidable presence. Opening up the universe required students to read and analyze and experiment and think. Miss Connell valued achievement, and her students learned to demand more of themselves in order to achieve. No accident that Margaretville Central School Honor Society is the Marion Connell Chapter, named for its founder, who taught forty-four years, retiring in 1976.

Marian taught her students the value of community through her own energetic example. She was a stalwart of the Presbyterian Church, co-founder of the Fairview Library, and longtime member and secretary of the Margaretville Memorial Hospital Board of Trustees. I served on the latter board with Marian.

I can still hear her sonorous voice and measured cadence as she read the monthly minutes she had so carefully composed the month before.

James Oliver and Marian Connell: maybe we can have more than one patron of Catskill Mountain schoolteachers.

David Stradling's *Making Mountains*

UNIVERSITY OF CINCINNATI PROFESSOR DAVID STRADLING, his wife Jodie, and their two young daughters toured the Catskills a couple weeks ago. In many ways, the trip was a homecoming for the professor. His grandfather, Glentworth Haynes, grew up in Highmount. When Professor Stradling was little David Stradling visiting his grandparents in Kingston, his postal-worker grandfather told stories of his Catskill Mountain boyhood, taking the boy on numerous nostalgic road trips into the mountains. Professor Stradling grew up living outside the Catskills but feeling intimately connected to them.

It's perhaps not surprising, then, that Professor Stradling chose the Catskills as the subject for his second work of environmental history, that school of academic history that looks at the way human beings interact with the environment. (His first book was on urban air pollution.) It is fortunate for those of us who live in the mountains that this grandchild of the Catskills is the author of the first comprehensive history of our area since 1972.

Alf Evers' *The Catskills: From Wilderness to Woodstock* was published that year by Doubleday, a major mainstream press capitalizing on the interest in the Catskills generated by the 1969 Woodstock concert. Ten years later, the regional Overlook Press republished Evers' book, which has been the definitive Catskill Mountain history for 35 years now. Lots of locally published regional history has appeared since, but Evers' book is the national standard source.

Move over, Alf. David Stradling's *Making Mountains: New York City and the Catskills* was published in 2007 by Weyerhaeuser Environmental Books, an imprint of the University of Washington Press, an academic publisher. It is good. Very good. Professor Stradling traces the history of the mountains through an analysis of changes in the landscape, both the actual landscape of the hills and valleys, and the imagined, envisioned landscape we all carry in our heads.

The professor's thesis is timely: that the Catskills have always been intimately connected to New York City, and that city dwellers and mountain folks collaborate in the creation of both our idea of the landscape and its reality. In fact, both the professor and his grandfather are representative of the many people who have close connections to the mountains while living, most of their lives, outside of them. In other words, we don't divide neatly into mountain folks and city people—so many of us, in important ways, are both.

Making Mountains is very inclusive history. Stradling begins with a look at the six generations of his family—he is a Haynes—who settled Haynes Hollow up Dry Brook in the early 1800s. He is able to see the mountains as land to be tamed, natural resources to be exploited as his ancestors and their fellow settlers built a life out of lumber and hides, bluestone and butter.

The historian is also sensitive to the ways artists and writers have shaped visitors' view of the Catskills. Each chapter begins with a quote from John Burroughs, who helped shape our mental concept of these mountains through his vision of nature at the border where civilization meets the wilderness. Stradling credits Hudson River School founding artist Thomas Cole with the creation of our mental image of the Catskills, one where nature is overpowering but reassuring, wild but restorative.

What makes Stradling's book so good is that it looks at the history of the mountains in a systematic way, one that poses an understanding of the past that can help us sort out the confusing present. I love Alf Evers, and The Catskills: From Wilderness to Woodstock will always hold an honored place on my shelf, but Alf was mostly telling stories, wonderful stories, one after the other, with little real narrative thrust. This new book applies the rigor of academic history to produce a highly readable, engaging, and interesting story of deforestation and reforestation, of a wilderness landscape turning into an agricultural landscape and back again, of hotels and reservoirs and second homes, of change, change, change.

Change is the one constant in this Catskill Mountain history, as writers and artists create an image or vision of what mountains are, city dwellers come to the mountains looking for that vision, and locals try to earn a few dollars by providing it. Sometimes the mountains are wild forest, sometimes fresh milk and eggs, sometimes hillside viewsheds of man-made lakes.

Whatever the mountains are to us at any given point, they are nurtured and protected, developed and conserved by the people who love them. Those of us who love them—including, I think, the late Alf Evers— are fortunate that this 2007 environmental history of the Catskills was written by someone who loves them.

You love the Catskills. Go get this book.

An Old-Fashioned Skimmelton

I WITNESSED A SKIMMELTON IN 1971. Visiting in the home of friends, a newly married couple, late one evening, we were startled by a loud ruckus outside the house. We needn't investigate long. A crowd of mostly young neighbors and friends had arrived outside with a tractor and wagon—or was it a pick-up truck loaded with hay? They banged on the door, banged on the pots and pans they carried, invaded the house, and, in high spirits and boundless good nature, "kidnapped" the newly-weds for a mock serenade, a hay-ride through the village accompanied by lots of noise and lots of razzing of the young couple. It was fun, although, as I remember, the couple themselves were less than thrilled.

I haven't heard of another skimmelton in the more than a third of a century since that time. There must have been a few, but the old custom seems to be largely dying out. As American culture becomes more and more homogenized, traditional local customs like the skimmelton fade away.

Such customs remind us that we live in a very particular place, with a history and a set of traditions particular to that place. Such customs remind us that a community and way of life precede us, and that *here* is bigger than just *now*.

The skimmelton was a very local custom. The word itself—with a variety of alternate spellings—was identified in 1949 as current in a well-defined region stretching from the Housatonic River in Connecticut to the upper Delaware in Pennsylvania and northwestern New Jersey, centering on the Catskills and the Hudson Valley in New York State. A similar custom, but with more harmonious music, called the Chivaree, has been identified out west.

When I moved to the mountains, there were lots of reminders that the culture of this place was different from the mainstream. In the little mountain village where I lived, men still gathered daily in the General Store to kibitz and gossip and trade insults and talk. The year was punctuated by seasons and activities new to me: haying time, and sap season, cider-pressing, and hunting camp. Area juke boxes largely featured country music—Tammy Wynette rather than Blood, Sweat, and Tears—and Round and Square Dances were frequent events.

The Catskills are beautiful, and the purity and beauty of the natural environment is a great draw to our region. But, for me, it was the mountain culture that I found fascinating. There was something here that seemed better, purer, more humane than the urbane suburban lifestyle in which I had been raised. There was something different about life in the mountains.

Several years before I got here, a friend who grew up in the Catskills, was telling me a story. He started by identifying the subject of the story: "My father's best friend," he told me, "is a truck-driver." I stopped him right there. See, I knew that my friend's father was a doctor, a professional man. "Wait a minute," I interrupted, "Your father's best friend is a what?" I have great respect for both doctors and truck-drivers, but where I came from the two would be unlikely to even know each other, much less be best friends. In the mainstream culture I knew, doctors and truck-drivers ran in very different circles. I had to see this place where those circles intersected.

The late Harriet Smith of Roxbury told me a story that illustrates that intersection. Helen Gould Shepherd, the daughter of Jay Gould, was a wealthy, cosmopolitan, and cultured woman who spent summers at Kirkside, her Roxbury home. Each evening, dinner would be served at 8, evening clothes required.

Harriet told me that it was not uncommon for a man to deliver coal or milk or plumbing repairs at the back door of the big house during the day, only to return, in a dinner jacket, at 8 that evening to the front door, his wife in her evening best, for dinner with the Shepherds.

Helen Gould was 45 years old when she surprised everyone, in 1913, by marrying Finley Shepherd, an employee of her family's railroad empire. The wedding was a lavish affair that took place in January in the family's Westchester County estate, Lyndhurst. I wonder if the locals gave the couple a skim-melton when that arrived in Roxbury that summer. Seems only right.

Rafting the Delaware

FOR YEARS, my brother in Philadelphia and I have talked—it's always been just talk—about taking a raft from my house to his house down the Delaware. While the rain that falls on my roof soon swells the river that runs by his, those who patrol the New York City reservoirs would certainly not welcome our raft. It's merely a fantasy.

From the late eighteenth-century to the early twentieth-century, rafting the Delaware was much more than a fantasy; it was an annual rite of spring. When the river rose with spring rains and snow melt, mountain loggers would lash together timber to be floated down the river for sale at Philadelphia or Trenton. These rafts were both commodities to be sold—the timber itself—and means of transport. Rafters would load cargoes of wheat, whiskey, and wool, bluestone and potash. (Potash, an important ingredient in the manufacture of soap, glass, and fertilizer, is made from hardwood ashes, a common by-product in clearing the land.)

The Delaware River is 360 miles from its sources to the sea. The West Branch begins in Schoharie County, up near Jefferson, and runs by Stamford, and Hobart, Bloomville, Delhi and Walton, before being impounded in the Cannonsville Reservoir. The East Branch rises in Grand Gorge, runs by Roxbury and Margaretville, where it is impounded in the Pepacton Reservoir, the largest in the New York City water system.

Below the dams, the two source branches meet at Hancock where the river, which had been flowing largely west, turns south, dividing New York from Pennsylvania, Pennsylvania from New Jersey, New Jersey from Delaware, before broadening into the great Delaware Bay and emptying into the sea.

The Delaware rafting industry is an interesting example of the resourcefulness of early settlers in the mountains. The annual swelling of the rivers is a fact of life in the Catskills, recurrent floods a hazard. Why not take advantage of the river's regular annual increase in carrying capacity? Transportation beckons.

A fellow named David Skinner was the first Delaware River raftsman that we know about. In 1764, Skinner floated six 80-foot straight pine spars down river to the Philadelphia shipyards where he got $20 apiece for them for use as ships' masts. Walton became a center of the mast-spar trade in the 1790s, providing the spars for *Old Ironsides*, the *USS Constitution* of War of 1812 fame, still a commissioned ship in the US Navy, the oldest commissioned warship in the world.

Skinner lived over near Hancock, and his pioneering trip down river made him a sort of godfather to river raftsmen who came after him. He was known as "The Admiral of the Delaware," and it is said that anyone who wanted to make the trip after him had to pay tribute to the Admiral—a bottle or two would usually do. David Skinner died in 1801.

Delaware River rafting grew as an important mountain industry throughout the nineteenth-century, reaching its commercial high point in 1875 when more than 3000 rafts were floated down the river. But by then, the competition of railroads and better roads began to eat into the river's transportation value. The Delaware was a one-way stream. Railroads could bring products back into the mountains as well as out. By 1903, only 150 rafts went downstream.

As the industry grew, a cadre of skilled steersmen emerged, men capable of taking a raft down river, not just in the spring swell, but throughout the non-frozen year. Like Mississippi river-boat pilots, Delaware River raftsmen became memorable characters in the American mosaic.

Raftsmen were known as a hard-drinking, hard-fighting, two-fisted bunch. Characters like Boney Quillen and Rastus Chute were regionally notorious "Delaware water-dogs," steersmen who knew how to negotiate the rapids and rocks of the river, while "fussin' and fightin' and "makin' jollification" all the way to Philly.

The raftsman, largely native-born mountaineers, hated the railroad, which both put up bridges that obstructed the way, and, they knew, promised their ultimate demise. The largely immigrant Irish railroad workers made an inviting target, and the late 1800s saw some real antagonism between the two groups.

The last raft down the Delaware was the last trip of the last steersman, a guy named Len Rowland from Corbett on the East Branch. Rowland hit a snag on the river, had a heart attack and died. No raftsmen were left to take his place. By the fifties, the reservoirs were going in and the raft era was definitively over, rendered impossible by the dams.

Simpler Times

DONALD W. BOUTON of Greene County's Halcott Center has written and published a wonderful memoir chronicling the changes in Catskill Mountain life over the 150 years of the family farm. Don's great-grandfather settled in the Halcott Valley in the 1850s. His grandfather, father, children and grandchildren have all made a home—and a life—in what Don lovingly calls "this special place in the Catskills."

By *The Light of the Kerosene Lantern* traces five generations of mountain life in a beautifully designed and printed book that contains numerous historic and contemporary black-and-white photographs. The author was moved to write by the questions of his grandchildren, questions spurred by the things of the past that seem so foreign in our day: What's that for, "Goompie"? or, How do you put shoes on a cow?

Organized like a grandfather sharing memories with the kids, the book is comprised of 45 stories on topics like "Stone Walls" and "Maple Syrup, "Steam Tractors" and "Milking Machines," "Cauliflower" and "Medicine Shows." What makes this book so special is that this grandfather can really write. His stories are beautiful little essays, personal yet communal, full of striking detail and homespun wisdom.

The star of the tale is Don's father, the late Marshall Bouton, a man whose presence on the farm seems palpable years after his death. Reading about Marshall Bouton reminds me of those many Catskill Mountain men I first encountered thirty-five years ago, men of deep intelligence and practical skill who, without benefit of a lot of education, seemed to me smarter than a lot of people I met in college.

While we tend to think of multi-tasking and the many faceted multi-job career as particularly modern phenomena, Marshall Bouton and his contemporaries were making a living and a life out of multiple endeavors all along. Besides operating a large dairy and poultry farm, Marshall was a farm machinery selling agent, a fertilizer dealer, a sawmill operator, a steam-powered machinery service provider, an insurance agent, a town clerk, and a notary public.

One of my favorite stories in the book is called "Big Trip." It tells of the

More cows than people described the Catskills in simpler times.

yearly journey Don and his brother made with their father to Catskill to pick up election supplies, one of the duties of the town clerk. I'll go to Kingston at the drop of a hat, the forty mile distance only a challenge as gas prices rise. Don recounts the day when a trip to the Hudson Valley was a trip to someplace else, an all-day affair that challenged the endurance of both the travelers and the 1920 five-passenger Dodge sedan in which they traveled.

The trip was such a big trip that a rest stop was required. Each year, the boys and their Dad would stop in Boiceville at the little country store and souvenir shop located there. The shop itself was constructed to look like a log cabin. Behind the shop stood several tall statues which purported to be Indian totem poles, highly visible on the hill just above the road. The statues attracted tourists and passers-by to stop; the souvenir shop sold Indian-themed trinkets.

That shop and those statues still stand, the shop now a business no longer selling souvenirs, the statues now hidden behind a growth of trees and brush. Look up to your right as you approach Boiceville from the Kingston side just beyond Bread Alone and The Boiceville Inn. You'll get a glimpse of a tall be-feathered native warrior stretching his cemented arms to the sky.

Native American imagery has long been used in the Catskills as symbols of our wilderness soul. While the native peoples themselves were largely part-time residents of our mountains, camping here seasonally to hunt and fish, the symbolic use of Native American artifacts and mythology has long been a mountain staple. I remember a boyhood neighbor friend returning to our suburban home town from a Catskill Mountain vacation with a souvenir pair of "Indian moccasins."

Today, many people are discovering Native spirituality as a road toward awareness of the soul and the deeper meaning of life. A number of Native American spiritual centers have opened in our midst—one at the old Smith Farm in New Kingston—and there is a growing interest in the sweat lodge and other Native American avenues of spiritual growth.

Sometimes this serious interest in the power of Native culture and the symbolic use of Native American artifacts and imagery merge. Such was the case recently in Arkville where the wilderness symbols of fire, forest, feather and fur were put to use in a symbolic initiation called "Ooga Booga." Conducted by the campfire as dusk descends on the forest, "Oooga Booga" is a rite created by flint nappers, men and women who work flint into arrowheads in the manner of the native people. One need not be a napper to be an Oooga Booga, but one must recognize the value of Native symbolism in the creation of community in harmony with the natural world.

Such community and harmony have long been important Catskill Mountain traits, as Don Bouton's book make abundantly clear. Oh, how do you put a shoe on a cow? Very carefully.

Mountain Tanning

MY FATHER was in the leather trade. His narrow wooden warehouse and office was on Gold Street, downtown by the Brooklyn Bridge, in an area of Manhattan known as the Swamp, because it had once been marshland. As a small boy exploring piles of soles and heels and leather strapping, I never imagined the connection between that place in the city and my future home here in the Catskills.

While the Swamp was the national center of leather manufacturing and sale, the Catskills were the nineteenth-century center of the tanning industry, a fact that had a profound effect on the nature of our mountain environment.

The preparation of animal hides for human use has a history that goes back to the beginning of recorded time. Skins were scraped, trampled upon, stretched, soaked, and smoked to make them pliable, durable, and useful. The ancient Hebrews discovered that soaking hides in a mixture of water and crushed oak bark made a permanent, heavy, pliable leather. That ancient method became the standard for a millennium or two.

In 1800, Sir Humphrey Davy, an Englishman, conducted a series of industrial experiments to find alternate vegetable products that could be used to tan leather. Among other vegetable agents, Davy discovered that hemlock bark contained sufficient tannins to make durable leather.

Oak trees tend to grow in mixed deciduous forests: a couple of oaks, a few maples, some beech, a varied bunch. That reality made oak tanning necessarily a small scale operation, often a backyard cottage industry. Hemlock, on the other hand, grows in extensive stands, its dense low-hanging canopy blocking the light, preventing other plant species from encroaching on the hemlocks' territory.

When Hendrick Hudson's men first saw the Catskills from the river, they called them the Blue Mountains, the extensive hemlock cover of our hills giving them a decidedly blue cast. The Catskills were full of hemlock, and entrepreneurs from the Swamp—long before my Dad —descended on the Catskills to take advantage of the plentiful hemlock so close to the city.

Their business plan was simple: bring the hides to the hemlock, using the Hudson River to transport raw animal skins to the mountains, many imported from as far away as South America. Once processed, the tanned leather would be transported downriver to the Swamp for manufacture and sale.

The first Catskill tanneries were established in 1817. Jonathan Palen set up a large tannery on the Kaaterskill Creek in Greene County, on a site that took advantage of both the hemlock forest and the stream's waterpower for grinding the bark. The ground bark was mixed with water. Scraped hides, hairless, were soaked in that mixture, often warmed by wood fires to release the tannins, creating a hard, tough leather. That tannery operated until the 1850s. Today Palenville marks the site.

Colonel William Edwards also established a tannery in 1817 on the Schoharie Creek, the town that developed around his operation first called Edwardsville and later Hunter. Other tanneries popped up in Tannersville (duh!) and Haines Falls.

Later, when the hemlock was used-up on the Schoharie, Colonel Edwards built a "Bark Road" through the Stony Clove to get at the Hemlock that grew to his south. That Bark Road has become State Route 214 today.

The champion tanner, of course, was Zadock Pratt, who, in 1825, established his massive tannery on the Schoharie Creek in the place now called Prattsville. Pratt had grown up in the business, working in his father's tannery, and operating, in partnership with his brothers, a small tannery in Lexington. His new operation was designed to be on an unprecedented scale, a kind of Wal-Mart of tanneries, with 300 soaking vats and a mill that ground a cord of hemlock bark an hour. In the twenty years Pratt operated his tannery he processed over a half million hides.

By the 1850s, over 250 tanneries operated in the mountains.

The tanners decimated the hemlock forest. Bark peeling could only be done in the spring, when the connecting tissue between bark and wood was weak. Bark peelers would take to the woods for a month or two at a time, building hemlock huts from the denuded logs their peeling created, working from first light to last. It was hard, dirty, and odiferous work; it's said one would smell a bark-peeler before one could see him.

While they seldom clear-cut, cutting and peeling only the largest trees, bark-peelers left the forest full of downed wood debris, inviting fire and rotting wood. Twenty years or so of working a hemlock woods led to depletion of the resource, deforestation, and a second-growth forest that was quite different from the first. The Civil War created strong demand for hemlock-tanned leather, a red, waterproof, hard material suitable for rough use in boots and saddles. By the 1870s the hemlock was pretty well gone.

Soon after, an American chemist discovered that chromium salts made an excellent tanning agent, and the demand for bark diminished. Business continued in the Swamp, but the Catskills were no longer blue.

Manor Houses

THE CATSKILLS were once an experiment in American feudalism. The experiment failed, thankfully, but it is useful to remember that many of our homes, fields, woods and farms were once the property of fabulously wealthy men who rented out parts of their great estates to tenants, who owed them yearly payment in both goods and service.

The 2,000,000 acre Hardenbergh Patent, granted to Johannis Hardenbergh by Queen Anne in 1708, stretched from the Rondout Creek to the West Branch of the Delaware, from Albany County in the north to a line somewhere around present-day Monticello in the south. Bought up by the Livingston family in the middle 1700s, the patent was divided into a number of Great Lots, each owned by a family member or business associate.

Often, the proprietor of that multi-thousand-acre Great Lot would build a house to serve both as the proprietor's residence when in the mountains, and as the central point of authority for the rented lands that surrounded it. The Armstrong house in present-day Fleischmanns, now the property of the Moshe Y'oel Yeshiva, was such a great house for the 8000-acre Armstrong Tract.

I understand the original big house on Lake Delaware, between Bovina and Delhi, has been torn down. I believe Livingston descendents still own a portion of the estate that was once the center of the Great Lot in that part of the mountains. Edward Livingston's big house once stood just east of Arkville, on land across Route 28 from DeBari's carpet store. It's said that Livingston lost that property to a French count in a New Orleans card game. Later, the house became the Locust Grove Hotel.

A trip up Route 30 to the Lansing Manor in Schoharie County can take us back in time to see what a great house was like in the days of the patent-owners. Owned and operated by the New York State Power Authority, Lansing Manor is on the same parcel as the Blenheim-Gilboa Power Project Visitors Center. It makes a great destination for an afternoon day-trip, particularly with children as summer wanes and they prepare to return to school. The promise of a swim at the Minekill State Park pool next door might add a little inducement.

Lansing Manor was the manor house of the 40,000-acre Blenheim Patent, granted in 1769 to John Weatherhead, an English civil servant, by King George III. Weatherhead never made it to his American lands, which passed into the hands of John Lansing at the time of the Revolution.

John Lansing was a prominent Albany lawyer, a delegate to the 1787 Constitutional Convention in Philadelphia and to the State Ratification Convention the following year. He went on to become the chief judge of the New York State Supreme Court.

Lansing built his manor house in 1819 for his daughter, Frances, and son-in-law Jacob Livingston Sutherland. (Man, those Livingstons were everywhere!) Interestingly, Judge Lansing himself disappeared one December night in New York City, where he had gone on business. Leaving his hotel at nine in the evening, he never returned. His disappearance caused a sensation. It's believed he was murdered, perhaps by political adversaries.

Lansing Manor is a grand and beautiful home. One enters an entrance hall lined with family portraits and framed documents, including the original deed for the 40,000-acre Blenheim Patent. A ladies' parlor, gentlemen's library, and drawing room are furnished both with original Sutherland pieces and period furniture. It's the 1840s all over again!

Upstairs, the master bedroom contains a big canopy bed and large chests of drawers, one original to the house. A nursery, girls' bedroom, and a boys' room give us an idea of how prosperous children lived back in the day. In one upstairs room, a table is set for a meal. Children, in those days, were to be seen and not heard, which meant that they often ate upstairs with a governess, rather than downstairs with their parents.

The coolest part of the house, both literally and figuratively, is the cellar, dominated by a large brick and stucco walled kitchen. All the cooking was done in the open fireplace. The original iron crane-work still holds big iron kettles and pots which would simmer or boil over the log fire. A brick oven to the side of the hearth was used for baking.

A long plank farm table holds a variety of implements used for food preparation. Other tools, including a tin sausage stuffer, are in the adjoining pantry. Down a basement corridor is a cozy family dining room with a wine cellar next door.

The Sutherland family stopped collecting rents before most of their fellow patentees did, but, sadly, they continued to hold slaves even after emancipation came to New York in the late 1820s. Jacob Sutherland died in 1845 and the property was soon sold to the Spring family who used it as a dairy farm. The Visitors' Center is in the large dairy barn they built.

In 1911, Floyd Mattice bought the farm from Edmund Spring. His son sold it to the Power Authority in 1971 and six years later the house was reborn as the Manor house it was built to be. We're lucky to have it.

The 3500 Club

WHAT'S the highest mountain in the Catskills? How many Catskill peaks exceed 3500 feet? How many people have climbed them all?

The answers to these questions are tied up with the Catskill 3500 Club, the leading hiking organization devoted specifically to climbing our mountains. Founded in 1962, the Catskill 3500 Club is open to anyone who meets the club's strenuous requirements of outdoor accomplishment.

An aspirant for membership must reach the summit of all 35 Catskill peaks over 3500 feet in elevation and must make a second winter climb of four mountains: Balsam, Panther, Blackhead, and 4180-foot Slide Mountain, the highest peak in the Catskills. At last report there are 1700 members.

The club actually grew out of concern not for hiking and mountain climbing but bird-watching. In the early sixties, Dan Smiley, scion of the family that founded the Mohonk Mountain House in New Paltz, was studying the Bicknell's thrush, a bird difficult to find because of its choice of summer habitat: balsam fir at elevations over 3500 feet. To locate specimens of the thrush, Smiley and his fellow birders compiled a list of peaks over 3500 feet.

Now, it is not as easy as it might seem to determine which mountains meet that 3500 foot standard. Multiple peaks in close proximity might be considered one mountain or several. Smiley's bird-watching list contained 32 Catskill Mountains determined to meet the standard. The list was published in a nature journal.

It was then that hikers saw their opportunity. Bill Spangenberger, President of the Cornell Steamboat Company, and his wife Kay, a New York editor, had first broached the idea of forming a Catskill Mountain climbing club as early as 1948. They wanted to do something similar to the Adirondack Forty-Sixers, a club organized that year for hikers who had climbed all 46 Adirondack peaks over 4000 feet. The smaller Catskills would require a 500 foot reduction in elevation.

The Spangenbergers climbed all the peaks they could find, but were unable to develop any sustained interest from others. In 1962, Bill climbed Doubletop Mountain with Brad Whiting, chair of the Mid-Hudson Chapter of the Adirondack Mountain Club. Inspired by the Smiley bird-watching list, Whiting suggested the formation of a high peak climbing club. The Catskill 3500 Club was born.

Scene at Big Indian with Balsam Mountain., 3619 ft., in background.

The list of eligible peaks was refined through the adoption of criteria established by the Adirondack group. To qualify as a separate summit, a mountain must be either one-half mile from a neighboring summit or must have a 250 foot drop between peaks. Using this standard, the club identified 34 Catskill Mountains over 3500 feet. In 1990, the previously unnamed Southwest Hunter Mountain was added to the list by membership vote, bringing the total to 35.

Wanting to encourage winter hiking, the founders of the club added a wrinkle that is unique among Northeastern climbing clubs: the winter climb requirement. Aspirants for membership must climb the four above named peaks between December 21 and March 21 for a total of 39 climbs. Canisters are hung in trees at the summits of several mountains so climbers can sign-in to prove their accomplishment.

To get the club off the ground, the founders offered charter membership to anyone who made the required climbs before the end of 1965. There are 27 charter members including Father Ray Donahue, former pastor of the Downsville and Margaretville Episcopal Churches, who brought attention to the club to many climbers in the central Catskills.

The Catskill high peaks are divided up into three regions: northern peaks, central peaks, and southern peaks. Hunter Mountain at 4040 feet is the highest of the 15 northern peaks, with 3980-foot Black Dome, 3940-foot Thomas Cole, and 3890-foot Blackhead Mountain not far behind.

Among the central high peaks, 3868-foot Graham Mountain and 3860-foot Doubletop are the highest of a group of 11 mountains that includes Panther Mountain, Balsam Mountain, Big Indian Mountain and Halcott Mountain.

In the southern Catskills, Slide, Cornell, and Wittenberg Mountains are contiguous and Peekamoose and Table Mountains are nearby. All exceed 3750 feet.

Fourteen of the 35 high peaks are trail-less, meaning climbers must bushwhack through the brush to find the summit. Members are prohibited from marking their way up, in order to allow the next climber to make a trail-less climb.

Want to become an aspirant for Catskill 3500 Club membership? You can download an Aspirant Registration Form at www.catskill-3500-club.org. Subscribe to their quarterly newsletter "The Canister" for $10 and reduce your eventual membership registration to $5 when you complete your 39 hikes.

An annual membership dinner is held every April. There, new members receive a card, certificate and blue and yellow hiker's patch reflective of their climbing accomplishment. Interested?

Jay Gould of Roxbury

JAY GOULD'S REPUTATION IN HISTORY was shaped on September 24, 1869, one of several "Black Fridays" in American financial history, this one a day when the price of gold dropped over 20% from $169 to $135 an ounce. Gould, President of the Eire Railroad, and his partner, Jim Fisk, had begun buying gold in August of that year in an attempt, it was said, to corner the gold market. When the price fell, Jay Gould took much of the blame.

His reputation wasn't enhanced two years later when he posted bond for the jailed Tammany Hall political leader, Boss Tweed, or three years later when English bondholders in the railway forced him out as president over accusations the Eire Railroad had issued fraudulent securities.

Gould died of TB in 1892 at age 56. Had he lived as long as his contemporaries—men like Andrew Carnegie and John D. Rockefeller—he might have been able to give away enough money to restore his reputation, at least a bit. Modern biographers like Edward Renehan (*The Dark Genius of Wall Street: The Misunderstood Life of Jay Gould, King of the Robber Barons, New York*: Basic Books, 2005) have re-evaluated Gould's business career, finding constructive results despite questionable methods.

In the late 1870s, Gould bounced back from losing the Eire when he gained control over the Union Pacific and Missouri Pacific Railroads, among others. By 1881, he controlled over 10,000 miles of track, 15% of total American mileage at the time, and he held a controlling interest in the Western Union telegraph company and in New York City's elevated railways. At his death, his wealth was estimated at 72 million dollars, billions in today's money.

Jason "Jay" Gould was a son of the Catskills, born May 27, 1836 on his family's West Settlement farm in Roxbury. The house is still there. His father, farmer John Burr Gould, was also born in Roxbury, 44 years earlier, son of a sea captain and grandson of a soldier killed in the Revolutionary War. Jay Gould's mother, Mary More Gould, was a descendent of the founders of Moresville, today's Grand Gorge.

The youngest of five children, little Jay was a gifted scholar, first at the Meeker Hollow school, then at a school over the hill in Hobart, and finally at the Beachwood Seminary a half mile below the family farm. There, he was a classmate and friend of the young John Burroughs, and a student of James Oliver, the inspirational schoolteacher who profoundly influenced both boys.

Jay Gould's first business venture, at age 16, was a partnership with his father in a corner hardware store in Roxbury. Today, an art gallery occupies the store. Jay kept the business ledger and was the firm's buyer, traveling to Albany and New York City to procure the inventory.

Always fascinated with geometry and logarithms, young Jay, in 1852, contracted to survey Ulster County. From that experience, Gould decided to make and market his own maps. After a couple semesters studying at Albany Academy, he conducted a survey of Delaware County, having hired a couple of surveyors to facilitate the job, and created a detailed map of the county. An original Jay Gould map is a collector's item today. Several hang in Delaware County public buildings, one in the former Superintendent's Office at Margaretville Central School.

In 1855, Gould wrote a history of Delaware County, losing the first completed manuscript in a fire, and re-writing the entire thing. The following year, he entered into partnership with Zadock Pratt in establishing a tannery in Pennsylvania in a town that soon became known as Gouldsboro, down around Stroudsburg.

Gould was in the tanning business for four years, managing the rural tanning end of the business while associates in New York City procured the hides and found buyers for the finished leather. He also got involved in the lumber business and in banking.

In 1863, Jay Gould married Helen Day Miller. Through his father-in-law, Daniel S. Miller, Gould became manager of the Rensselaer & Saratoga Railway, which he soon bought and re-organized. He soon added the Rutland & Washington Railway to his portfolio, selling both at a handsome profit, before moving to New York City where he began to buy and sell railroad stocks. It was then that he entered American history.

Jay and Helen Gould presided over one of America's castles, Lyndhurst, down in Westchester County, where they raised their five children: George, Edwin, Helen, Anna, and Frank. But home for Jay Gould always meant Roxbury. Soon after he died, on December 2, 1892, his children built Roxbury's Jay Gould Memorial Reformed Church in his memory.

Perhaps, Gould's reputation was best characterized by his boyhood friend, naturalist John Burroughs. "Jay has got himself a whole lot of enemies," Burroughs wrote his father in 1871 at the height of Gould's notoriety, "Everybody seems to think he is the worst kind of man since Judas. I tell them he ain't nearly so bad as is made out. But nobody listens."

Dr. Orson M. Allaben

IN THE YEAR 2000, the Village of Margaretville marked the 125th anniversary of the incorporation of the village with a celebration at the old Margaretville pavilion. I served as master of ceremonies, the first choice for the job having turned it down. My role was to make some introductory remarks and introduce the various dignitaries who would offer their own comments. We'd then enjoy some food, beverage, and neighborly conversation.

What do you talk about when trying to sum-up 125 years of community life? Being a guy who likes to understand the history of things, I did a little research into the history of Margaretville. That's when I discovered Dr. Orson M. Allaben, one of those people few remember but to whom many are indebted.

Orson Allaben was born on August 5, 1808, in what was then the Town of

Delhi, today the Town of Hamden, on a farm in what is now the hamlet of DeLancey.

When he was a year old, his father moved to a farm in the Town of Roxbury where little Orson attended the district school. He was a good student, and, evidently, a good farm hand, as well.

When Allaben was 16, he suffered an accident on the farm which made manual labor difficult for him. So, he became a school teacher, working for the next several years in one-room school houses. When he was 19, Orson decided he wanted to be a doctor. He went to work in the office of Dr. Cowles in Roxbury. In those days of primitive medicine, an apprenticeship with a physician was an acceptable entry to the study of medicine and surgery. But young Orson wanted more: he wanted to go to medical school.

Medical school required a knowledge of Latin, a subject generally unavailable in the one-room grammar schools of the day. So, Allaben left Roxbury for Delhi where he attended the Delaware Academy until he had mastered enough Latin to qualify for medical school. He was accepted at the Waterville Medical College in Waterville, Maine. Off, he went.

When I started teaching in Margaretville in the early 1970s, I met a number of kids who had never been much out of the mountains. Imagine what it must have been for a kid born in DeLancey, raised in Roxbury, a farm boy for whom study in Delhi was an adventure, to go off to Maine, of all places, to become the doctor he dreamed of being. He arrived in Waterville in November 1827, pursued his studies there for four years, and got his M.D. in June 1831.

Dr. Cowles having the medical franchise in Roxbury, the new Dr. Allaben settled instead in the Town of Middletown, next door. He established his practice, and, in October 1832, married Thankful Dimmick, daughter of Noah Dimmick who owned the sawmill and tavern in what was then called Dean's Corner's. It was that tavern that gave Arkville its name. During an autumn flood—a "pumpkin freshet"—the low-lying ground filled with floodwaters, leaving Dimmick's tavern on the hill the only dry spot. "Look at Noah's ark, above the waters," people said, and Arkville was born.

Dr. Allaben quickly became a respected member of his new, albeit very small, community. He was elected Supervisor of the Town of Middletown in 1839 as a Democrat. The following year he was elected to the State Assembly. In 1843, Dr. and Mrs. Allaben moved to the place on the East Branch of the Delaware where the Binnekill branches out, the spot that is today the Village of Margaretville. At the time, there were only three buildings there.

In 1846, Allaben built his house, a house on the corner of present-day Main Street and Walnut Street where he was to practice medicine for the next 45 years. The following year, he opened a store there, the first store in the new hamlet. In 1848, Dr. Allaben traveled to Washington at his own expense to petition for the establishment of a post office. He served several times as postmaster.

Orson M. Allaben served as supervisor of the Town of Middletown for seven terms. He was a New York State Senator in 1864-65, established the first school in town, and on July 7, 1863, began publication of *The Utilitarian*, the first newspaper in town and a precursor of the *Catskill Mountain News*. In 1871, he procured the necessary legislation for the establishment of the Ulster & Delaware Railroad, just as, in 1840, he had procured the legislation for a turnpike from the Ulster County line to Delhi.

In 1875, Dr. Orson M. Allaben was a leader in the call for the incorporation of the Village of Margaretville, and served as the third president, or mayor, of the village. In 1876, he was a delegate to the Democratic National Convention that nominated for president New York Governor Samuel Tilden.

He helped establish the old Margaretville Fair by purchasing 26 acres of land on what is today called Fair Street. In 1889, the Catskill Mountain Agricultural Society had its first fair in the last week of August, with O. M. Allaben serving as president.

Dr. Orson M. Allaben died in 1892, 61 years after he established his medical practice in the village that he, more than any other individual, helped create: Margaretville. He is buried on the hill in the old Margaretville Cemetery.

American Presidents Around the Catskills

I HAVE ON MY COMPUTER A PHOTO, sent to me by a friend, of former President Bill Clinton, his wife, then the junior senator from New York, and Ike Phillips of Woodstock radio station WDST standing in a crowd of onlookers on Tinker Street in Woodstock. The former president and the senator came to the Catskills in August in an unannounced visit that was a surprise to most of us and a mountain vacation for them.

The first reports of the Clintons' upstate vacation appeared on August 13 when the couple ate lunch at the Beekman Arms Tavern in Rhinebeck. The next day they appeared, unannounced, in the Corner Cupboard in Woodstock for coffee, and then took a walk along Tinker Street, taking in the sights, as so many Catskill Mountain tourists—and residents—do. That's when Ike caught up with them.

They stayed overnight in Shandaken at the Emerson Inn. I understand the former first couple had the premier accommodations of the Inn: the Imperial Suite, a luxury duplex that normally rents for a gazillion dollars a night, although I certainly have no inside information as to their personal arrangements. If I were the innkeeper, I'd probably put them up for free.

That's because the accommodation of a president can be a publicity bonanza. When I arrived in the Catskills over 35 years ago, the Delaware Inn in Stamford was on its last legs, a run down "hotel" that was, by that point, really a neighborhood bar and grill. Yet a sign outside still proudly proclaimed, "Teddy Roosevelt slept here". The 26tth President, who served in the White House from 1901 to 1909, actually stayed in Stamford in the 1880s when he was a young state assemblyman, but a president is a president in hindsight.

In the late 1980s, my boss, the principal at Margaretville Central School, arrived to work one Monday morning excitedly asking each person she saw, "Guess who was in church with us yesterday? Jimmy Carter!" The former President, a dedicated fly fisherman, was fishing the Beaverkill, and Sunday morning. He and his wife attended the little church that serves that valley. I don't think there's a sign there saying "Jimmy Carter worshipped here."

There are few celebrities that have the cachet of a president. One who did was Babe Ruth. Both the Andes Hotel—still doing a brisk business—and the recently demolished Phoenicia Hotel, boasted of visits by the Babe, who frequented the Catskills to hunt and drink. The Babe understood his celebrity. When told by Yankee management that the post-market-crash salary he was demanding was more than President Hoover made, the Babe famously replied, "I had a better year than he did."

We've never had a Catskill Mountain resident as President, although a couple of our close neighbors held the post. Martin Van Buren, "The Little Magician" of Kinderhook, just across the river, was our eighth President, serving from 1837 to 1841. Van Buren learned his politics in the tavern his father ran on the Albany Post Road, a popular way station for state politicians traveling between New York City and Albany. It was even rumored that he was actually the secret son of Aaron Burr, America's third Vice-President, a rumor that author Gore Vidal put to use in his novel *Burr*. After serving in the White House, Van Buren retired to a grand house he purchased for his retirement, a house he called Lindenwold, which is open on State Route 9H for sightseers today.

Sightseeing at the home of our other neighbor President was reported to be one of the things that drew the Clintons to our region. President Franklin Roosevelt's home in Hyde Park is one of Bill Clinton's favorite spots. As President, he made three visits there, including a 1995 meeting with Russian President Boris Yeltsin.

FDR, a life-long country squire on his Duchess County farm, began his political career running successfully for the State Senate in our across-the-river neighboring county, and returned to Hyde Park whenever he could as governor form 1929 to 32 and president from 1933 to his death in 1945. He was a real upstate guy.

Perhaps, our Catskills came closest to having a president during the run-up to the 1956 Democratic Convention when New York Governor Averill Harriman was a candidate for his party's nomination. Harriman's family owned the Gerry Estate, Broadlands, in Lake Delaware, and he was a frequent second-home resident in the Catskills, particularly during ski season when he often skied Belleayre. Harriman had the important support of former President Harry Truman, but dropped out of the race before the convention.

Maybe there is a boy or a girl in one of our Catskill Mountain schools who will be president one day. Then we can create a sign that says "Home of the President of the United States."

Mountain Drovers

UNDERNEATH STATE ROUTE 28, between Margaretville and Arkville, where the Hess gas station and convenience store and the Delaware National Bank stand on one side of the road and the Meadows Golf Center on the other, is a cow pass. A cow pass is a tunnel, and this one, back in the fifties and sixties, allowed Glen Vermilyea's cows to cross safely from the barn on the south side of the road to the pasture on the north side. I walked through it not long ago, although I'm guessing I probably wasn't supposed to be in there. I'd plead research!

When that cow pass was built, it was a major safety improvement, keeping cattle off the state highway. The Delaware County Catskills were dairy country. It was common, well into the 1970s, for motorists to have to wait patiently while a herd of cows crossed the road in front of them. Any travel at milking time was bound to be so delayed.

The widespread proliferation of dairy farms began to wane when the processors and the state mandated farmers change from milk cans to sanitary bulk-tanks to store their product on the farm. Many small operators couldn't afford the expensive new equipment the changeover entailed. The number of farms further shrank with a government buy-out program in the early 1980s. President Reagan's supply-side economics sought to raise farmers' income by reducing the overall national supply of milk. The government bought herds for shipment to impoverished areas overseas. Rumor had it that a milk cow, at the time, was worth more as a MacDonald's hamburger than as a local income producer. Many Catskill Mountain farmers sold their herds and sought another line of work.

Sheep once dotted the Catskill Mountain landscape.

But, once, these mountains were redolent with the smell of cattle. Mountains and hillsides that are heavily forested today were, not too many years ago, cleared to the summit for pasture and hay. I remember a trip to the Adirondacks in the early 1970s when my overall impression was the profound difference between the two New York State mountain regions: the Adirondacks wild and heavily forested, the Catskills extensively "meadowed" and agricultural.

In the late 1800s and early 1900s, the Delaware County Catskills were a major producer of cattle and sheep for sale in distant markets. Every other summer Tuesday, a cattle train would travel the Ulster & Delaware rail line picking up cattle in Stamford, Hobart, Arkville and other rural stops, to go to market. Sometimes the train would be comprised of as many as fourteen cattle cars, some double deck. That's a lot of livestock!

In 1958, the late Jeanne Palen interviewed her uncle, Jimmy Winter, the last of the Catskill Mountain drovers, the men who gathered and drove those herds of cattle from the farms of the sellers to the train, and from the train to the buyers.

Jeanne Palen was born and raised in little agricultural New Kingston, the only child of Ruthven and Lillian Robertson, went to nursing school in Poughkeepsie, worked at the old Margaretville Hospital, and married Dr. Gilbert Palen, the surgeon and general practitioner after whom the Margaretville Family Health Center's building is named.

Jimmy Winter and his brother Frank took over the droving business their father, Rob Winter, started in New Kingston in 1876. The Winter boys gathered stock from surrounding farms in the valley and from places like Bovina and Dingle Hill, keeping the animals in a large pen located next to New Kingston's general store. From there, they would drive the cattle or sheep along the road to the train station at Arkville.

"I've often taken cattle as far as Connecticut," Jimmy Winter told his niece. "You could always sell cows there for a good price. The trip took five days. We'd start out early in the morning from New Kingston with a big drove, and by night we'd be in Pine Hill, 23 miles away. There'd be four or five of us along, and the roads were not too good. It was hot and dusty in the summer, and the mud was deep in the spring."

Jimmy Winter was born in 1864 and died in 1958. He told his niece that farmers, in the old days, kept summer cows which they bred in the fall. Once breeding was done, bulls were sold for slaughter. "I remember when our yard in New Kingston was packed with nothing but bulls," he told her. "Some were so vicious that we had to blindfold them to drive them along the road." Move over Pamplona!

Once the cattle reached the train in Arkville, the drovers would ride with them to Kingston, in order to make the last leg of the trip to Connecticut or another final destination. "I've driven many a herd right down the middle of Broadway in Kingston," Jimmy Winter boasted. "I'd like to see you try it today!"

Jimmy Winter was 43 years old when he made his last drove. "The last bunch went in 1905," he remembered at the end of his life. "That was the end of the drovers' business around here." He never explained why.

Today, New Kingston's Winter Hollow memorializes his family's name, and the redoubtable Fran Faulkner, provider of the Jeanne Palen interview, keeps his, and her valley's, history alive.

Slabsides and Woodchuck Lodge

A COUPLE OF WEEKS AGO, coming home from a visit with a friend in the Hudson Valley, I visited Slabsides. Slabsides was the Hudson Valley woodland retreat of naturalist and essayist John Burroughs, the Roxbury boy who left our mountains to seek his fortune in the middle of the nineteenth century and became an icon to millions of nature-observant spiritual seekers at the beginning of the twentieth. His picture hangs on the wall behind me as I write this.

I hadn't been to Slabsides in years, since the time, years ago, when my friend and teaching colleague, Nat Ciccone, and I invaded the semi-annual Slabsides Day celebration with an early shoulder-mounted VHS style video camera and microphone, intent on making *Slabsides: The Movie*, a projected teaching aid for school. Our bulky equipment and seemingly presumptuous manner turned us into a spectacle and led to an embarrassing moment or two—the country bumpkins among the urbane, knowing, and confident Burroughs in-crowd.

That's a feeling John himself must have felt a few times when he left his native Catskills with his wife Ursula in the middle 1860s to seek employment in wartime Washington. He was a country kid, an aspiring writer who had published a couple of essays so close in style and subject to those of Ralph Waldo Emerson that he was once suspected of plagiarism. Having spent his entire life in the Catskills, John wanted to be a poet in the wider world. He had published one good poem, "Waiting," which contains the line that, years later, became his epitaph: "I stand amid the eternal ways, / And what is mine shall know my face."

Burroughs chose Washington not only because steady government employment was available there, but also because his literary hero, Walt Whitman, lived there. Burroughs had read Whitman's revolutionary American poem *Leaves of Grass*, and wanted to meet the poet who seemed to speak so eloquently in the language of the common person. He did. They became fast friends, John and Walt, and it was Whitman who told Burroughs, "Publish your personality," a bit of oblique wisdom that took the country boy a while to figure out. Write about what you know and love: in Burroughs' case, the outdoors, the mountains, meadows, woods, and streams, birds and fishes that he knew so well. He went on to create and master the nature essay.

In 1874, John got himself transferred closer to home as a Treasury Department bank examiner for upstate New York. He and Ursula bought a fruit and berry farm on the Hudson River in West Park, Town of Esopus, Ulster County. They built a home there, which they called Riverby. The Burroughs had a difficult marriage, held together largely by their shared devotion to their son Julian, born in 1878.

**John Burroughs, his fur coat,
and his Woodchuck Lodge.**

It was that difficult marriage that led to Slabsides. Ursula and John had trouble occupying the same space. She was a meticulous housekeeper, a tough taskmaster, and did not support or understand John's preoccupation with writing.

He tended to neglect household tasks, and seemed, somehow, less than properly presentable. Bad marriages often lead to unintended good results. Perhaps, we owe Ursula a debt of gratitude for driving her husband ever outward, toward nature, away from her. John kept building retreats farther and farther away from his wife.

First, he built "The Bark Study," a small outbuilding near the family home where he would go to write. When Julian was 16, he and his father built Slabsides, a mile or so distant from the house, up-hill from the river, in a rock-ledged boggy ravine, next to a celery garden. Visiting Slabsides today, one is impressed by the sheer isolation of the one-and-a-half story rustic house which appears suddenly to the eye as one approaches up a sloping path into a rocky crag of forest. The house gets its name from its siding; row upon row of tree-slabs give it an organic look.

Roxbury's Woodchuck Lodge may also owe its interesting history to the Burroughs' difficult marriage. With Julian grown and off to college, John, perhaps, felt free to wander farther a-field in his search for pleasant surroundings away from his wife. Around the turn of the century, he obtained an old tenant house on the family farm in Roxbury, then owned and operated by his brother Curtis. John redid the house in his signature rustic style, renamed it Woodchuck Lodge, and used it from 1910 to 1920 as his regular summer home and sometime retreat.

Woodchuck Lodge has faced some tough times lately. The five member Board of Trustees, led by its able board President, Diane Galusha, strives mightily to maintain the building, but nature seems to get in the way. Last winter, a tree fell through the roof. Structural repairs are needed. Money is tight. (I should tell you: I, too, am a member of that board.) Necessary maintenance and repair projects go undone because they are unfunded. Donations to support Woodchuck Lodge, Inc. are gratefully received at Box 492, Roxbury, NY 12474. (Shameless, aren't I?)

And Slabsides? That seems to be on firmer financial footing, from the looks of the building and the property the other day. Slabsides is worth a visit. Travel south on Route 9W from Kingston until you get to West Park. Follow the signs directing you to turn right just beyond the Holy Cross Monastery. Slabsides is open only twice a year: the first Saturday in May and the first Saturday in October.

Leave behind the VHS camera and the microphone.

Delhi and Tannersville's Candace Wheeler

A COUPLE OF YEARS AGO, I drove out to Lenox, Massachusetts, in our neighboring Berkshires, to visit The Mount, the magnificent summer mansion and gardens of Edith Wharton. Wharton, who lived from the 1860s to the 1930s, was a major American writer, the author of over a dozen novels, including The House of Mirth, a great book, and *The Age of Innocence*, an important novel that, fifteen years ago, was turned into a big movie by director Martin Scorsese.

I was surprised to discover that this writer of fiction chronicling the lives of the wealthy old-money society families of nineteenth-century New York got her start in interior decoration. Wharton's first book was The Decoration of Houses, a book that argued for simplicity, balance, and architectural harmony in interior design, a break from the heavy-handed over-dressed rooms of the Victorian Age. Her design ideas seemed fresh and modern at the beginning of a new century and Wharton used interior design to help usher in a more modern age.

It turns out that Edith Wharton was not alone among wealthy society women who turned to the decoration of homes as a way to achieve social and cultural change. Another was Candace Wheeler.

Candace Wheeler was born on a farm in Delhi in 1827, one of eight children of a Delaware County farmer and cap-maker named Thurber. It is said she learned the arts of the home-spun age at home: spinning thread, weaving cloth, sewing and knitting clothes and household linens in domestic manufacture. By the age of 17 she was married to Thomas Wheeler and living in New York City. Mr. Wheeler must have been pretty successful because, by 1854, the couple had a house out in Jamaica, Queens, a house named *Nestledown* (if a house has a name, it must be quite a place).

They also had two children, and Candace Thurber Wheeler devoted much of her considerable energy to motherhood. By the 1860s, though, she had time to take art lessons from George Henry Hall, a prominent American painter of the romantic Pre-Raphaelite school. After the Civil War, the Wheelers traveled widely in Europe, and Candace may have taken more art classes in Germany.

Her story sounds familiar: a talented, ambitious, and energetic woman seeking an opening to express her energy to the world. Almost. Almost. Then, at age 49, Candace Wheeler's life was changed by an exhibit at the 1876 American Centennial Exhibition in Philadelphia. The English Royal School of Art Needlework presented an exhibition of artistic needlework done by underemployed, economically strapped, middle-class English women who had been taught how to turn the arts of domestic manufacture into cold, hard cash.

Candace Wheeler saw the opportunity to help American women in the same way, to provide an economic outlet for the creative energies of women, and seek commercial value for "women's work." In 1877, she founded the Society of Decorative Art of New York to "encourage profitable industries among women who possess artistic talent and to furnish. . .a market for their work".

Within a couple of years, the Society was something of a rage, having mounted a very successful, and well-connected, exhibition of the decorative arts in New York and having spawned related societies in Chicago; St. Louis; Hartford; Charleston, SC; and Troy, NY.

In 1879, Candace Wheeler went into business with Louis Comfort Tiffany, founding one of America's first firms in interior design: Louis C. Tiffany and Company Associated Artists. When the partnership dissolved in 1883, Wheeler took Associated Artists as the name of her firm, designing and producing demins, silks, velveteens, embroideries and taspestries, as well as providing interior design services.

She became not only a successful businessperson and social reformer, but an important textile artist, as well; important enough to get her own show at the Metropolitan Museum of Art in New York. Of course, that didn't come until years after her death in 1923. In October 2001, the Met mounted the exhibit *Candace Wheeler: The Art and Enterprise of American Design 1875-1900*.

In 1887, Candace Thurber Wheeler of Delhi returned to the Catskills when she and her brother bought 2000 acres just north of Tannersville for the summer retreat and artists' colony that became Onteora Park. Her privately printed 1914 book, *Annals of Onteora*, is posted online—you can read it on your computer screen. Readers will enjoy her description of looking for and finding the perfect mountain location to build her dream mountain house.

The Catskills had always had a place in Candace's imagination. As a child, the blue mountains in the distance "between our valley and the Hudson" were a place of romance, her "Delectable Mountains," named for a fictitious range in the only romance allowed in her father's austere puritan library. Her Delawares, as she called her native Delhi-area hills, were a western spur of the Catskills, and, building Onteora, she was going home.

Take a ride to Tannersville and turn left at the red light, up Route 23C. The road will wind up the hill, carrying you up the ridge to Onteora Park, a community of private homes where architecture, history, and great views merge. The park's stone church is particularly impressive.

Anti-Rent War (#1)

I AM LOOKING AT A MAP of the Catskill Mountains and Hudson Valley in 1750. The two-million-acre Hardenbergh Patent contains most of the Catskills, including half of Delaware, Greene, and Ulster Counties, and three-quarters of Sullivan. This huge land-grant, given to a group of speculators by Queen Anne in 1708, stretches from just southwest of the village of Catskill to just north of the village of Monticello, from the West Branch of the Delaware to just beyond today's Ashokan Reservoir.

The Hardenbergh Patent is merely the largest of dozens of land grants that appear on the map of colonial New York. I count 23 patents, 13 manors, and a host of tracts, forming a jig-saw puzzle of land ownership in New York province under British rule. Some seem familiar. Kingston Patent, Hurley's Patent, Marbletown Patent, Rochester Patent, and New Paltz Patent formed the basis of towns in our region. Other's seem a bit strange: Chesecock's Patent and Kakiate Patent don't exactly roll off the tongue.

This hodge-podge of patents, manors, and tracts came to dominate land-ownership patterns in New York due to several historic factors. The Dutch government claimed the lands Englishman Henry Hudson explored in 1609, an expedition financed and controlled by Dutch business interests. In order to spur development, the Dutch offered huge tracts of land to developers who would sponsor immigrants, foster settlement, and exploit the resources of the new world. Because the river was the center of the colony, land grants were long stretches of shoreline, typically many miles, and all the land beyond the river for miles and miles inland.

By far the largest of the Patroonships, as the Dutch called these huge estates, was Rensselaerwyck, granted by the Dutch government in 1629 to Killiaen Van Rensselaer, "Patroon of the North River of New Netherland." His manor stretched 24 miles "above and below Fort Orange, on both sides of the river." Fort Orange is today's Albany, and the Patroon's land comprised all of today's Albany and Rensselaer Counties, 726,000 acres.

The English conquered New Netherland in 1664, with a mostly bloodless show of force that led the practical Dutch to cut their losses and turn administration over to their more powerful rivals. The English King Charles, whose father had been beheaded in a rebellion fifteen years earlier, had recently been restored to the English throne after a period of puritan republican radicalism in London. He wasn't interested in New England-style colonial communities. He turned New Netherland over to his brother, James, the Duke of York. James appointed governors who sought to create an outpost in the New World that reflected the land-ownership patterns of the Old World.

A series of colonial governors converted the Dutch patroonships to English manors and granted manors and patents to one wealthy British aristocrat or striving wannabe after another. By 1698, a colonial official complained that, "This whole province is given away to about thirty persons."

The proprietors of these large tracts all agreed that their land would remain forever intact, never "alienated in fee simple," legalese for sold outright. Instead, a novel legal form was created: the "lease in fee," a perpetual lease that granted use of the land and inheritance rights for the settlers while maintaining the enduring ownership interest of the lord of the manor. Settlement terms were often attractive: the first seven years of rent was free, followed by an annual rent of, maybe 10 to 14 bushels of wheat per 100 acres farmed. Of course, the landlord retains all mineral rights and water rights forever.

By 1785, the price of wheat was high and land-hungry sons and daughters of New England farmers flocked into Albany, as many as 500 families a day, migrating to New York's wilderness looking for land. Like the adjustable rate sub-prime mortgages of our day, the proprietor's lease in fee was powerfully seductive—no money down, no payments for seven years, followed by a low, low annual fee, and wheat prices soaring! Lots of settlers settled on leaseholds, over 3000 on the Manor of Rensselaerwyck alone.

In fact, inspired by American republican principles and the smart-business desire to keep his tenants productive during a later period of falling wheat prices, Stephen Van Rensselaer III, had rarely collected rents from his tenants, many of whom were second or third generation on the same farm when Van Rensselaer III died January 26, 1839. His heirs, his two sons, were forced to begin rent collection that year, in order to pay the many debts the estate owed.

Lease-holding farmers had already suffered under the New York state-specific "lease-in-fee" legal justification of feudalism. They largely missed out, in the mid 1830s, on the growth opportunities provided by rising agricultural prices because their lack of clear land-title made it impossible to raise capital by mortgaging their land. This sudden collection of long-dormant rents was the last straw.

On the Fourth of July, 1839, tenant farmers in the Helderberg Mountain section of the Rensselaerwyck Manor held an angry assembly in the Albany County village of Berne. They published an Independence Day Proclamation, publically equating their lease-holds with "voluntary slavery" and proclaiming to the world, "we can no longer endure the infamy of tamely entailing upon future generations such wretchedness and unhallowed bondage as, inevitably, awaits them if we, any longer, submit ourselves to be thus unjustly, unrighteously, inhumanly oppressed and imposed upon."

The Anti-Rent War had begun. It would not end until our own Delaware County was in open insurrection.

Anti-Rent War (#2)

THE 1838 MID-TERM ELECTIONS were a real challenge for incumbent President Martin Van Buren and his Democratic Party. His party had been in power for the past ten years nationally, the past thirteen in the President's home state of New York, where Governor William Marcy, after whom the Adirondack's highest mountain would later be named, was running for re-election. But the economy was not in his favor.

The financial Panic of 1837 had spun the country into recession. For the first time in a long time the opposition was united in a strengthened Whig Party that was ready to compete for the votes of the "common man," votes the Jacksonian Democrats had always relied on.

In New York, the Whigs were led by William Seward, a thirty-seven year-old lawyer from Auburn who had been General Counsel for the Holland Land Company, a major developer of settlements in central and western New York.

Seward was a terrific speaker, inspirational to his many adherents, appealing, as he did, to their sense of idealism and hope. He espoused a forward-looking policy of government investment in internal improvements, government encouragement of commerce and credit, government-led social reform to encourage economic growth and equal opportunity.

This approach was in sharp contrast to the Democratic Party, which espoused traditional Jeffersonian republicanism: #1, the only legitimate function of government is the protection of individual rights, especially property rights, and #2, the best government governs least.

It was a shock when Seward beat Governor Marcy. He was sworn in as governor on January 1, addressing a joint session of the State Legislature later that day. In a State-of-the-State message that set the standard for those that came after, Seward proclaimed the responsibility of government to promote democracy and progress, even happiness and social enjoyment, to shape society according to "the democratic principle" and "the law of social improvement." All very idealistic: government activism on behalf of the little guy.

So, when the eighth patroon of the Manor of Rensselaerwyck, Stephen Van Rensselaer III, died 25 days later, and, seven months later, the tenant farmers of Albany County's Heldeberg Mountains held a Fourth of July Anti-Rent Rally to inaugurate a rent strike, Seward was kind of boxed in. He had publicly placed himself on the side of progress, change, and social equality. He was clearly sympathetic to the anti-rent side of this dispute. Yet, he had sworn to uphold the law. He couldn't, as governor, support the violation of law that a rent strike entails.

In September, mob violence in Albany County threatened rent collection agents, process servers, and law enforcement officers attempting to enforce the law. The Democratic county sheriff called for the governor to call out the state militia to protect him and his citizens' posse. Seward did so, but not without some political encouragement for the anti-rent forces.

Seward called for land reform. He asked the legislature to abolish the "lease in fee" that allowed landlords to keep a title interest in perpetually leased farms. But how do you take thousands of acres of land—property—from one class of citizens to give it to another? There was no legal procedure to do so. Developing a formula to transfer ownership to tenants and to compensate the landlords would take political negotiation and compromise.

And the Democratic Party was still smarting from their unaccustomed defeat at the polls at Seward's hands. They had long been the party of landowners and land wealth. The Democratic Party traditionally stood for the protection of property rights and the sanctity of private contractual arrangements, such as the legally executed contract between landlord and tenant. They had a dog in this fight, too.

Thus, the rent issue became a bit of a political football, and, over the next few years, the Whigs and the Democrats traded a few elections back and forth on either side of the issue; sometimes, probably, on both. With the political leaders unable to develop a political solution, the anti-rent troubles took to the streets.

Anti-Rent societies sprang up each of the affected counties, first in Albany County, then in Rensselaer and Columbia Counties, then in Schoharie County, and finally down into Delaware County where land on the East and West Branch-es of the Delaware River was still owned by landlords with names like Livingston and Montgomery and Lewis and Verplanck. Anti-Rent Societies were political action groups, whose members urged "Victory through the Ballot." They had meetings and officers and passed resolutions and worked for change.

But these political action groups had underground activists as well, men organized in local "tribes" who showed up at property auctions dressed in cali-co print "Indian dresses" wearing identity-hiding leather masks, harassing law enforcement, intimidating potential buyers from bidding on property being auc-tioned to cover the unpaid rent. The sheriff and collection agents would, at the landlord's compliant of unpaid past-due rent, arrive at the leasehold farm of the rent-striking tenant, to auction off livestock, farm implements, and other per-sonal property of the farmer to cover the amount of the rent owed.

These underground Calico Indians were generally some, although not all, of the members of the local Anti-Rent Society. When one "Indian" spotted law enforcement traveling to a striking farm, he would blow his tin horn, the kind previously used to call him in to dinner. One horn call would lead to another until the hills reverberated and the Indians would stealthily make their way to the auction site. Often their mere presence provided enough intimidation to stop the sale. Sometimes the horrible torture of tar and feathers was applied.

Until, one day in August 1845, their presence led to America's first notorious case of "Who shot the Sheriff?"—the climax of six years of down-rent, up-rent controversy, a confused hail of gun fire, and a dead Delaware County lawman.

Anti-Rent War (#3)

ON AUGUST 27, 1845, New York State Governor Silas Wright declared Delaware County "to be in a state of insurrection."

For the previous three weeks, since County Under Sheriff Osman Steele was shot and killed on Dingle Hill in the Town of Andes, anti-rent activists had been harassed, chased, and arrested by a vengeful posse of over 300 citizens, impressed, by the Sheriff, into law-and-order service from towns with up-rent majorities, towns like Walton, Franklin, and Delhi, the county seat, which was Osman Steele's hometown.

The posse rode roughshod through down-rent towns: Andes, Middletown, and Roxbury, especially. Years later, John Burroughs would remember being a boy of eight, watching the posse pass his family farm in a hurricane of dust. Anti-renters scattered into hiding, afraid of the murder charge that seemed to threaten anyone who might have been part of the unruly mob of calico Indians that had showed up the first Thursday in August at the rent-collection auction of the personal property of farmer Moses Earle—his small herd of cows, a few pigs, some tools.

Moses Earle withheld his rent with his eyes open. A deeply religious man in his early sixties, Moses Earle was a tenant-in-perpetuity of Charlotte Verplanck. He also owned, outright, 100 acres contiguous to his leasehold farm. Earle lived with his wife on this small farm a mile up Dingle Hill on the Tremperskill side. His hired girl, Parthena Davis, was a rabid anti-renter. She urged her boss to refuse to pay his rent to make a point, strike a blow for freedom. Earle had the cash to pay. He just wanted to do the right thing.

He decided the right thing was to refuse to pay. Mr. Earle allowed Sheriff Green Moore to conduct a sale rather than submit to the rent. Allies of the landlord, agent John Allen and lawyer Peter Wright, were prepared to bid on Earle's cows and pigs to recoup Miss Verplanck's losses. A mob of over 200 disguised anti-rent calico Indians gathered threateningly to see that such bidding did not occur.

The anti-renters were in violation of the law simply by appearing in public in disguise, an act criminalized by statute designed to combat the terror the calico Indians had created. For years, these masked men had harassed land agents and law enforcement officers who attempted to enforce the law by collecting legally owed, unpaid, and overdue rents.

Perhaps, the day was lost as soon as the keg was tapped. The combination of anger and alcohol, gunpowder and politics proved explosive.

Osman Steele was one of those guys you either really liked or really didn't. He was a hot-headed, red-headed, boisterous and confident fellow who had many friends and lots of enemies. He was a notorious opponent of the anti-rent movement, a law-and-order Democrat, a lawman who went out of his way to go after the calico Indians, cowards, in his view, who hid behind dresses and masks.

Earlier in the year, three calico Indians from the Towns of Middletown and Roxbury—Silas Tompkins, Lewis Knapp, and Anson Burrell—had been sent to Sing Sing Prison after being unmasked in a confrontation with a Steele-led posse.

A fourth, Ezekiel Kelley, was merely fined when he changed his plea from "not guilty" to "guilty." Anti-renters felt persecuted for the very act of defending their political point of view: that the left-over colonial leaseholds were un-American and invalid.

So tensions were extremely high on the morning of August 7, 1845, when Osman Steele and his sidekick, Constable Erastus Edgarton, arrived in Andes, stopping for a drink with breakfast at the Hunting Tavern on the main street.

Tavern keeper Ephraim Hunting, an up-rent, law-and-order man, warned his friend, the Under Sheriff, not to go up to the Earle farm, that rumor had it the calico Indians would show up in force, and that Steele, himself, was a marked man.

"Lead can't penetrate Steele," the loud-mouth is supposed to have said, and he's supposed to have dumped gunpowder into his drink before he chugged it. Now, every police officer I know is all too aware how easily lead does penetrate, so it sounds a bit made-up-later to me, but when Steele and Edgarton made their way up Dingle Hill Road, there were men in disguise on either side of them, and everybody had had a chance to get a little liquored-up, as some did, and the auction started and stopped and started again, and someone shouted, and someone yelled, and someone shot, and shots fired, bang, bang, bang, bang, and smoke and dust fogged everything, and when the air cleared, Osman Steele, Undersheriff of Delaware County, in the course of his official duties, was down, bleeding, shot.

They carried the lawman into Mr. Earle's house, and laid him on Mr. Earle's couch, and men and women on both sides of the conflict tended to him, and he slowly died all that afternoon until eight o'clock that evening when he was dead. Then all hell broke loose.

A posse was formed. Sheriff Moore felt he had to re-establish the rule of law. Vengeance was the goal of Sheriff's Deputy James Howe, the martyred Steele's brother-in-law, who spoke for both the family and the law enforcement brotherhood who felt betrayed by the anti-renters, traitors all!

Known anti-renters took to the hills. Some left the mountains for other parts, but many, literally, took to the hills, sleeping in caves and huts up behind their farms, food run to them by supportive family. Villains to some, heroes to others! Men were chased and caught. The governor called out the state militia to aid the posse. Three new log jailhouses were quickly erected in Delhi.

Hundreds were imprisoned. As many as 60 faced criminal charges related to the incident. Two, Edward O'Connor and John Van Steenbergh, were convicted of murder on flimsy evidence and condemned to be hung. Later, their sentences were reduced to life imprisonment, and, in 1846, they were pardoned by newly elected Governor John Young, a Whig elected with strong anti-rent support.

That flashpoint moment on Dingle Hill was the climatic moment of the Anti-Rent War. Over the next several years, the leasehold system withered away, although, surprisingly, a few rents were collected right into the early 20th century.

Margaretville Memorial Hospital

WHEN I FIRST CAME TO THIS PART OF THE CATSKILLS, Margaretville Hospital, on Route 28, was still referred to as "the new hospital." Forward-looking men and women of the Upper East Branch Valley had conducted major community fund-raising a few years before, raising astounding thousands of dollars for the effort. The new hospital was a source of community pride: a bricks-and-mortar example of what a community can accomplish when focused on a tangible goal.

It was also, then as now, a wonderful little hospital, one of six independent rural community hospitals in Delaware County at the time. Walton's Delaware Valley Hospital, Delhi's O'Connor Hospital, The Hospital of Sidney, and MMH are still in business, although all are presently affiliated with a larger, stronger entity. Stamford Hospital and Hancock Hospital are no longer with us, victims of the precarious nature of the health-care business.

The hospital boasted a team of outstanding nurses, a cadre of women who provided each patient a level of care, commitment, and concern that was the hospital's calling card. Joanie Asher, Betty Griffin, Bucky George, Barb Kapitko—mentioning some leaves out others, but many readers will continue the list from memory.

The hospital attracted physicians and surgeons to practice here. Dr. Spector delivered babies. Doctors Halim and Abrahao did surgery. Dr. Abe Rotkov had a general practice in Fleischmanns. I loved his practical approach to medicine: "A guy gets hit over the head with a beer bottle," I heard him once say, "he doesn't need a bunch of tests. He needs a bandage!"

Margaretville Memorial Hospital was founded in 1931 in a two-story frame farmhouse located at the western edge of that village. Eight years later the new central school would be built on the field just below the hospital.

There had always been a rudimentary system of medical care in the rural Catskills. From the late nineteenth-century through the early twentieth-century, general practice physicians made house calls, midwives delivered babies, and a few area nurses provided 24-hour sick care in the patient's home. In those days, patients needing surgery or hospitalization had to travel to Kingston City Hospital or to Oneonta.

Dr. Gordon Maurer, a surgeon, settled in Margaretville in 1926, and began to provide surgical services in the operating room of his clinic, located in several village houses the doctor rented. In 1931, he purchased the farmhouse of Sinclare Archibald to establish a proper hospital. Margaretville Hospital became a memorial to Dr. Maurer in 1938. The young doctor, an avid hunter, was killed in a tragic early morning hunting accident in November of that year. The impressive monument to Dr. Maurer in the old Margaretville Cemetery has been featured in a book of American epitaphs.

In the post-war years, Margaretville Memorial Hospital flourished under the medical leadership of Doctors Gilbert Palen and C. Ray Huggans. A surgeon and an internist, the two delivered a sophisticated level of medical care to their rural patients. Dr. Palen, a pilot as well as a surgeon, made Margaretville one of the first hospitals to use modern anti-biotic drugs. He would fly his small plane to Philadelphia to pick up the medicine, then fly it back here, landing, he once told me, on the old fairgrounds by the river.

Recently, I was told the story of the two doctors, back in the 1950s, building a small bonfire of invoices for medical service provided, invoices they knew their economically-strapped patients would not be able to pay. I'm told the two doctors burned-up over $100,000 worth of bills.

My friend, the doctor's son, used to tell me how the family table was often graced with a string of trout, or leg of venison, or dozen eggs that the good doctor had been given in payment for services rendered.

Money has always been an issue in providing health-care. Back in the seventies, the new hospital always seemed on shaky financial ground. Some waited for it to fail, planning for future uses of the building as a middle school or community center. But the wise among us knew that the hospital could not be allowed to fail. Without it, we are simply too far away.

One used to be able to become a life member of the hospital for a total donation of something like $50. Life-members met in an annual meeting—in good years in a church basement with twenty or so people in attendance. In years of controversy, several hundred life members would gather in the school gym. The life members would elect the Board of Directors, who ran the hospital.

In 2001, the life members put themselves out of business, merging the hospital into the health-care system generated by the Kingston Hospital, Health Alliance.

Clarke Sanford

I'VE BEEN SPENDING A LITTLE TIME LATELY IN THE 1930s with the *Catskill Mountain News*. Weekly newspaper issues published between 1902 and 1937 are posted on line. A couple of weeks ago, I got to thinking about the market crash of 1929 and the Great Depression that followed it. I know a lot of people were thinking about that historical precedent, a couple of weeks ago. So, I visited the Catskills in the thirties.

The Historical Society of the Town of Middletown coordinated the microfilming and digitalizing of the *News'* archive. Go to http://history.catskill.net. You can use the search engine on that page to find newspaper references to a particular topic, word, or phrase: "hardware store" or "John Burroughs." I like to click to the list of digitalized issues, click on a year, pick an issue close to this year's calendar date, and read the paper like it was this week's, front to back.

Interestingly, in 1929, the *Catskill Mountain News* was a four-page newspaper, eight columns a page. By 1936, the paper ran regularly 12 pages. Part of the change is clearly a new printing press. Sometime in 1935, the *News* takes on a brighter, cleaner look, with print so crisp you can almost feel the texture of the ink through the computer screen. Five broad columns display a brighter, clearer printing of the news.

In those days, the *Catskill Mountain News* was housed upstairs over the Galli-Curci Theater. Both were enterprises of Clark Sanford, founder of the paper as we know it today, and grandfather of the present publisher. Clark Sanford grew up on a farm in Dunraven, went off, after high school, to the Normal school in Oneonta, now the State College, and took his first job as a reporter with the *Oneonta Star*.

In 1904, Clarke's parents informed him of the estate sale of one of Margaretville's two weekly newspapers, the *Margaretville Messenger* and *Catskill Mountain News*. They urged him to come home to buy it. I think he got the paper for 50 bucks or so. In 1918, he bought the other village weekly, *The Utilitarian*, founded in 1869, and merged it with his own.

Clarke Sanford became a highly successful business man. Besides the newspaper and the movie theater, he was the local Chevy dealer, the showroom for his cars in the front of his theater, just below his printing press. He was a master of what business schools call today "synergy": win a new Chevrolet by selling the most subscriptions to the newspaper which runs the movie schedule on the front page. He became a leader within the Republican Party, a civic leader within the community. He was a principal in the People's National Bank in Margaretville; his brother, Courtney, was bank president.

And as the Depression-era thirties marched on, his newspaper seemed to get bigger, busier, with more news and, most importantly, more advertisements. Such a business expansion during historic hard-times seems counter-intuitive. It is not what we expect.

Reading through these depression-era papers, one gets the sense that the local economy was fairly robust, that local trading was brisk in everything from coal to timber to truckloads of cabbage, that Main Street stores provided local consumers nearly all their needs. Perhaps, as the broader national economy offers fewer opportunities for economic activity—investment, sales, and purchases—the local economy picks up the slack. Perhaps, folks stay closer to home during tough economic times and, perhaps, the local economy benefits.

Whatever the explanation, the thirties newspapers are full of store ads for liver pills and mackinaw coats, canned goods, and new cars, especially new Chevrolets. An Exchange Column allowed readers to offer to buy or sell all sorts of things, kind of a print flea market.

Its fun to follow the politics of the time as well. Delaware County was solidly Republican, as was the paper, which predicted dire consequences should Roosevelt be re-elected in 1936. The weeks leading up to that election saw meetings and rallies on both sides. The Republican Woman's Club met in Dugan Hall, now the Granary Building, one week, followed by the Roosevelt Democratic Club the next.

After Roosevelt's landslide win (he carried Fleischmanns, by the way), the Democrats organized an impromptu Thursday-after-Election-Day parade of about 50 cars down Main Street in Margaretville. They had an old outhouse propped up on a trailer with signs attached to it reading "Republican propaganda" and "Independent Coalition of American Women." People were peeved! Public apologies had to be made, and neighbors stopped speaking to each other. When I got involved in local politics in 1973, there were still bruised feelings over the incident. That was 37 years later!

Clarke Sanford was publisher of the Catskill Mountain News for 60 years, until his death in 1964. Once, near the end of his long life, Mr. Sanford was in the local drug store. The pharmacist, on seeing him, said, "Mr. Sanford, Everett Herrick is looking for you." Everett Herrick was a prominent local businessman, one of the first to see the economic benefit of developing unimproved land for the second-home market. Mr. Herrick was also the local funeral director.

"Oh, Herrick," old Clarke Sanford replied to the druggist. "He's been looking for me for a long time."

Poetry on a Rock: Dr. Gordon Maurer

USUALLY, I do my research before I write. Usually. A couple of weeks ago, I took a short-cut. Writing about the founder of the hospital in Margaretville, Dr. Gordon Maurer, I mentioned that his epitaph appeared in a book of American epitaphs. Dr. Maurer was killed exactly 70 years ago in a November 1938 hunting accident. He is buried in the old Margaretville Cemetery.

It's not that I made anything up. It's just that, in the midst of a busy week, I didn't go to the cemetery to look for the headstone to read the epitaph myself. Instead, I took the information about it from Ethel Bussy's classic 1960 book *History and Stories of Margaretville and Surrounding Areas*, lent to me a couple of months ago by my accountant (in the midst of a national financial crisis, it seems reassuring to use the phrase my accountant).

The other day, I corrected my mistake. I spent an hour or so wandering through the terraced old cemetery looking for Dr. Maurer's headstone. It is a wonderful cemetery, an old fashioned park-like rural resting place that contains the names of many who figure prominently in the history of this part of the Catskills. A tall granite obelisk marks the grave of Orson Allaben, Margaretville's founder, and that of his wife, Thankful Dimmick, daughter of Noah Dimmick, Arkville's first citizen. Ray Marks, elected Delaware County Treasurer in 1932, rests there. I found several graves of people I had known.

The cemetery is on a side hill, and reaching the top requires a bit of a climb, but at the very top of the hill, on the uppermost terrace, I found what I was looking for. It was worth the effort! Gordon Bostwick Maurer, 1899-1938, is memorialized by a massive double-wide granite slab on which is inscribed a profound and moving poem of remembrance and respect, written by Dr. Maurer's friend, Clarke Sanford, and published originally in the *Catskill Mountain News* in Sanford's column, "The Mountaineer."

Standing next to the headstone, one looks directly across the East Branch valley at the hill on the other side, looking directly at the Margaretville Hospital, founded by Dr. Maurer and dedicated as a memorial to him. What is uncanny, and a bit magical, is that that hospital was not located there until 30 years after Dr. Maurer's death. His interment in a spot that directly overlooks the hospital he founded is, at least, a delightful coincidence. Perhaps, it is more.

And the epitaph! If you can, take the hike to the top of the cemetery hill and see it for yourself. It tells the story of a young man who graduated first in his class as an undergraduate engineer, and then, at Yale Medical School, number one in his class once again. More importantly, it tells the story of the connection made by an individual and a community.

Let the Mountaineer give us his remembrance. The headstone reads as follows:

> Thirteen years ago there came here a city chap, trained in one of the great universities.
> The other members of his class went to 'big towns.'
> He, with the best records of them all, wanted to begin the practice of medicine in a country village.
> He had compiled a list of prospective communities. He looked over several and chose us.
> An untried city college boy—with magic hands, a keen vision, and uncanny knowledge of both the human body and the soul which activates it.
> Soon after arrival he was called upon to care for a life given up as lost.
> He saved it.

He began to save others. He worked day and night. When he did not have proper apparatus or appliances he built some. When the snows kept him from patients he constructed a snowmobile.

Neither storm nor night nor mud nor snow kept him from the sick.

He took people into his home. It became a veritable hospital.

The fame of the boy spread throughout the section. Men and women from all walks of life asked for his attention.

The community built a hospital that he and others might the better care for those who needed care, medication and operation.

He continued. When a tired body all but gave up, he took a year out and returned to Yale for special work that he might come home and serve better.

He had tired of city pastimes. The lure of the country had been breathed into his soul. Camp, rod and gun, open fires, life in great outdoors gave zest, relief, happiness.

He loved our hills, our mode of life; he knew our ambitions, he smiled at our shortcomings

He gave freely. Much of the work he did was without charge. Few knew the extent of his help to those who needed help. He served as few had ever served here before.

He was physician, parson, priest, confessor—we told him both our physical and mental troubles and he put us back on the road to reason and living.

Thirteen years he served. It was a life work worth while.

Today our hearts are numb at his loss, our senses befogged to know how to live without him. May we turn from the tragedy of the golden Indian summer morning that knew his death.

And in the bleak days of the approaching Thanksgiving season thank God for those thirteen years.

The deer in the woods inspired both the young doctor and his elegy-writing journalist friend.

Ivan Miller

I stopped a former student of mine the other day in the store where she works. I told her that I had recently held in my hand a little book of poems put together in 1932 in the Shaver Hollow School. There were poems in the booklet by children who shared her family name, children she identified as her father and her aunt.

The publication of student work, especially their creative and expressive work, is a feature of our most creative and progressive classrooms today. Providing children the joy and responsibility of authorship is progressive education in any era. The fact that it was done in a one-room school house in 1932 seems surprising, although only surprising to people who did not know the teacher in that depression-era Shaver Hollow School: Ivan Miller.

Ivan Miller was born in 1909 in Shaver Hollow, Town of Andes, just above Union Grove, one of several Upper Delaware Valley villages drowned by the 1954 damming of the East Branch of the Delaware River to create the Pepacton Reservoir. Arena, Pepacton, and Shavertown were others.

Ivan attended that one-room Shaver Hollow School himself, went on to high school in Downsville, attended Union College in Schenectady, my alma mater, and got a Masters Degree from the University at Albany. He taught at Andes Central, where he soon became principal, leaving the principal's job in 1959 to become guidance counselor at Margaretville Central.

The field of Guidance & Counseling was brand new at the time, and Ivan was a pioneer in the field. In 1971, he went to the State Education Department in Albany where he helped develop the policies and practices that were to shape school guidance for a generation.

Ivan was one of the smartest people I've ever known. I met him as the new kid on the faculty he had just left. We shared an interest in politics and history. I was beginning my career in education as he was winding his down. We became friends.

I used to love his election day stories: how the Republicans would hold a big lead in the votes from Andes village, votes which were always counted first in the village-located town hall, where folks waited for the Shavertown results to come up the Tremperskill by train, votes that were invariably more heavily Democratic.

In 1948, those votes helped Ivan Miller overcome a 4 to 1 Republican registration advantage to be elected supervisor of the Town of Andes, one of the few Democrats ever to hold that office. He did it by knocking on every door in the town, often in the company of a local supporter, a neighbor of the resident who answered the knock to receive a pencil, a request for support, and some common-sense thinking form the 39-year-old candidate.

I wonder if the GOP/Democratic split between the two sections of pre-reservoir Andes town goes back to the Anti-Rent unpleasantness. The river front farms on the East Branch were, perhaps, more likely to be owner-occupied and, hence, loyal to the old Jefferson-Jackson Party of land owners, while the hill farms around the village might be more likely leased farms and, hence, down-rent. I wonder.

The climax of the nineteenth-century Anti-Rent upheaval occurred, of course, in Andes, on Dingle Hill. On Labor Day weekend 1945, the Town of Andes commemorated the 100th anniversary of the shooting of Delaware County Under-Sheriff Osman Steele with a centennial re-enactment, parade, and historical symposium. J. D. Frisbee of Andes and Ivan Miller of Union Grove were appointed co-chairmen of the event by the Andes Men's Community Club, the group spearheading the effort. Ivan wrote the script for the re-enactment.

A friend of mine recalls being a very small boy watching the line of costumed re-enactors—all locals— straggle up the Dingle Hill Road to the site of the Moses Earle farm where the shooting was to be staged. He remembers vividly a team of oxen, cows pulling a cart to a little boy who had never seen oxen in his modern 1940s life. The sight of those oxen is still vivid to him these 63 years later!

Over 80 different people participated on the various committees that planned and orchestrated the event. Many wore costumes for the re-enactment. Fred Ruff played Osman Steele. Fred drove school bus for years, so everybody in town knew him. E. A. Van Keuren played Moses Earle and the Reverend R. V. Wright, Walter Sprague, and Howard Frisbee were among a dozen featured re-enactors.

The evening symposium in the school cafeteria featured the noted historian of Delaware County, John D. Monroe, and Henry Christman, author of *Tin Horns and Calico*, then the definitive book on the Anti-Rent War. Who rode in the parade with those two worthies on a horse-drawn wagon? Ivan Miller. That was three intellectual heavyweights in a wagon driven by a young Wayland Gladstone behind a team of horses from the Gladstone Brothers farm.

A square dance and fireworks display rounded out the centennial celebration.

Ivan died in January 2000. At the time of his death he had over 90 periodicals delivered to his Margaretville home. According to his son, Steve, he read every one.

SUNY Delhi's Outdoor Education Center

WE have a little gem of a park right nearby. Maybe the word park is less than clearly specific here. I have a friend who often reminds us that, here, we live in a park—all lands, public and private, inside the Blue Line boundaries of the Catskill Park (basically, Johnson Ford, Kingston to Bridge Street, Margaretville) are lands inside a park.

The gem I have in mind is a little 50-acre park well west of the Catskill Blue Line: the SUNY Delhi Outdoor Education Center a few miles below Delhi Village on State Route 28. It is marked by a little, unobtrusive brown sign that reads "SUNY Delhi EDU." At first, I wasn't sure what EDU stood for—until I stopped thinking road sign and started thinking Internet: the web suffix for educational facilities. But this EDU is not virtual; it is natural, and a magical place.

It is also a working classroom. Delhi College offers Associate Degree programs in Adventure Recreation, Park and Outdoor Recreation, and Environmental Studies. This piece of land along the Little Delaware River is groomed and manicured by Delhi students for the express purpose of providing the public with a little bit of recreation, education, and adventure in nature's outdoors. A regular hands-on learning lab.

And a great place for a walk. The trails are wide swaths that wind down the hill from the ample parking area to the flat below. There is a butterfly garden and a fire circle, a sundial, and a sugar shack. Rustic benches are tucked away in private copses of trees and on knolls overlooking natural vistas. Outdoor tables invite a picnic by the Little Delaware, in warmer weather, anyway. A couple spots on the river are groomed for fishing access in season. It is a really nice place.

The star attraction, I think, is the large labyrinth cut into the meadow that sits on the flat at the base of the park's side hill. A labyrinth is an ancient construction. According to Greek mythology, Daedalus the artificer, a kind of early engineer, built for King Minos of Crete an elaborate spiral structure to hold the Minotaur, half-man, half-bull, and all-dangerous. The path from the outside to the inner circle of the Labyrinth was so intricate, that Daedalus himself almost couldn't find his way out.

A labyrinth is different from a maze in that it has no false passageways, no puzzling dead-ends. Rather, the path in a labyrinth twists and turns, doubles back on itself, sometimes seemingly away from the center destination, but leads inexorably to the center.

That's what makes walking a labyrinth such a reflective, even spiritual, experience. In the twelfth and thirteenth centuries, the Labyrinth became a feature of the great medieval cathedrals, a circular path that spirals its way inward, toward a center. Walking the labyrinth became a kind of compact pilgrimage, a spiritual journey that could be taken right on the cathedral floor.

Labyrinths became a feature of monastery gardens. Walking the labyrinth was a tool for meditation. Devotees would pray, meditate, and reflect as they walked, step by step, the intricate labyrinth path.

New Age spiritual seekers rediscovered the labyrinth sometime in the late sixties.

Today the labyrinth is enjoying a wave of interest and popularity. Walking the labyrinth is seen as a constructive exercise by both traditional religions and contemporary spiritualists.

The walker in the labyrinth often cannot see the way forward. Just taking the next right step, the next step forward, is enough. Because the path goes only one way, twisting toward the center, just taking the next step forward is enough to get you, eventually, to your destination.

Some pretty powerful lessons in that experience!

The labyrinth at the SUNY Delhi Outdoor Education Center is the nicest one I've ever seen. It begins under a wooden arch, somewhat Japanese in style, with bright orange suns painted on the arch supports. Bluestone flags lead your feet into the labyrinth.

I walked it in an inch or two of snow one cold November morning. This labyrinth is a good fifty feet in diameter, and the late-autumn remains of its path-lining shrubs, bushes, and wildflowers make following the path in your mind's eye difficult. You have to let your feet find your way. You cannot see your way forward. You wind your way, often seeming to backtrack on your trail. Let the center be your reward.

The walk out of the labyrinth retraces your steps. The walk back up the hill to the car provides a few pleasant visual surprises: an old four-wheel cultivator in the woods under a tree, a modernist bluestone bench in a natural alcove off the trail.

Oh, your dog is welcome to some outdoor education here, too.

Catskill Mountain Books

"SHOP LOCAL!" we're told, particularly this holiday season with world recession squeezing local economies. We want to help, want to do the right thing, want our holiday dollars to circulate in our mountain towns. But we also want to buy Christmas and Hanukah gifts worth giving. Happily, many regional retail outlets now stock Catskill Mountain themed books, books that just might be perfect holiday gifts this year.

A great gift any year is Diane Galusha's *Another Day, Another Dollar: The Civilian Conservation Corps in the Catskills* (Black Dome Press, 2008). Galusha is one of our top mountain historians, the author of four previous Catskill Mountain themed books including *Liquid Assets, the Story of New York City's Water System* (Purple Mountain Press, 1999) and *When Cauliflower was King* (Purple Mountain Press, 2004), the tale of the rise and fall of a cash crop that was, in the mid twentieth century, a major mountain commodity.

Today, with the economy struggling and a new administration coming to power, the 1930s Depression-era New Deal is attracting renewed interest. Might the programs and policies put in place by Franklin Roosevelt in 1933 be a blueprint for programs and policies to confront today's difficulties? Galusha's book on the Civilian Conservation Corps could not be better timed.

The CCC was established in the first weeks after Roosevelt's inauguration in March 1933. It's purpose was twofold: to provide employment to millions of unemployed youth, and to confront the major environmental problems of the day: deforestation, soil erosion, and frequent floods.

Things moved fast. On April 6, 1933, the first recruit to the new all-male "Forest Army" enlisted in Pennsylvania. On April 17, the first CCC camp was established in Luray, Virginia. By July 1, 275,000 corpsmen were housed in 1300 CCC camps throughout the US. By the end of its nine-year run, over three and a half million men served in 4500 CCC camps in every state of the union.

The corps was organized along military lines: the corpsmen wore surplus World War I uniforms, slept in tents and barracks, and were commanded by experienced military officers. In New York State, 210,000 corpsmen worked out of 161 camps, planted over 221 million trees, battled insect pests and diseased plants, built 19 fire towers, 1200 ponds, and almost 400 miles of forest access roads.

In late June 1933, the first CCC camp in the Catskills was established in Boiceville, on a strip of rented land between State Route 28 and the Esopus Creek where the Boiceville Market now stands, across the street from the present Onteora School, built twenty years later. The corpsmen were charged with battling the spread of the gypsy moth, but also worked to remediate stream erosion problems, build hiking trails, and plant tress. Soon, other camps were built in Tannersville and Margaretville, in Breakabeen and Masonvile and in six other Catskill Region towns.

The CCC cleared the first Catskill Mountain ski trails at Simpson's hill in Phoenicia. They prepared the ground for the Belleayre Ski Center, built the Woodland Valley Campground, turned the old Catskill Mountain House grounds into the North Lake State Campground, created Gilbert Lake State Park.

Another Day, Another Dollar is beautifully illustrated, a pleasure to hold and to look at, a great read with first-class production values: a book you'll be happy to own and to give.

Martha Frankel doesn't write about the mountains, but she lives here, a writer of national reputation who has interviewed and profiled celebrities and artists for publications like *Cosmopolitan*, *The New Yorker*, and *Fashions of the Times*.

Martha was featured along with her husband Steve Heller in Jane Smiley's 1988 book *Catskill Crafts: Artisans of the Catskill Mountains* (Crown Publishers, New York). Steve crafts furniture and sculpture at Fabulous Furniture on Route 28 in Boiceville.

It was there that I bought an autographed copy of Martha Frankel's memoir *Hats and Eyeglasses: A Family Love Affair With Gambling* (Jeremy P. Tarcher/Penguin, New York, 2008). The book is a candid exploration of the author's descent into obsession and loss, with on-line poker the culprit that finally turned a family legacy of gambling into a destructive personal Jones. It is a brave book, available at a good price at Fabulous Furniture (or full-price on line).

In the 1970s, Big Indian was the world center of the movement of the spiritual teacher Swami Rudrananda, known as Rudi. Rudi established an ashram, store, and restaurant in Big Indian, and had numerous disciples and students, some still living here in the mountains. He died, in a plane crash I believe, in 1973. Later, the movement he began relocated to Portland, Oregon.

At the Emerson Resort shops, I bought a copy of *Rudi: In His Own Words* (Rudra Press, Portland, OR, 1990). The book offers a look at the Swami's teachings in chapters with titles like "Growing" and "Detachment" and "Surrender." The spiritual seeker, or the merely curious, who receives this gift book will appreciate the brief snippets of teaching that can be read quickly now for further thought later. So, shop local. Catskill Mountain books might be just the gift you're looking for.

Beach, Guyot, and Steuding

MENTION THE CATSKILLS to someone from somewhere else and often they think first of the Sullivan County *Borscht Belt*. In the 1940s, 50s, and 60s, the big hotels down by Monticello and Liberty seemed to be the epicenter of the mountains.

Yet, the Sullivan County Catskills seem downright "hilly" to residents of the high peaks. One of my sons came home, once, from college in Pennsylvania complaining of a classmate from Monticello who claimed the Catskills as home.

"That's not the Catskills," he sneered, defensive of his home turf.

Yet, just a couple of generations before, my son's own claim to Catskill Mountain residence would have been challenged and denied by conventional geographic thinking. For the first hundred years of American independence, the Catskills Mountains were understood to be only that range of high peaks extending back from the escarpment that rises from the Hudson at North and South Lake, the Mountaintop of Haines Falls, Hunter, Windham, and Tannersville.

The Catskills were limited to the Mountaintop for economic as well as geographic reasons. Charles L. Beach was the proprietor of the first great resort hotel in America, the Catskill Mountain House, built on the escarpment in the 1820s. From its Pine Orchard location a couple thousand feet above the Hudson River, the Mountain House commanded a magnificent view. "If you want to see the sights of America, go to see Niagara Falls, Lake George and the Catskill Mountain House," the writer James Fenimore Cooper told his European audiences on a mid-nineteenth century speaking tour.

Beach did not want to share his Catskills with any possible competitors. He jealously guarded his franchise, claiming an extra 750 feet or so in elevation for his hotel and insisting that the highest peaks in the mountains, the authentic Catskills, were those mountains that surrounded his hotel.

He got away with it for half a century. The mountains south and west of the Esopus Creek were called the Shandakens, a separate, and, by inference, inferior region that lacked the cachet of the Catskills, and so remained an unexplored, unheralded backwater.

Enter Arnold Henry Guyot, Professor of Physical Geography and Geology at Princeton. Guyot had been surveying the southern Appalachians when the Civil War broke out. Research impossible in the south, Guyot came to New York's mountains in the summer of 1862 with a team of surveyors. He and his team spent the next 17 summers measuring, plotting and mapping every peak, every hill.

Guyot's 1879 "Map of the Catskill Mountains" and ensuing article in the *American Journal of Science* disclosed significant scientific truths. The Catskills are part of the Appalachians, although they run in the opposite direction. The Catskills extend farther than previously thought, comprising the traditional northern section, and, south and west of the Esopus Creek, the southern Catskills. Most significantly, the highest peak in the Catskills was not Charles Beach's Round Top, but Slide Mountain, formerly of the now-defunct Shandakens.

Bob Steuding tells this story and more in his book *The Heart of the Catskills* (Fleischmanns, Purple Mountain Press, 2008). Bob is, perhaps, our leading Catskill Mountain writer, the heir to the late Alf Evers. An accomplished poet

The Catskill Mountain House.

and historian, Bob has been the Poet Laureate of Ulster County, and is the chronicler of the Catskills south and west of the Esopus Creek.

His 1985 book *The Last of the Homemade Dams: The Story of the Ashokan Reservoir* (Fleischmanns, Purple Mountian Press) tells the story of the 1906 drowning of the way of life that had animated the broad Esopus Valley for a hundred years before. In this new book, Bob explores that way of life.

This is a social history of that part of the Catskills that still contains great expanses of wilderness, an area that still presents residents with everyday-living challenges. Beginning with first settlers, William and Ann Denman, Steuding traces the history by telling the stories of the people who lived that history. Tanners and bark-peelers, farmers and hunters, Steuding's people are a fascinating lot. I'm saving Big Indian's Jim Dutcher for a future column.

Good friends of mine live down on the Hudson near the estate of Judge Alton B. Parker, the Democratic candidate for President who ran against Teddy Roosevelt in 1904. Turns out, Judge Parker was one of the founders of the Winnisook Club, located on the little lake of the same name at the top of the divide between the Esopus and Neversink Valleys, up above Oliverea.

That club was founded by a group of prominent New York Democrats. (Who knew?) Seems that William Jennings Bryan, the populist 1896 Democratic candidate for President, made an arduous and out-of-the-way journey to Winnisook shortly after he won the nomination in Chicago. Conservative New York party leaders were cool to Bryan's candidacy, so they weren't making this

113

peace-making meeting easy for him, perhaps hoping he wouldn't come. Bryan went to Winnisook, party leaders remained cool, and he never became President.

It's all in Bob Steuding's book.

Night Before Christmas

WHEN I WAS A KID, Christmas Eve meant putting up and decorating the tree. My widowed mother was a traditionalist and, since in her Staten Island childhood the tree never went up before Christmas Eve (and came down on Epiphany, January 6th) that's the way it was going to be for her three sons as well. Made Christmas Eve a busy day. Mother would be cooking while my two older brothers and I untangled strings of lights, wrapped the tree in garlands of glass beads and tinsel, and kept track of who dropped and broke the largest number of fragile ornaments. Generally, it was me.

At five o'clock in the afternoon, we'd turn on *The Early Show*, a CBS afternoon movie that used to be the last broadcast of the daytime TV schedule before the evening news. This was in that innocent time before broadcasters discovered the advertising goldmine that is today's 5 o'clock live-at-five local news and infotainment.

The movie every Christmas Eve was *A Christmas Carol*, the Reginald Owen version, made in 1938, with a frighteningly bandaged and manacled Marley, a pathetically hobbled Tiny Tim, and a big open-faced Ghost of Christmas Past who led Owen's tight-lipped Ebenezer Scrooge on the journey of a night-time. Years later, as a teacher, I found George C. Scott's 1984 Scrooge more relatable for students, but, for me, *A Christmas Carol* will always be in grainy black and white.

That's the way it is with the holidays. Whether we celebrate Christmas or Hanukah (or both!), or, perhaps, the more recently created Kwanzaa, each of us has specific holiday memories and rituals that, along with the deeper reality of the spiritual meaning of each holiday, create an individual continuity of observance for each of us.

It's said we are all kids at Christmas. Perhaps. Or, perhaps, the truth is we all try to recreate the Christmas we remember as kids. On the night before Christmas, it's a pleasant self-indulgence to see ourselves as "the children…nestled all snug in our beds" rather than as "mamma in her kerchief" or any other tired, responsible, holiday-providing adult seeking "a long winter's nap."

These "visions of sugar-plums" come, of course, from what may well be

America's most famous and enduring piece of holiday literature, "A Visit From St. Nicholas," better known as "The Night Before Christmas."

That poem first appeared anonymously in the Troy, New York, Sentinel on Christmas Eve, 1823. It was widely reprinted in newspapers and almanacs over the next several years, until it became a holiday staple, credited with the creation of the image of St. Nick as the sleigh driving, chimney-dropping Santa we know today. People wanted to know who wrote the poem.

In 1837, credit was given to Clement Moore, Professor of Oriental and Greek Literature at what was then Columbia College. Mystery solved. Or not.

It seems that all of the children of Henry Livingston, Jr., of Poughkeepsie, remembered vividly their father reading them the very same poem as far back as Christmas 1822, the year before it was first published anonymously. Henry Livingston died in 1828, so he was unable to contest Clement Moore's authorship claim. But his children were certain.

Henry Livingston Jr., of course, was a member of the Livingston family that once owned two-thirds of the Catskill Mountain Hardenbergh Patent. Born in 1748, he was a direct descendent of the first Robert Livingston who established the family as Hudson River patricians, and a cousin of the Robert Livingston who served on the committee with Jefferson to draft the Declaration of Independence.

Henry served as a major in the 1775 invasion of Canada led by his cousin Janet's husband, General Richard Montgomery. His six-month enlistment ran out and Henry returned home before the New Year's Eve death of Montgomery in the failed siege of Quebec. Wasn't really the soldiering type.

Henry spent the rest of his life presiding over his farm estate, Locust Grove, which later passed into the hands of Samuel F. B. Morse, of telegraph and Morse Code fame. Henry also wrote and published poems, often anonymously, in newspapers and periodicals in New York and Poughkeepsie. His poems displayed rhyme schemes and metrical patterns similar to "The Visit of St. Nicholas."

Contemporary author Don Foster pretty much confirmed Livingston's authorship after an extensive investigation. Even a quick web search uncovers plenty of evidence bolstering the Livingston claim.

We shouldn't be surprised. In Henry's first known publication, in the September 7, 1787, *Country Journal and Poughkeepsie Advertiser*, he seemed to declare his lack of interest in claiming credit to gain fame. In his poem "The Soliloquy of a Careless Philosopher," Henry declares, "I rise when I please, when I please I lie down / Nor seek, what I care not a rush for, renown."

By his own poetic proclamation, Henry Livingston Jr. cared "not a rush" for fame. Good thing. He still doesn't get any credit for the most famous Christmas poem in the English language.

Roads

A GOOD FRIEND OF MINE, long a stalwart member of the community, first came to the Catskills on summer vacations with his parents in the fifties. They'd stay at John and Martha Hewitt's Denver Valley farm, boarding in the big farmhouse for a week or two, living the country life of fresh air and outdoor exercise. The car trip from Long Island's Nassau County to the Town of Roxbury took over six hours, my friend remembers today, much of it winding through villages and hamlets up the old, narrow, twisting Route 28.

Route 28 was widened and straightened in the late 1950s, a widening and straightening that made the road much more a state highway and much less a country road. Old-timers report that the old road was quite rustic as it rose through Stony Clove just west of Kingston making the ascent into the mountains.

Once in a while, I like to try to capture the experience of traveling the old Route 28 by turning off the present 28 every time a portion of the old road appears, often signaled by a little green road sign reading "Old Route 28." I'm not sure that system gives the old road justice.

Maybe a better way to get the feel of the old entrance to the mountains is by riding the bus from Kingston west. While the bus-route follows State Highway 212, not 28, the slow winding path through each of the mountain towns – Woodstock, Shady, Mount Tremper, Phoenicia – provides an old-fashioned feeling of the long slow experience of getting up into the hills.

Living out in the mountains requires a lot of time on the road just getting where we need to go. Roads are mighty important to country living, and their history, I think, is both important and interesting. John D. Monroe's classic 1949 book *Chapters in the History of Delaware County New York* (Delhi: Delaware County Historical Association) is particularly good at presenting the history of roads in our part of the world.

"The earliest known road west of the Hudson River south of Albany," Monroe reports, "was the Minisink Road, otherwise [known as] the Old Mine Road, leading from Kingston to Port Jervis, said to have been constructed by the Dutch to reach mines in Warren County, New Jersey." State Route 209 follows the trail of that road, built sometime in the late 1600s to facilitate the shipping of copper from the Delaware River mines to the Hudson. The road stretches 104 miles from Kingston to Kittatinny Point at the Delaware Water Gap. It is said to be the oldest continuously used roadway in America. I've driven its length. It seems to go on forever.

State Route 28 follows the route of the old Ulster and Delaware Turnpike. That turnpike was chartered in 1802 by the State Legislature when they incorporated the Ulster and Delaware Turnpike Road Company to build a road from Salisbury Connecticut to the Susquehanna River at Jericho, now Bainbridge.

The turnpike was chartered to run from the state line through Pine Plains to Rhinecliff on the east bank of the Hudson. There it would meet up with the ferry, owned by John Radcliff and Moses Cantine, which would carry traffic to Kingston on the west bank.

From Kingston, a road 33-feet wide passed via the old "Red Bridge" over the Esopus Creek, then followed that stream-bed west to Shandaken, up over Pine Hill, followed the Bushkill stream—then called "The Tweed"—to the East Branch of the Delaware up to the Little Stone Schoolhouse in Dunraven.

Let Monroe tell the tale. He does it better than I can. "Near the Stone School House the road crossed the East Branch of the Delaware and ran up the Plattekill, over Palmer Hill to Andes, then over Cabin Hill to Delancey, then to near the bridge at Hamden, and so to Walton and thence to Bainbridge. From Dunraven to Hamden the road was all new road to be built through the wilderness. Doubtless Morgan Lewis, who was Governor of New York from 1804 to 1807, and owned the north one-half of Great Lot No. 39, Hardenbergh Patent, had much to do with fixing the route through Andes."

Regular readers will not be surprised to recall that Morgan Lewis was married to a Livingston!

Route 28 was constructed as an automobile road on the similar path to the old turnpike beginning in 1900. Construction and reconstruction went on in one form or another until 1935.

In 1912-13 the road from Andes to Delhi was built and the route changed to carry traffic that way rather than over Cabin Hill. By 1935, a good road ran from Kingston to Delhi: 74 miles of good road.

That road is the lifeline of this part of the Catskills.

Mountain Speech

A BANKER IN CINCINNATI is on the phone with a banker from another part of the country. After finishing their business, the Cincinnati banker asks, "Is there anything else we can do for you?"

"No," comes the reply, "but, you are not from Ohio, are you?" The Cincinnati banker allows that she is not. "You are from New York," she is told. "In fact, you are from upstate New York."

The Cincinnati banker, born in Mexico, was raised and educated in the Catskills. Having learned her English from teachers and classmates in upstate New York, she developed a pattern of pronunciation—in this case the way she sounded her A's—that gave away her upstate New York roots.

We all do it. The way people speak English varies in pronunciation, vocabulary, and grammatical structure. People make sense, and sentences, in a manner that reflects their social and regional background. We're all familiar with the "southern accent" that lets us know we have crossed the Mason-Dixon line, or the Cockney dialect of London that Liza Doolittle learned to replace with the Queen's English in the American musical *My Fair Lady*.

We tend to be less aware of dialect variations in ourselves. When I first came to the mountains, my students made sport of the way I said the word water. I guess I sounded my A's in a distinctly downstate manner. Gradually, I'm sure, my pronunciation changed.

A dialect is a variation of a language, a variation that develops as spoken language grows and changes within an interconnected group of people, a speech community. Today, that speech community may be a virtual community, connected on-line, but not very long ago, when people tended to stay put, speech patterns were more likely to develop regionally.

The study of American dialects, dialectology, had its high point in the period between the two world wars, when a monumental linguistic atlas project attempted to map the dialectology of the eastern US. That project, based locally on a 1940 Vassar College thesis, included the Catskills in the Hudson Valley dialect area.

Well, any trip to Kingston makes it clear that's not correct. Catskill Mountain folks speak differently than the people of the valley, that was immediately clear to me, just as it was clear to my mountain students that I sounded "downstate."

Looking for a research topic in my mid-eighties graduate school years, the dialect of the Catskills seemed like a natural. Living in a mountain hamlet, I was surrounded by the talk of men and women who had spent lifetimes wresting a living out of the hard Catskills soil, men and women whose talk resonated with a connection to the past and a love of place. Their Catskill Mountain speech was distinctive and memorable. Clearly not of the Hudson Valley, their Catskill Mountain speech was worth studying.

A local oral history project recorded the memories of dozens of local residents in the late seventies and early eighties. The project was sponsored by the old Erpf Catskill Cultural Center, now a part of the Catskill Center in Arkville, which had a wonderful folklore program working for a few years. People were recorded with an interest in preserving what they said. I listened to the tapes with an interest in *how* they said it.

Walt Wolfram, a Professor at North Carolina State, had, with colleagues, identified the grammatical structure of the dialect spoken in the southern Appalachians, a dialect they call *Mountain Speech*. Armed with a chart (it would be a spreadsheet today), I listened to the tapes looking for those specific features.

I found them. Remember, if you are old enough (or watch re-runs), *The Beverly Hillbillies*? Remember how Grandma would say things like "Jed is a-fishing." Well, that's an actual grammatical feature of Mountain Speech, called "a-prefixing." It has real meaning, a continuity of action that has a different shade of meaning than "Jed is fishing."

I found what I'll bet is the northernmost example of a-prefixing in the dialect literature right up in Haynes Hollow.

Right up in Haynes Hollow. In a landscape that is folded up and down in hollows and hills, a degree of geographic specificity might be expected. Double-prepositioning, the combination of several words of direction and placement, is a Catskill Mountain speech feature I identified. You got a house on Dingle Hill, you really are *back up in*. Double-prepositioning, an important feature of Catskill Mountain Speech, makes sense.

Yes. Yes.

The dialect of the Catskills is a mountain dialect, related in grammar and structure to the dialect of our southern Appalachian cousins. Like all regional and social variations, our mountain dialect changes as our speech community changes. But we can still hear the speech of the mountains if we but listen to each other.

Zena R. Travis

ZENA R. TRAVIS. I must have walked by an inscription of that name thousands of times. You may have walked by it, as well. Her name appears on a commemorative plaque in the front hall of the Roxbury school, of the Margaretville school, of the Stamford school, of the Gilboa school, of the Windham school. . . .

Zena R. Travis was the longtime Superintendent of New York State's Fourth Supervisory District of Schools, the district that comprised much of the central, western, and northern Catskills. Supervisory districts are sub-regions of the state created by the Legislature back in 1910 to improve the overall supervision of local schools. The state commissioner of education was authorized by this legislation to divide the rural part of the state—municipalities of fewer than 4500 people—into supervisory districts.

These districts did not have the authority to provide educational services. That was the job of locally elected boards of education. Rather, the Supervisory Districts were designed to improve educational quality through greater supervision and assistance. Each district was headed by a district superintendent, who was a state official with salary paid by the state.

In the early part of the twentieth-century, most rural education occurred in one-room schoolhouses. High Schools were found only in the larger villages, but every hamlet and hollow, every valley and crossroad seemed to have its own little eight-grade schoolhouse. As late as 1940, there were over 4000 small independent public schools throughout the state. Today there are a little over 700 public school districts.

As you drive through the Catskills, you'll notice a certain similarity in the central schools that serve our towns. The Downsville School looks a little bit like the Tannersville School, the Stamford School reminds one of the Windham building.

Each were built as projects of the infrastructure re-building Works Projects Administration of Franklin Roosevelt's depression-fighting New Deal. Zena Travis presided over much of the 1930s centralization that combined little Catskill Mountain districts into gleaming new Central Schools. Hence, her name on the plaques.

Zena Travis was quite a Catskill Mountain success story. She was born around 1890, raised on a Meeker Hollow farm in the Town of Roxbury, graduated from the old Roxbury High School. Roxbury, Margaretville, Fleischmanns, Andes, Grand Gorge, Stamford and other mountain villages established high schools where village children were educated in grades 1 through 8, and high school education was offered to those few who chose to pursue it. Zena was an excellent student, graduating high school at the top of her class.

We can piece her story together through newspaper clippings. In 1909, she appears in the *Catskill Mountain News* as a student home on school holiday from the Oneonta Normal School, precursor to today's State College. By 1912, she is spending the summer in Meeker Hollow, home from a year teaching in the public schools of far-off California, preparing to return for a second year. What an adventure!

By 1916, Zena Travis is listed as a teacher at the old Margaretville High School, probably teaching village children in one of the paired grades: grades 1 and 2, 3 and 4, 5 and 6, or 7 and 8. In 1919, she is listed as the teacher in one-room School #14, perhaps the Meeker Hollow school she had attended as a child.

And then, by 1921, the 29-or-30-year-old schoolteacher from Roxbury has been elected District Superintendent. And from that point forward, she is everywhere. She visits schoolhouses in Bovina one week, on Dingle Hill the next, up Redkill one day, Montgomery Hollow the next.

In 1922, she publishes a newspaper article urging local schoolteachers to monitor their pupils' nutrition. Children cannot learn if they are hungry, Miss Travis points out. Provide malnourished children with a quart of milk per day. We thought concern with student nutrition was forward-thinking and progressive in the 1970s. Zena Travis was focused on children's health and nutrition in 1922!

I knew lots of Catskill Mountain folks who got their education in a one-room school. I never heard anyone complain about the lack of opportunities there. On the contrary, many boasted that their one-room schoolhouse education was a good one, with a real focus on reading, writing, and mathematic skills, and a cooperative learning environment among children of varying ages. I think that emphasis on quality and cooperation is a tribute to Zena Travis, who helped set the standards high and the school climate inviting.

In 1936, Miss Robinson, teacher in the Meeker Hollow School, took sick. Who substituted for a week? The District Superintendent, Zena R. Travis.

Miss Travis set the standard for Catskill Mountain country schools for three or four decades. The quality of education that many of us found here is, I think, a tribute to her. She made sure Catskill Mountain kids had a chance.

In 1960, Zena Travis was the guest speaker at the Fleischmanns High School graduation. By that time, she had been pursuing and urging excellence for over fifty years.

Election of '36

WHEN THE FIRST JANUARY INAUGURATION took place in Washington, D.C., this part of the Catskills was roiling in resentment, anger, and neighbor-against-neighbor ill feeling. It was January 20, 1937.

For the first 150 years of our republic, the transfer of power from one president to the next, and from one Congress to the next, took place on March 4, a full four months after the November election. In an era when distance mattered and transportation was difficult, the long period between election and inauguration was designed to give newly elected officials a chance to put their affairs in order and make the often arduous trip to Washington.

No one seemed to mind this long inter-regnum much, as long as the new presidential and congressional policies promised to be pretty similar to those of the out-going president and congress. Most years, the country's problems seemed like they could wait for new leadership.

This "lame duck" period first proved to be a problem in 1861, when southern states, one after the other, passed Articles of Secession in response to the election of Abraham Lincoln. Lincoln, required to wait four months to take power, found himself unable to respond to the growing crisis, since, as President George W. Bush said, during the 2008 financial crisis, "We only have one president at a time."

Anxiety over the long wait arose again as the election of 1932 approached. The Great Depression was in full swing, President Hoover was wildly unpopular, and public opinion was anxious and eager to replace him. Congress proposed an amendment to the Constitution eight months before the election, and by the beginning of the following year it had gained ratification through the approval of the states.

The 20th Amendment did not take effect until the end of the year it was ratified, so the first transfer of presidential power at noon on January 20th took place after the next presidential election: the election of 1936.

That campaign was a hot one here in the mountains. The legacy of the Civil War had made our area solidly Republican. After all, the Democratic Party had been the party of the south. Lincoln's Republicans had won the Civil War and ended slavery. The Catskills were rural and overwhelmingly Protestant, and Democrats were identified with cities, saloons, former-slave holding southerners, and largely Catholic immigrants: "Rum, Romanism, and Rebellion" in the words of one late- nineteenth-century Republican broadside.

Franklin Roosevelt, a Democrat, ran for a second term in 1936, and the campaign here in the Catskills was hard-fought. Roosevelt's New Deal was controversial, and the President, our across-the-river neighbor, was either loved or hated here. Most supported his opponent, Kansas Governor Alf Landon. A metal Landon sign hangs on my barn, a generous gift from a friend who took it off his New Kingston garage where it had hung continuously since 1936.

The Roosevelt Democratic Club carried on a vigorous campaign here, holding a late October rally in Margaretville's Dugan Hall, now the Granary Building. That rally followed a rally for Landon, organized by the Independent Coalition of American Women, an organization that became the Republican Women's Club after the election.

Women were very active in the campaign, 1936 being only the fifth presidential election in which women had the right to vote. Fanny Hubbell of Kelly Corners led the Roosevelt Club, organizing a campaign luncheon for 60 at the Andes Hotel. *The Catskill Mountain News* was strong for Landon. The campaign was hard fought. Polls predicted a Landon victory. Roosevelt won in a landslide.

Jubilant Democrats celebrated, perhaps a bit too much. On the Thursday after election, a line of 50 automobiles paraded down Margaretville's Main Street in what the News described as "a kind of gasoline fan dance to the truck of Ray Shultis," blowing horns and making merry. On Ray Shultis' truck, the celebrating Roosevelt supporters propped an outhouse. On the outhouse was a sign that read "Independent Coalition of American Women." Another sign on the truck read "Republican Propaganda."

Well! The next day people were peeved. No, more than peeved, downright angry. The out-house was deemed not just vulgar, but an insult to Republican women, and in the old-fashioned chivalry of the day, an insult to the wives and mothers of Republican men. "Life long friends met on the street the next morning with an icy stare, business places were boycotted and the streets were filled with excited groups of people talking and making gestures," the *News* reported. The *Oneonta Star* reported that the trouble threatened to tear the town apart.

It was a big deal.

Stanley Bussy was one of the few Democratic businessmen in town. His grocery, Bussy's, became the focus of the boycott.

Trouble continued through the weekend. On the following Monday, the Democratic Town Committee met to issue a public apology. Republicans met soon after, first the Women's club, then the Men's. Amid a lot of hard feeling, and strong words, cooler heads prevailed, agreeing to accept the apology. "Life returns to normal in the Catskill Mountain village where surely it would be impossible to be at odds with neighbors," the *Catskill Mountain News* opined on the front page.

Forgive, maybe, but forget? Thirty-six years later, I got involved in local politics and people still talked about the outhouse parade of 1936. Surely, hurt feelings, anger, and resentment were still fresh when Roosevelt was sworn in for a second term that January day in 1937. Tough business, mountain politics.

Mr. Fleischmann Comes to the Catskills

IN 1883, one of the richest men in America bought 60 Catskill Mountain acres to build a summer colony for his extended family.

Charles Fleischmann was a 32-year-old master distiller and yeast production superintendent on the estate of an Austrian nobleman when he first visited the United States in 1866. He came to New York City to attend the wedding of his sister Josephine.

The story goes that Fleischmann was aghast at the poor quality of the baked goods served at the wedding. Austrian yeast breads and pastries were lighter and better. French scientist Louis Pasteur had recently discovered the role of the one-celled yeast fungus in fermentation, and Charles had become expert in the process in carrying out his duties: producing spirits and yeast for his aristocratic employer.

Opportunity knocked. American bakers had long relied on sour dough, or malted and sugared potato flour, or brewers' yeast skimmed off fermenting ale. No commercial yeast production existed in the United States. The door was open for a new American industry.

Charles and his brother Max immigrated to the United States, first working in a distillery in New York, then moving to Cincinnati, Ohio, where they found a financial backer to establish a yeast production plant on the banks of the Ohio River. To promote their product, they opened Viennese-style bakeries in New York and Philadelphia.

The 1876 American Centennial Exposition in Philadelphia provided a breakthrough. Fleischmann's Yeast created a sensation. Bread and cakes were lighter, smoother, more flavorful. The brothers developed an efficient distribution system, getting their product both to commercial bakeries and the home kitchen. Fleischmann's packaged yeast helped make home bread-baking a staple of American life. The alcohol produced as a by-product gave the brothers a second product: Fleischmann's Gin.

The family prospered. Yeast quickly became a product everybody bought, used, and bought again, and Fleischmann's Yeast was so much the best and most widely-distributed yeast that it became the only yeast. Think Bill Gates and software and you get an idea of the Fleischmann brothers and yeast.

Charles developed respiratory problems and his doctors recommended a mountain climate to avoid the humid heat of the Ohio Valley in summer. In 1883, the family discovered the Catskills and the little hamlet of Griffin's Corners on the Ulster & Delaware Railroad. From local farmer, John Blish, Charles bought 60 acres on a hill just west of the village. There, he established his summer colony.

Perhaps, Charles had a second motive for establishing a new summer resort for his family rather than seeking a summer home in an already established community. In 1877, Joseph Seligman, a wealthy Jewish banker from New York, was rudely and unceremoniously turned away from the Grand Union Hotel in Saratoga, a hotel he and his family had frequented in the past. A new wave of anti-Semitism spread through the resort and spa areas of the time, and one could never be sure what indignities might await. I'll bet Charles Fleischmann was determined that not happen to him.

When he arrived in Griffin Corners, the little village sat at the base of a hill on its east end, Armstrong Park, the August retreat of the Hudson-Valley-Roke-by-Farm Armstrong branch of the patrician Livingston family. I have visions of the immigrant Jewish Fleischmann seeing the wealthy old-family estate sitting on a hill east of the village and saying, "I'll take the hill on the west side!"

And quite a colony he built. The family compound was on top of the hill, four or five houses that provided a ten-week summer home for Charles and his family as well as the families of a variety of relatives. He surrounded his home with a deer park, well-stocked trout pond, spring-fed heated swimming pool, baseball field, and riding stable. The baseball field is today's Fleischmanns Park and the stables are visible behind today's West Wind Motel.

The station at Fleischmanns. Carriages from the hotels await arriving guests.

The family built a railroad station to serve their colony, a station called "Fleischmann's." Friends, cousins, and business associates of the Fleischmann family flocked to Griffin Corners. Soon, other Jewish immigrants from the old Austro-Hungarian Empire came. Wagner Avenue was built as a grand boulevard of summer mansions, and hotels and boarding houses sprang up. A thriving Jewish summer trade made the little village a hub of activity every summer.

In the early 1900s, the Fleischmann family withdrew from the village, donating the ball field for a park, accepting the renaming of Griffin Corners in their honor.

The Village of Fleischmanns remained a vibrant resort, attracting a large Jewish clientele, right into the 1960s and 70s. Gradually, that clientele died off, and, in an era of air-conditioning and cheap airfares, few came to take their place.

But, ahh, what Fleischmanns once was!

I See Ya, Joe DiMaggio

IWAS AMUSED a few years back by a cover story in *New York* magazine. The August 2003 article was about the Catskills second-home real estate boom that followed the horrible events of September 2001, when hundreds of New Yorkers discovered the Catskills and many bought homes and acreage here in the mountains.

What amused me was the notion that the Catskills were kind of a new Hamptons, the seaside resort-towns where many New Yorkers have traditionally summered. "It's the old Hamptons lifestyle without the new Hamptons scene," the article said of our mountains, "though there's certainly no shortage of beautiful people."

Well, at least they got that right. I'm sure the magazine wasn't referring to the Converse sneaker-wearing, Dickies-work-clothes-and-Carhartt-jacket crowd that I found so compelling when I came here from the suburbs thirty some-odd years ago. Nonetheless, the Catskills are filled with beautiful people.

How do you capture the sensibility of a people? What made Catskill Mountain folks so, I don't know, interesting to the many of us young people who flocked here in the wake of the back-to-nature sixties and seventies?

A Joe DiMaggio story I once heard captures some of it. It seems the great Yankee Clipper, perhaps the greatest baseball player ever to play the game, was a passenger in an automobile driving through our area on the way to the Baseball Hall of Fame. Somewhere south of Cooperstown, the driver got lost. Spotting a farmer on his tractor at haying, DiMaggio's friend pulled over to the side of the road to ask directions.

The farmer got off his tractor and walked slowly to the passenger side of the car. He leaned in the passenger side window, looking and talking across the famous, and highly recognizable, ballplayer to give directions. "Cooperstown?" he said, eyes on the driver. "Just head straight a few miles until you come to an intersection," the mountain farmer began. His focus was on the driver, describing turns and landmarks, until he interrupted himself momentarily, patted DiMaggio on the arm, said, "I see you, Joe, I see you," and then went right back to direction giving.

No fuss. No celebrity gushing. Just the quiet human dignity of one person letting another know he matters, but on an equal plane, and within the context of the task at hand: getting the driver to Cooperstown. For me, that's the Catskills.

I got to thinking about this last week at a workshop I attended that focused on the great writer and naturalist John Burroughs. Each of us who participated in the session focused on Burroughs as the writer of over thirty books, Burroughs as the master of the nature essay, Burroughs as literary critic, Burroughs as keen observer of the natural world. And John Burroughs was all of those things.

Yet, somehow, coming away from the workshop, I felt as if the John Burroughs I have come to admire and love was missing. That was the John Burroughs who was friends with the poet Walt Whitman and the President Theodore Roosevelt – two pretty different types of guys. The John Burroughs who used to stop at the neighbor's to take a quick nap, tuckered out from the long walk home up-hill from the Roxbury post office. The John Burroughs surrounded by a bevy of Vassar girls who loved the old man.

That John Burroughs was a Catskill Mountain guy, a lot like the farmer who refused to objectify Joe DiMaggio.

Elbert Hubbard, a long-time friend of Burroughs, tried to capture the essence of the man in his little book *Old John Burroughs*, now out of print. Hubbard was a writer and thinker associated with the early twentieth-century Arts and Crafts Movement. Not being a Catskill Mountain guy himself, he gushed a bit over Burroughs. But he also captured a bit of the mountain sensibility that makes John Burroughs so attractive even today, decades after his death.

Of Burroughs, Hubbard wrote: "He is a piece of elemental nature. He has no hate, no whim, no prejudice. He has no airs, and he believes in the rich, the poor, the learned, and the ignorant. He believes in the wrongdoer, the fallen, the sick, the weak, and the defenseless. He loves children, animals, birds, insects, trees, and flowers. You would confess to this man – reveal your soul and tell the worst, and his only answer would be, 'I know! I know!' and tears of sympathy and love would dim those heaven-blue eyes."

Now there's a description of the Catskill Mountain beautiful people we can all aspire to.

Jim Dutcher

IN THE LATE 1800s, "the best known and most reliable guide" in the Catskills, was James W. Dutcher of the Big Indian-Oliverea Valley. So stated the *Commemorative Biographical Record of Ulster County*, published in 1896.

Jim Dutcher was born in 1838 up in Prattsville. Like many in that part of the northern Catskills, Dutcher family prosperity was tied to the tanning business. Zadock Pratt's huge tannery closed in 1845. Young Jim's father died a few years later. When his mother remarried, young Jimmy, just 13 years old, decided it was time to move on. So he walked to Shandaken.

Tanning in those days was dependant on an abundant supply of hemlock trees, the bark of which contains tannins that, when mixed with water, produces a strong, reliable tanning agent. Hides soaked in hemlock-bark-solution become tough, durable leather, a major Catskill Mountain product right up through the Civil War.

But it took a lot of trees, a devastating number of trees. Bark-peelers would take to the woods in spring when the sap started running. That sap-run produces a slime just below the bark that makes efficient bark-removal feasible. Teams of bark-peelers would cut hatchet-gashes around a hemlock trunk, twice scoring the bark deeply the entire circumference of the tree, the two gashes about four feet apart. They would pull that four-foot section of bark off the standing tree, then cut the tree down. The felled trunk was stripped of bark in four-foot sections, the bark piled into cords for sale to the tanneries, the stripped hemlock wood often left to rot on the forest floor.

Bark-peeling destroyed the hemlock forest. Today, stands of first growth hemlock are prized. Forestry expert Michael Kudish identifies only 16 such stands throughout the Catskills, all but two located above 2400 feet, elevations that made them difficult access for Bark-Peelers. Several are on the shoulder spurs of Slide Mountain, a couple on Giant Ledge, one up Rider Hollow, and one up McKinley Hollow. All areas Jim Dutcher knew well.

Jim Dutcher walked to Shandaken because he knew he could find work there. Tanning and bark-peeling was a moveable beast, the life-span of a tannery about 30 years. When the hemlock was depleted in one part of the Catskills, the industry moved to another. Young Jim knew where he was going. As 25 tanneries closed up on the Schoharie Creek, 17 operated along the Esopus.

He got work as a bark-peeler, tough, dirty work that went 15 hours a day from first sap-run to the fourth of July. Soon, his pluck and energy and natural intelligence facilitated his rise, at age 17, to contract-agent, the guy who hired and housed a team of peelers, arranged the transport and sale of the bark, and worked for profit rather than wage.

In 1860, Jim Dutcher married Mary Andrews. They had 11 children, fostering a family line that still today brightens the Esopus Valley. Sometime in the 1870s, Jim and Mary Dutcher built the Panther Mountain House, a summer boarding house and hostelry at the head of the Oliverea Valley. The building is gone now, but, I understand, it stood on a side hill up behind today's Full Moon Resort where the road begins its climb up to Giant Ledge and Winnisook.

It was through his hotel business that Jim became a celebrated Catskill Mountain guide, well known for his intimate knowledge of Slide Mountain, where he blazed one of the first trails up that tallest Catskill Mountain, and built a stone step-way and an observation tower to make his guests' mountain hike easier and their views more imposing. Through his activity in the Republican Party, Jim became postmaster, a position akin to mayor-in-chief in many Catskill hamlets, right up to the re-organization of the Post Office Department in the 1960s.

Bob Steuding's wonderful book *The Heart of the Catskills* (Purple Mountain Press, 2008) contains several photographs of Jim Dutcher, who seemed equally at home on the trail leading a party of well-dressed female hikers or, swilling a drink, shotgun in hand, sitting by a rock ledge with a trying-to-be-hard-boiled group of male hunters. He seems to have had the gift of easy company.

Jim Dutcher left the Catskills after the death of his wife, following two of his sons to the Far West, where he died in 1913 in Washington State. Several of his descendants continued to reside in Shandaken. One, the late Hooper Dutcher, had a gift for horticulture, creating, along with his wife, Lisa, a lush garden and nursery on the banks of the Esopus, on land that had stood fallow and unproductive for years.

A hundred years ago, Jim Dutcher, postmaster, hotelier, mountain guide, was called Slide Mountain's "guardian spirit." I like to think he still is.

Melvin Mayes' House

I LIVE IN MELVIN MAYES' HOUSE. He built it himself in 1925, raised his family here, and sold it when he moved to Florida in the early 1980s. The house changed hands twice before I bought it in 1996. I like to point out that, I believe, it was the only house sold in Fleischmanns that year.

There's nothing too remarkable about any of that, except maybe the dearth of home sales in Fleischmanns in the mid-90s, until one learns a little bit about Melvin, a self-employed carpenter and builder who grew potatoes in the backyard and kept chickens and a cow in the big shed out back.

Melvin liked to write. He loved history, particularly the history of his home village.

Here I am, living in the house he built, sharing many of the same interests. Like Melvin, I like to write. Like Melvin, I love history, particularly Catskill Mountain history. Is there something kind of mystical about that?

I never met Melvin Mayes. After he moved to Florida, Melvin carried on a brisk correspondence with Lewis and Jackie Grocholl of Fleischmanns. They were kind enough to lend me his letters, which Jackie has preserved meticulously. In his rounded, flourishing, fountain-pen inscribed hand, Melvin begins his letters with comments on the weather and the current state of his health, before diving into memories of life in Fleischmanns in the days of his youth.

Those days were the first decades of the twentieth-century when Melvin and his boyhood friends—Harry Tubbs, Harold "Jimmy" Judd, Harold and Ray Slover—lived in a world of horse-drawn wagons, and .22 rifles, and fishing in the Vly Creek that runs out of Halcott, then known as the Portertown Creek.

In an early letter, Melvin wrote of a funeral procession which began in the Slover cabinetmaking shop on Main Street, Fleischmanns. Jackie Grocholl is a Slover, so Melvin was gearing his story to his audience. In those days, a furniture shop also made coffins, so the Slover furniture wagon served as the local hearse.

The Slover building later housed Halpern's Supply, a once-famous hardware store that advertised the lowest prices around in the 1930s and drew bargain hunters from distant points, a kind of early destination shopping outlet. Later, artist Alfredo Santos had his 1970s studio in that building. Santos' work enjoyed a retrospective gallery exhibit and sale in Fleischmanns just last year. He is a highly regarded artist who created a mural in San Quentin during a youthful bid in that prison. Today, Bud Sife owns the building that once housed the Slover furniture shop.

Melvin tells the story of a funeral procession that lasted nearly a full day, beginning in the morning at Slover's, heading up the Redkill Road, over the Denver-Vega pass to a cemetery in Roxbury. It was nearly dark by the time the furniture wagon and the little procession got back to Fleischmanns. It's fascinating that a trip I take nearly every week—it takes 17 minutes or so—once consumed the better part of a day. That's history.

Jackie also has a complete collection of the *Fleischmanns Flyer*, the little four-page newsletter that Wray and Loni Rominger of Purple Mountain Press published between 1975 and 1977. In it, the Romingers told the news of Fleischmanns: clean-ups of the Bushkill, meetings of the Chamber of Commerce, hotly contested mayoral elections, arson and fires, urgent meetings to "save our village."

Particularly heart-wrenching is the issue headlined "Black Friday" that announced the sale of the Williamson Veneer Plant on Depot Street to the Weyerhaeuser Corporation which immediately closed it, putting 70 people out of work. The next two issues contain an exchange of letters, one from Wray to the corporation asking for hope that the plant might re-open, the other to Wray from the corporation making it clear there was no chance the plant would operate again.

The Flyer contained an occasional feature called "Memories of Fleischmanns," written by an anonymous author. Having read Melvin Mayes' letters, I notice enough stylistic similarity that my hunch is that he was that writer. I think my hunch was affirmed when I read Wray's dedication to Melvin in a 1991 rebirth of the *Fleischmanns Flyer*.

Melvin Mayes, Wray wrote, "made us feel welcome in our new home" and "shared with us his extraordinary memory of the village in its heyday." He went on to write that Melvin was in the habit of writing "witty, anonymous poems in the *Catskill Mountain News*."

And I write, although not anonymously, in the *Catskill Mountain News*, as well. I think there might be something to this house sharing.

Jake Moon: Man and Restaurant

SO, I'm driving to Albany, going to see a movie—there are a lot of high quality, grown-up movies out right now, but, living in the Catskills, you have to travel a bit to see them. I decide to take a cross-country route to the Capital District, looking for a little mountain adventure on a gray, ground-hog's-seen-his-shadow late winter day.

I drive up Route 30, through Grand Gorge and North Blenheim, Middleburgh and Schoharie, to the intersection of Route 30 and Route 443, just beyond the Old Stone Fort in Schoharie. There, I turn right onto Route 443 toward Gallupville.

It's an unfamiliar route to me, but the map tells me I'll enter Albany on Delaware Avenue, site of the theater. It also just seems right, approaching the capital, as I am, from the upper Delaware River and all.

Route 443 winds its way through Gallupville and West Berne, Berne, and East Berne, climbing through the Helderberg Mountains, and the villages and hamlets known as the Hill Towns of Albany. It's a pretty ride. The road seems to follow the hill-tops, through rugged backcountry, along the ridge of the Heldebergs, with fewer dramatic variations of elevation than in our Catskills.

Just to my left, a few miles north of my route, the Heldeberg Mountains rise majestically from the wide, flat lowland geologists today call Lake Albany, a sandy fossil-rich expanse surrounding the city, formed by an ice-age glacier that created a now-dry inland sea. The Heldeberg Escarpment is a 200-foot rocky rise that forms the northern edge of mountainous terrain above the flats of the Mohawk Valley, and curves south to form the western border of the Hudson River lowlands, as well.

John Boyd Thatcher State Park straddles the escarpment. Signs direct the traveler from Route 443 to the park, and it's well worth the trip. Thatcher Park is one of the most beautiful places in the state, and it's right in our side yard. On a clear day, one can see from the Park's escarpment trail, the Adirondacks to the north, and Vermont's Green Mountains to the east, as well as the Mohawk Valley and Capital District at one's feet. It's a great place.

But I had a movie to catch, and, being unfamiliar with the route, was unsure of how to gauge my time. Thatcher Park would have to wait for another day. I followed Route 443 east, past the signs for the park, into Clarksville, a little country hamlet not unlike many in our own mountains. That's when I saw the sign: *Jake Moon Restaurant and Café*.

It was unmistakable. The sign would be instantly recognizable to anyone familiar with the former Jake Moon Restaurant in Big Indian, precursor to today's vibrant and delightful Peekamoose Restaurant, successor to the inventive and original now-long-gone Rudi's Big Indian. I caught the sign out of the corner of my eye: the yellow and burnt umber color scheme, the long, narrow-faced bearded mountain man in a soft, wide-brimmed felt hat, the squinty, narrow-eyed stare. It was Jake Moon! I had to stop, turn-around, pull-in. The movie could wait.

Chef Dan Smith grew up in Woodland Valley, learned his craft while serving in the Army in Europe, where he earned a degree in Restaurant Management and graduated from La Varenne School of Cuisine in Paris. He honed his skills under chef Eugene Bernard, a Basque who stressed the use of fresh local produce. Dan was executive chef at Rudi's Big Indian, and bought that restaurant in 1994 establishing the first Jake Moon.

Jake Moon himself was a legendary Catskill Mountain Man and Dan Smith's great-great-great granduncle. Of both Native American and European heritage, Jake Moon was one of the first settlers of Chichester. He stood 6 foot 6 inches tall, was a bark-peeler and railroad man, and a local character.

Once, he was night watchmen at the rail yard in the Stony Clove Notch above Chichester. Asleep in the guard's shack, he was suddenly awakened by a landslide that carried him and the building he was in down hill onto the railroad tracks, into the path of an ill-timed on-coming train. I'm not sure how he survived, but he did, starting his family when in his seventies. A number of his descendants, direct and collateral, still live here in the mountains.

And one, Dan Smith, "retired" to Clarksville where last month he opened his new version of Jake Moon. I had lunch, a terrific grilled chicken sandwich on homemade dill bread with a wonderful handmade coleslaw. Dan serves breakfast and lunch daily, weekend dinners, and Sunday breakfast and brunch.

Like the Catskill Mountain Cuisine he refined in Big Indian, Dan uses fresh local ingredients including dairy products from a farm just down the road from his place and grass-fed beef from another Albany County farmer. The food is great.

Jake Moon Restaurant and Café is at 2082 Delaware Turnpike (Route 443) about 25 miles from Route 30 north of Schoharie, about 11 miles this side of Albany.

If you are looking for a pleasant ride and a taste of home away from home, try Dan Smith's new digs. It's good.

And I made the movie!

The Professor: Frank Russell

FRANK RUSSELL was my friend. He was also *a rare bird*, as Frankie himself might say.

Born in 1894, Frank was already an old man when I met him at a wedding in the late sixties, wearing his dress converse high-tops and a short, wide, hand-painted tie. I'd never met anyone quite like him, and, as it turns out, so hadn't anyone else. Frank was a character.

He lived in New Kingston, had lived his whole life in a house in the middle of that village that has been, now, the home of his nephew's family for over 25 years. The house had been the home of Frank's grandparents, and, as he told me many times (Frank had a tendency to repeat his stories) when he was a *wee lad*, his mother, about to give birth to a younger sibling, sent Frankie next door to stay with his grandmother and, well, he never went back home. Stayed right there. *Yes, yes.*

The house itself was amazing. Right up to Frank's death in 1982 his house had no running water. Frank lived the old way, the way everybody lived in these mountains until electricity and indoor plumbing brought modernity to the Catskills in the twenties and thirties. He had a chamber pot beneath the bed, an outhouse out back. From about April to October, Frank bathed in the Plattekill Creek out behind his house. From October to March, your guess is as good as mine.

What was really remarkable was the front room, the parlor, in Frankie's house. Sometime in the 1870s or 1880s, an itinerant painter from Kingston had made his way up into the mountains and sold his services to Frank's grand-mother, hand-painting borders and designs on the walls of the parlor in the lat-est, late-Victorian style. New furnishings finished the room: a rug, round center table, velvet upholstered settee, and side chairs.

On her deathbed, Frank's grandmother made him promise that he would preserve and protect her prized parlor, and Frank was a man of his word. Noth-ing was changed in that parlor during Frank's lifetime. He kept the room shut, in the traditional way, only opening it on special occasions. In the olden days, the parlor was never used by the family, but reserved for visits from prominent guests, like the local minister, whom Frankie still referred to as *The Dominee* in the old Dutch manner.

One such special occasion was the New Kingston Whoop-de-doo, a last weekend in August celebration of country life that was held for four or five years in the mid-and late-seventies to raise funds for the New Kingston Presby-terian Church.

On Whoop-de-doo Saturday, hundreds of people would line up to wind their way through that parlor, amazed that this relic of the nineteenth century was so beautifully preserved late in the twentieth.

Now, don't get the impression that Frank was some kind of relic or rube himself. He was anything but. Called *The Professor* by his many friends, Frank was a schoolteacher of wide reputation in these mountains, an intelligent man who taught a couple of generations of Catskill Mountain kids in the one-and two-room schools that dotted these mountains in the early part of the last centu-ry. As a teacher, Professor Russell was much in demand, his services vied for by the various school boards responsible for providing a teacher for the children of their town, valley, or hollow.

"What are you teaching these kids over in school?" Frank would ask me. "I ask 'em who discovered the Hudson River?" Like many an old teacher, Frank was never quite satisfied with the manner of education that followed his time. He loved history and geography, especially that of New York State. The late Howard Davis, a former student of Frank's, summed up his teaching style: "Frank would teach like hell all morning long, then put his feet up in the after-noon."

Frank graduated from the old Margaretville High School in 1912. One of his favorite stories was traveling by train to Downsville to play that village's high school team for the Delaware County baseball championship. Frank's Mar-garetville team won.

Frank boarded over in Margaretville to attend high school, staying in the old Ketchum house on the Margaretville Mountain Road during the week, returning home to New Kingston on weekends. In *them-there* days, the seven miles between the two villages was a considerable distance.

After high school, Frank attended the Oneonta Normal School to become certified as a teacher. He taught for 26 years or so, retiring when the local schools were centralized in 1939 only because he didn't apply for a position in the new central school, so used to being pursued by school boards coming to him to seek his services.

For the next forty years, *The Professor* was the unofficial mayor of New Kingston, telling the old stories, keeping alive the old ways. I miss him. Anyone who knew Frank Russell misses him, too.

Reginald Bennett

A FRIEND AND FORMER COLLEAGUE is the principal of the Reginald Bennett Elementary School. That's the school in the Town of Olive, up on the knoll behind the Onteora High School-Middle School on Route 28.

Reginald Bennett was the founding Superintendent of the Onteora School District, a post-World War II super-centralization that combined numerous one, two, and four-room districts into the second largest school district, in terms of area, in the state. Onteora serves students from West Hurley to Highmount, from Lanesville to Oliverea. That's a lot of Catskills!

Bennett himself was much more than the name over the entrance to an elementary school. Along with Phoenicia pharmacist Phil Gordon and a handful of others, Reg Bennett was the driving force behind the founding of the school district, which opened for business in 1953.

A friend of mine, a member of the first graduating class of Onteora High School, remembers his older sister rising before dawn to travel to high school in Kingston, returning home, often, long after dark. That arduous day was common for Ulster County Catskill Mountain kids seeking a high school education in the years before Onteora was there.

Reg Bennett himself never attended high school. He was born in Chichester in 1896, a bright mountain kid who excelled at the local elementary school, read voraciously, and found himself teaching his younger neighbors in the Chichester school at the age of 16. He qualified for admission to the State Teachers College at Albany, got a college degree without benefit of a high school diploma, and went on to get a Master's degree from Albany, as well.

And he came home to teach. He also hiked, fly-fished, pitched town team baseball, told stories, and wrote. He did all those things with a strong sense of ethics and ideals. I have read that, once, a fishing buddy challenged him on the curriculum: "What do you teach those kids up at the Sunshine Hill Schoolhouse?"

"To tell the truth," Mr. Bennett replied. The respect for this country school-teacher was such that he was Mr. Bennett to nearly all. Of course, by the time he became a district-founding administrator, he had taught most of the people he knew in Chichester, and in the surrounding hollows.

Chichester was a company town, and Reg Bennett wrote the definitive history of that place as his Master's thesis. Later, Purple Mountain Press published it as a book, *The Mountains Look Down: A History of Chichester, A Company Town in the Catskills* (Fleischmanns, NY, 1999).

Chichester's history begins in 1870, when brothers Frank and Lemuel Chichester bought the economically exhausted valley, stripped of trees by tanners who took the hemlock and left a wasteland: a wasteland of hardwood and waterpower. There, Stony Clove and Warner Creeks merge to form a pretty strong flow of water, and the Chichester brothers exploited that stream to power the chair factory they erected there. The coming of the railroad spurred their business, which increased dramatically when the brothers designed and patented a rocking cradle that became a big seller. Over 300 people worked in the factory.

In 1884, the Chichester brothers sold out to a New York City firm, William Schwarzwaelder and Son. Nine years later, the son, W. O. Schwarzwaelder, took over the direct supervision and operation of the factory. By the early 1900s, Chichester was jumping, with a large factory that produced a full line of office furniture, chairs, cabinets, and church furnishings. Workers' housing, a park, fellowship hall, company store, church, and bowling alley were all owned by the company.

W. O., known behind his back as *The Kaiser*, was an excellent businessman and concerned, paternalistic employer. He lived in a spacious mansion with his family, a house known locally as "the big house." Later, his son replaced it with an even bigger "Big House." It is still there, although the big houses built in the 1990s make it seem more medium-sized.

W. O. also built Tiskilwa Park, on the Ox Clove hill up behind his house, for the enjoyment and recreation of his workers. It is gone now, partially in private hands, partially state land, but much of the Tiskilwa stonework remains. Tiskilwa is a native-sounding word, either invented or discovered, meaning "Valley of Peace and Beauty."

All this was for the employees who worked in the factory, rented the company houses, took their leisure time in the park, bowling alley and clubhouse, and worshipped in the company church. Reginald Bennett's father, Rupert, was a foreman there, supervising the lumberyard and mill floor.

W. O died in 1924 and his sons were less successful executives than he. The depression of the thirties, and poor management, wore the business down. Workers' hours were cut, the payroll shrunk, orders reduced. Finally, in January

1938, the Schwarzwaelder Company filed for bankruptcy. A year and a half later, on October 28, 1939, the entire village was sold at auction, house by house, lot by lot. The company town was no more.

Today, a ride through Chichester reveals the company houses, altered and renovated over the past 70 years of individual ownership. The church and clubhouse, the big house, and the remains of the fountain that once graced its gardens, are still there.

The old company store now houses the post office, which contains an historical exhibit of the company town that once was. Across the street, an empty field and the ruins of brick kilns mark the spot where the bustling factory, now a ghost of prosperity past, once stood.

Abe and Mia

IGOT TO THINKING about Abe Savetman one day when the President of the United States was talking about the importance of setting high educational standards for our young people. Abe did not live in the Catskills very long, but, in one mountain public school, he went a long way toward establishing a standard of excellence that young people have pursued, now, for over twenty years.

Abe Savetman was already an older guy when, in 1982, he bought the former Mountain Star House up on Turkey Ridge in Greene County's Town of Halcott. Abe retired to the mountains with the love of his life, Mia Steiner, after what one local friend describes as "quite an adventurous life."

Abe had been an avocado farmer in California and a chicken farmer in Tennessee. He had lived in Israel for a while. An accomplished baker, Abe had tried to start a bakery in New Jersey, but problems with a partner or with financing or with government regulation had squelched that plan. Besides, the 70-something lifelong bachelor had fallen in love.

Mia Steiner, a holocaust survivor, was the widow of Abe's best friend. She was a smart cultured lady, an artist who painted in an impressionistic style, with a palette and technique inspired by the great French painter Claude Monet. Abe pursued Mia vigorously in her widowhood, and, finally, she relented, agreeing to accompany him to the Catskills where they would marry. When they discovered that the New Jersey marriage license they packed in their luggage would not be accepted for a New York wedding ceremony, well, they decided to leave well enough alone.

Abe brought Mia to their new home, the old Mountain Star House, a 30 or 36 room former boarding house that had once been owned by the grandparents

of Don Bouton, lifelong Halcott resident and author of a wonderful, and beautifully written, book of reminiscence *By the Light of the Kerosene Lantern* (privately published, 2001). Later that big house was owned by Myron Morse.

The Mountain Star was quite a house, a three-story, flat-topped, mansard-roofed Victorian with a tower that contained all the house's bathrooms. Abe and Mia filled the Mountain Star with books and music and art, and with the smell of bread baking.

Abe Savetman was "quite the character," in the words of one of his friends and neighbors, the mother of several small children whom Abe "harassed" with bits of song and poetry and with quotations from Mark Twain. Abe was

Mia Steiner of Halcott Center. and Abe Savetman tending his early season garden.

devoted to Twain, frequently quoting the great American author of *Huckleberry Finn*, the book the writer Ernest Hemingway credited as being the beginning of modern American literature.

He was also devoted to classical music, believing it was the only music worth listening to. Abe had a good singing voice, although untrained, and he regularly sang operatic arias, whether his friends wanted to listen or not.

Abe was equally devoted to natural foods and whole grains. He set up his commercial baking equipment in the house, and baked his dark, coarse loaves late into the night. He would give a loaf a bread to whomever he might visit or see the next day. More than one of his country neighbors found his bread unpalatable, "like cow feed," in the words of one.

Tragically, Mia Steiner died a few years into their Catskill idyll, and, soon thereafter, Abe's beloved retriever, Goldie, died, and then Abe himself was diagnosed with prostrate cancer. Knowing his own end was near, Abe Savetman brought a loaf of bread to a local attorney and asked him to draw up his will.

It was that will that had a profound effect on the education of a generation of Catskill Mountain kids.

After disposing of his tools and baking equipment, his books—including many first editions—and his real estate, after making a modest bequest to a loyal and true neighbor and friend, Abe Savetman left the residue of his estate, some $84,000, to the Margaretville Central School to establish a scholarship fund and, more importantly, a series of prizes to be awarded to students for outstanding scholarly or creative work. These prizes were to be awarded in honor and memory of his love, Mia Steiner.

The will was specific about the kind of work for which Abe wanted to reward students. Faculty members at the school refined those wishes to create a series of prizes and awards to which students might legitimately aspire. The *Mia Steiner Prizes* and *Mia Steiner Childhood Awards* were first given in the late 1980s, and have been an annual fixture of student achievement at Margaretville Central ever since.

Secondary students compete for Mia Steiner Prizes; elementary pupils for Mia Steiner Childhood Awards. There are Mia Steiner Prizes and Childhood Awards in Science, Math and Technology; in Social Studies and Community Life; in Visual Arts; in Creative Writing; in Performing Arts; and in Poetry. Kind of like an in-school mini-Nobel Prize program, with cash and savings bonds along with the prestige of the prize. Winners of Mia Steiner Prizes and Awards are justly proud.

Abe Savetman died in 1987. Soon after, his house burned to the ground, taking with it his library and Mia Steiner's paintings. But his legacy and hers live on in the poetry and paintings, the piano and flute pieces, the short stories and songs, the dioramas and dramatic readings of countless children and teens every spring at one little Catskill Mountain school.

Discovering the Common Schools

FOR MANY YEARS, Sonny Somelofski ran the Tremperskill Country Store, one of the few general stores left in the mountains—every little hamlet and valley used to have one—and a beacon for Catskill Mountain fishermen from April to October. The store was originally a one-room schoolhouse, it's an old building, and a few years ago Sonny and a friend put on a new roof.

They ripped off several layers of asphalt shingles, down to the original shakes, tore those off, and were looking through the rafters when Sonny's friend noticed something laying down in on top of the attic sheeting. "Reach down in and get it," Sonny told him, "Your arms are longer than mine." His friend pulled out a book, in good, readable condition, a book that had been laying in there for over a hundred years.

Lanesville-in-the-Catskills up Stoney Clove, the bridge and old schoolhouse.

The book was the *Department Register of 1891-92*, published by the State of New York Department of Public Instruction, Andrew S. Draper, State Superintendent of Public Instruction, and distributed yearly to each of the over 10,000 school districts throughout the state. Sonny's store was once School District Number 21 in the Town of Andes. The teacher had to sign for the school's copy.

Education in New York State began under the Dutch with the establishment of common schools, neighborhood schools designed to transmit literacy to as many people as possible. The English, perhaps not surprisingly, placed more emphasis on the establishment of academies to provide a classical education to the children of the elite. With independence, the common schools once again became the center of the new state's educational system.

Common schools educated children from about age 7 to about age 14, for 20 or 25 or 30 weeks a year, in reading, 'riting and 'rithmetic. Teachers, at the start of their careers, were often little older than their oldest pupils, with only a bit more education than the scholars they taught.

The schools were financed through a local land tax levy combined with state aid from a Common School Fund, endowed from the proceeds of state land sales and lotteries. Any costs not covered had to be made up by charging tuition, or rates. Rate bills kept many poor children out of school. After numerous attempts, rates were outlawed and public schools became free to all families in 1867.

Fourteen years earlier, a state law allowed one or more common school districts to form a Union Free School District, governed by a Board of Education, which could establish an "Academic Department" to provide a secondary education to students who desired it. This was the beginning of public high schools in New York.

The Department of Public Instruction supervised the common schools, dividing the state into 113 School Commissioner Districts. Delaware County, in 1891, was divided into two such supervisory units. The eastern, Catskill Mountain portion of Delaware County was the Second School Commissioner District, comprised of 170 common schools in 10 towns. Andes had 21 district schools, Middletown 23, Roxbury 18, Bovina 11 and Delhi 19.

The Town of Shandaken, in Ulster County's Third School Commissioner District, had 13 school districts, Olive 16, Woodstock 7, and Hardenburgh 9. Greene County's Town of Halcott had 4 schools, Lexington 12, and Prattsville 7.

The number of children in school in 1891 is even more surprising than the number of Catskill Mountain school districts. Today Andes Central School educates 120 kids, kindergarten through 12th grade. In 1891, 545 children were enrolled in the 21 schools throughout that town, the great majority in common schools that covered grades 1 through 8. Shandaken had 711 kids in school; Roxbury 543; the Town of Middletown had 812; Halcott 97. That's a lot more children than any of those towns boast today. A lot more.

The bigger mountain villages boasted graded schools, many union schools that offered a secondary education through an Academic Department. Roxbury and Margaretville, Andes and Hobart, Griffin's Corners and Downsville all had graded schools.

Delaware Academy in Delhi was the first secondary academy in Delaware

County founded in 1819. The Delaware Literary Institute, in Franklin, incorporated by act of the state legislature in 1835, was the second. Both transformed into the public central schools that serve their towns and surrounding communities today.

Throughout much of my own career teaching in the Catskills, I heard the drumbeat of criticism of our public school system, how we weren't doing as well as the Japanese. It was comforting for me to read the same concerns in 1891, how our New York State students were two years behind the French and the Prussians. Eek!

Our economy, tough as it is today, is still well ahead of the decades-long doldrums of the Japanese economy, and the Prussians, organizers of modern Germany, lost two World Wars to us, so perhaps we Americans haven't been doing too badly right along.

Corbett Acid Factory

TAKE A RIDE ON ROUTE 30 around the scenic Pepacton Reservoir to the lower East Branch of the Delaware River. Three miles south of Downsville, an impressive old green Roebling-style suspension bridge marks the entrance to Corbett.

Corbett's calling cards these days are that bridge and a 75 foot tapered red brick chimney that rises just beyond it, along with an impressive little white clapboard community center and pavilion a few yards up the road. Otherwise, the hamlet, in the Town of Colchester, is pretty similar to scores of other mountain villages: a couple streets, a bunch of houses, an out-of-business store or two.

The bridge itself might be enough to make Corbett interesting. There are very few suspension bridges in the Catskills. Suspension bridge building was the invention of John Augustus Roebling, a nineteenth-century German immigrant civil engineer, whose wire-rope suspension bridge design, made famous by the 1883 Brooklyn Bridge, revolutionized civil engineering.

Roebling's wire rope revolution began on the Delaware River. He built suspension aqueducts to carry the Delaware & Hudson Canal over the Delaware. Today, the Roebling bridge between Lackawaxen, Pennsylvania and Minisink Ford, New York, down on Route 97, is a National Civil Engineering Landmark.

The 170-foot Corbett Bridge was built in 1926, based on Roebling's design principles. It was built by Corbett and Stuart, the firm founded by a pair of families who built Corbett and owned the entire village for nine decades. In 1892,

Julius and Merrit Corbett, John Stuart and their wives bought, from farmer Bryan Landfield, 167 acres along Campbell Brook from Soules Hill to the river. Their purpose—build a wood acid factory. They ended up building what is said to be the largest acid plant ever built. That 75-foot chimney is all that is left.

Wood acid was a major industrial product a hundred years ago. A range of industrial solvents were extracted from the dry distillation of wood, a process of heating, cooling, distilling, and extracting that was one of the earliest manifestations of the emerging American chemical industry. Acetic acid, acetate of lime, wood alcohol, and charcoal were all produced by the acid factories.

According to the *McGraw-Hill Encyclopedia of Science & Technology*, "Many modern chemical engineering operations developed through the study of acetic acid production." Along the upper Delaware, Neversink, and Susquehanna Rivers, there were 45 acid factories in the 1890s. Seventy other factories operated in northern Pennsylvania. Dry wood distillation was big business in the western and southern Catskill region.

Wood distillation required massive quantities of timber for burning and a constant supply of water for cooling. That's why factories were located along our mountain streams, in places like Cadosia and Cooks Falls, Hale Eddy and Fishs Eddy, Shinhopple and Shavertown. From around 1898 to 1916 an acid plant operated in Arkville on the north side of the river near today's Pavilion Road.

But the Corbett factory was the biggest. Corbett and Stuart built a large plant with numerous buildings, retorts and ovens that exhausted through that tall brick chimney. They had a company store, a freight house and rail siding on the old Delaware & Northern Railroad, a telegraph office, and a Delco plant to produce electricity. Thirty-five company houses provided homes for workers. Corbett was a company town.

The company employed an army of woodcutters, mostly immigrants from Italy, Poland, Russia, and the Czech lands. They earned $1.20 to $3.00 per day, supplying the factory with the 60 to 80 cords of wood it consumed every day.

Such indiscriminate cutting decimated the forest. The discharge of waste by-products into the streams polluted the waters. In 1890, the New York Times reported on the efforts of fishermen and resort owners to stop the pollution. Naturally, acid manufacturers—Corbett and Stuart was not yet in business—claimed that "the destructive effects of their refuse is greatly exaggerated."

Corbett and Stuart's factory reached its height of production during the First World War. Critical to the production of gunpowder was one of its products: acetone, a volatile colorless industrial solvent similar to today's nail polish remover. After the war, business slowed, as other chemical products replaced their wood-based counterparts. In 1934, the plant closed.

But Corbett remained in the family. Leonard and Merrit Stuart, sons of co-founder John Stuart, owned the village. By 1972, Lenny's widow, Bula, was the lone landlord, renting the former company houses for $32 a month. In 1977, she decided to sell.

I remember when the hamlet of Corbett was for sale. It was a pretty unusual and interesting thing. The Institute of Man and Science of Rensselaerville, New York bought it, as a self-help rehabilitation effort, setting up a village corporation. The Institute's plans attracted the attention of CBS correspondent Charles Kuralt, and Corbett was featured on that network's Sunday Morning TV program in 1977.

Today, Corbett is a hamlet of the Town of Colchester. A photograph of the acid factory hangs in the community center, one of the few reminders of the company town that it once was.

Murder in Andes

IMAGINE TWO YOUNG MEN walking down the sidewalk in Andes, having just dropped off their dates at one o'clock in the morning after a Friday night dance at the fire hall. As they approach what is today the Ron Guichard Realty building, one, surprised at the appearance of activity in that building in the wee hours of the morning, says, "I think I see a light."

Suddenly, a voice from just a few yards away, toward the street, demands, "Throw up your hands!" One of the boys responds, "We are friends, don't shoot," but a shot rings out, and the young man described by some as "probably the most popular young man of Andes" falls, shot in the stomach, writhing in pain.

That's exactly what happened on October 28, 1905. Today's realty office was then the Ballentine National Bank, and the young man clutching at the grievous wound in his abdomen was Frank Graham. He and his running mate that evening, a surveyor on the Delaware & Eastern Railroad, had just walked Hazel Newman and Lillie Ballentine home, to the house of Dr. Gladstone, where they lived, located just behind the bank.

Frank Graham was shot on the sidewalk about ten feet east of the bank building next to the bank's wrought iron fence. Perhaps, his friend ran in fear, because it was Graham himself who struggled his way up to the Gladstone residence where they had just left the girls. Dr. Gladstone attended to his wounds, while Lillie and Hazel ran to the fire hall to wake the sleeping town by ringing the fire bell. David Ballentine, president of the bank, inspected his premises.

His investigation showed that someone had tried to pry open the rear door of the bank, failed, and moved to the front door, which they successfully broke open. Inside, the bank robbers had knocked the combination tumbler off the safe, drilled a small hole into the safe door, covered that with coats to deaden the sound, and used a small amount of explosive to blow open the safe. It didn't work. All the explosion did was blow off the outer portion of the lock, leaving the safe door snugly, and securely, closed.

Meanwhile, a posse was formed to find the criminals. Frank Graham reported, through the clenched teeth of his agony, that he had heard, right after he fell, one of the men say, "We must be getting out of this!" The robbers immediately ran.

But where? The posse headed up Cabin Hill, riding in their search all the way to DeLancey and Hamden. Two Hamden farmers reported encountering well dressed strangers, seven or eight of them, huddled around a campfire on Hamden Hill, but that lead went nowhere, and the posse found itself empty-handed.

Back in Andes, Dr. Wight and Druggist Norton worked with Dr. Gladstone attending young Frank Graham. It was clear his wounds were life-threatening. Delicate surgery would be required.

Commodore Elbridge T. Gerry happened to be at his summer home at Lake Delaware. Gerry contacted his New York City doctors, summoning them to the Catskills. At 5:40 on Saturday afternoon, Dr. Robert C. James and Dr. Adrian V.S. Lambert, eminent surgeons, boarded a train in the city, making connections to Walton. A special train met them there, taking them to Delhi, where Mr. Gerry's carriage carried the doctors to Lake Delaware where they spent the night.

Saturday morning the Andes Town Board had held an emergency meeting in which they voted to appropriate a $1000 reward for the arrest and conviction of the bank robbers who had shot young Graham. Many in town believed that these were the same criminals who, a month before, had shot Davenport storekeeper George Hotaling while attempting to hold-up his store.

A number of pieces of evidence were found at the bank, including a supply of dynamite saturated with nitroglycerine, some blasting caps and a fuse, a sledge hammer, chisel and a couple of screwdrivers. Several of these tools had been stolen from the shop of local blacksmith John Bretz. Also found at the scene was a holster for a Colt pistol marked with the initials E.H.M.

Turns out, several people had heard the explosion at the bank, had heard the shots that felled Graham, but thought little of it, as the Andes boys were known to shoot up the air while celebrating Friday night.

At ten Sunday morning, Drs. James and Lambert performed surgery on Graham at Dr. Gladstone's house, assisted by Andes physicians, Gladstone and Wight, and by Delhi's Dr. Gates. The surgeons discovered four holes in Frank Graham's intestine but could not locate the ball that had torn that organ so drastically that 30 stitches were needed to closes its oozing.

Commodore Gerry paid for the services of a trained nurse, Miss Olive Gray of Delhi, to attend to Frank Graham at Dr. Gladstone's where the 25-year old lay for the rest of the week. But he did not get any better. The following Friday, Frank Graham died.

His killers were never found. The crime remains unsolved, a cold case, as it were, 104 years cold.

How can one conclude such a tale? The words of the poet seem to fit. Robert Frost wrote, in his poem, "Out, Out"—which tells the story of the sudden death of another young man—lines which capture our human response to any such tragedy. Eventually, the people of Andes, "since they were not the one dead, turned to their affairs."

It is ever so.

Ethnic Catskills

THE CATSKILLS have always been a haven for immigrants. Something about the Catskills reminds people of home: the rounded mountain slopes, wide green valleys, narrow hollows, rushing creeks, and small lived-in villages. People from all over the world have long seen the familiar here.

The Borscht Belt of Sullivan County is, of course, the most well-known ethnic resort area in mountain history, perhaps in American history. Many of the famous Catskill summer hotels, there, began as boarding houses, designed to supplement the income of immigrant farmers. Lots of immigrant Jews came to the Catskills in the first years of the 20th century to farm.

In the late 1800s, Baron Maurice de Hirsch, a German-Jewish philanthropist, established an international movement to provide persecuted Russian Jews the wherewithal to emigrate and establish themselves as farmers. In 1900, The Jewish Agricultural Society was established in the United States as part of this movement. At that time, only 200 Jews farmed in the U.S. By 1938 there were 100,000.

Selig Grossinger was one of them. With his wife, Melke, Selig had come to Sullivan County to make a living as a farmer but, like many Catskill Mountain farmers, soon discovered that taking in summer boarders was more lucrative than selling eggs and vegetables, and a lot more predictable. The boom of the twenties put money in the pockets of immigrant Jewish workers seeking a vacation. Selig and Melke put their entrepreneurial daughter, Jennie, in charge of their boarding business. Plentiful kosher food, fresh air, and organized activities attracted summer visitors to their large farmhouse and 100 acres, which soon transformed into a major resort.

**"Summer fun among folks like you" was the unspoken promise of many
mountain resorts catering to specific communities and groups.
Here, the Takanassee Hotel pool in Fleischmanns.**

Grossingers, of course, was only one of the famous Jewish resorts of the
Catskills. Brown's Hotel, The Raleigh, Kutsher's Country Club, The Concord—
the list is endless. Bungalow colonies provided a lower cost alternative. A resort
at every economic level welcomed immigrant vacationers, and their American-
born children, to the Catskills.

And they weren't the only ones. It seems every immigrant and ethnic group
in America has found a part of the Catskills to call their own. The Villa Roma in
Callicoon and Villa Vosilla in Tannersville today cater to all kinds of people, but
began as self-consciously Italian-American resorts. Villa Vosilla still advertises
itself as being "nestled in the Italian Catskill Mountains."

The Oliverea Valley was long a German-American vacation stronghold, the
narrow valley, steep hillsides, and mature forest, perhaps, reminiscent of the
Black Forest or of Bavaria. One can still get wonderful German food at the Slide
Mountain Forest House at the head of that valley.

Friendship Manor was a 1960s-era resort catering to African-Americans. The
manor was located on the site of today's Belleayre Beach at Pine Hill Lake, in
what had been the old Funcrest Hotel. Mr. Reed ran a bustling ethnic resort,
attracting busloads of folks who'd come up from the city on weekends, where
friends recall a lively music scene.

Down in Kerhonkson on the edge of the Catskills, Peg Leg Bates operated
the Peg Leg Bates Country Club, a resort catering to African-Americans, from

1951 to 1987. Peg Leg lost a leg at the age of 12 to a South Carolina cotton gin, but went on to become an amazing tap dancer, showman, and entertainer who, it was said "danced better with one leg than anyone else could with two."

The Irish Catskills, up in East Durham along Route 145, are "the nearest thing to the old sod." In a former life, when my children were small, we spent a few days every summer at Mullen's Irish Spring Hotel, now the Blackthorne Resort. I remember talking with a nun, there, who ran a parochial school in the Bronx. She told me, "We have so many illegal aliens coming to register their children at our school, that we don't even ask for documentation anymore."

This was back in the '80s when wars and atrocities in Central America were on the front page every day. "Where are they coming from, Sister," I asked, "Nicaragua? El Salvador?"

"Oh, no, no," Sister replied. "Ireland."

She and other guests at the hotel always maintained the mountains reminded them of home.

It is not surprising, then, that participants in America's most recent wave of immigration have found a home in the Catskills, as well. Beginning in the 1980s, immigrants from Mexico began to come to the United States to find a better life for their families. Many, from the state of Peubla, came directly to Newburgh, N.Y. where they settled and found work. But Newburgh is a tough town, and the Puebla migrants were essentially country people. In 1986, Arturo Garcia bought a house outside Fleischmanns, and brought his family to live and grow in the mountains.

Others followed. Today, about 20 percent of Fleischmanns' 328 residents are Mexican-Americans. They own houses and operate businesses, pay taxes and send their children to the public school. They work hard.

Jessica Vecchione of Hamden has made a one-hour video documentary about the Mexican-American community of Fleischmanns. It is very good. (I should say that I am in it—my least favorite part of the film.) When you get the chance, go see *Beinvenidos a Fleischmanns: An Immigrant Community in Rural America*.

It is history we are living through right now.

Doug Faulkner: These Were Men!

"THESE WERE MEN!" That exclamation, almost Shakespearian in its emphatic simplicity, was the oft-repeated refrain of the late Doug Faulkner when talking about the generation that came before his. Doug was the longtime postmaster of New Kingston, a World War II Marine, self-made success as a businessman, logger, trader in real estate and rural artifacts, community leader, and keeper of a General Store.

He might have been talking about M. J. Faulkner, no relation to Doug (or, at least, not a close enough relation to recognize in a mountain community where, at one time, everyone seemed to be related, back a few generations, to everyone else). Right after the war, Doug went to work for M. J. in the New Kingston General Store.

Doug Faulkner's intelligence, work ethic, shrewdness and business acumen were the assets he parlayed into material success. He grew up on the New Kingston farm where he was born, was educated in the local one-room school, graduated from Margaretville High School. He didn't have any money, he didn't have a college degree. He had pluck and brains and he figured out how to make a dollar from the resources around him: timber and tomatoes, farms and furniture.

I came to the mountains from a New York City bedroom community, a place where men left the women and children in the morning to ride the train to do things that I, as a child, didn't really understand: sales manager, vice-president, marketer, account executive. When I got to the Catskills, fresh out of college, I met men, like Doug, who did things I could see and comprehend, men who milked cows, cut trees, hauled trash, trucked coal.

The path to success—whatever that means—in the world of my up-bringing was clear and linear: college plus job plus promotions equals career. Here I was in a place where success seemed to depend on looking for an opportunity, making an investment of money or effort or risk, and either reaping the rewards or taking a bath. Seemed kind of, I don't know, archetypically American.

Our Catskill communities still contain men and women who have parlayed mountain shrewdness, native resourcefulness, and hard work into material and financial success. I won't embarrass anyone by naming names, only remind them that they are part of a tradition of self-made Catskill Mountain successes. Of the generations that peopled the mountains before us, we can truly say, "These were men! These were women!"

I moved to New Kingston in 1972. By that time, Doug had left the general store, had moved the post office into a renovated portion of his house. I heard stories about Doug's abilities as a storekeeper, how he would study commodity future prices to determine how much coffee or frozen orange juice or bacon to buy, stocking up when futures prices were on the rise, so, at the height of price spikes, Doug could undersell the A&P. Or how, on Saturday evenings, he'd drive from farm to farm and house to house selling whatever produce he had that he didn't want to keep over until Monday.

Doug's daughter, June, and Barbara Condon each ran the New Kingston

General Store for a few years in the seventies, so I did get a chance to experience that traditional rural institution. They sold milk and butter and eggs, canned goods and groceries, coffee and tea, a little bit of hardware, some cloth and thread, with a gasoline pump out front. Most importantly, they sold neighborhood and community, although there was very little actual profit in that.

The General Store was a place where people hung out, especially men, who often, it seems, find it harder to find something to do at home than women do.

In the New Kingston store, retired farmer Marvin "Hap" Hosier was a mainstay, full of talk and good cheer and lots of gentle kidding of his friends, fellows like Guy "Sharky" Faulkner and Kenny Sanford, who hung out in the general store every day.

Bob "Buck" Russell might stop in on his way to or from work at the creamery in Roxbury or the Central School in Margaretville. His brother, Frank, "The Professor," would tell a story or two. The New Kingston General Store was a lively place.

We miss those kind of places, places where neighbors gather to talk and kibitz and just be neighbors. That's why we read of the collaborative effort to save Russell's Store in Bovina, to make it what it once was—the center of the community.

It just worked a lot better when there was a dollar or two in it for some smart, hard-working mountain guy like the late Doug Faulkner.

Basil Todd

WRITE DOWN YOUR MEMORIES TODAY. Tomorrow they become the stuff of history. In February and March of 1971, Basil Todd, then living in Arkville, wrote two long letters to the *Catskill Mountain News* detailing his memories growing up in and around Fleischmanns. My friend, Jackie Grocholl, always interested in the history of her home town, cut those letters from the paper, carefully pressed them into photo-album pages, and preserved them in her scrapbook of local history for, now, 38 years.

I love local history because I love the Catskills, but, I think, if I lived in Chicago I'd find myself fascinated with the history of Chicago. Local history is the most democratic branch of historical study. It is the history of everyday life, of social, cultural, economic, and political life at their most immediate, individual, personal level. Local history is democratic history, as well, because its practice is open to all of us: we are each capable of writing down our memories of the people, places, and things that fill our days, or, perhaps, talking them into a recording device. Those memories, sometime in the future, provide raw material for people looking to recall that past.

And memory goes back even beyond our living memory. Basil Todd (pronounced Bay-sil, like the spice, not Baa-sil like the Rathbone) was born in 1891 on Sunset View Farm, located on the east Redkill Ridge, looking west over the Redkill Valley. Today, the road leading to that boyhood farm bears Basil Todd's name. The memories in his letters include memories from before his birth, from his grandmother's time. A doctor's bill, for example, found among her papers reveals the price of two days of medical care provided by Dr. John M. Banker in May 1873—four dollars!

There were four doctors in Fleischmanns in Basil Todd's day, three drug stores, four grocery stores, two barber shops, 32 hotels and boarding houses. As a 16-year old, Basil helped build the dam that created Lake Switzerland. Just a couple of years ago, the State of New York demolished that dam and returned that artificial lake, located across from the Regis Hotel, to the Vly Creek streambed.

Lake Switzerland was built by Charles Vermilyea in 1907 for summer recreation—boating and swimming—and winter ice harvest. The dam was destroyed in the early twenty-first-century to prevent catastrophic failure and the destructive flooding such failure would bring.

Basil Todd experienced catastrophe himself when he and his young wife went away for a few days in October 1912. At that time, they lived in a house on the road to the Fleischmanns' train depot, near today's Hasay Realty office. Their house burned to the ground while the young couple was out of town, destroying all their earthly goods. Just a few weeks back, quick work by the Fleischmanns Volunteer Fire Department on a Sunday night, prevented another fire in the same neighborhood from becoming such a catastrophe.

Signing his letters, B. C. Todd, Basil seemed to revel in the fact that he and Bill Morrison were the "oldest surviving 'Natives' of Griffin Corners and Fleischmanns and vicinity." His memory went back all the way to Matthew Griffin, pioneer founder of that settlement, who was a 95-year old dealer in wool and hides when Basil Todd was a boy. Matthew Griffin was also a "pettifogger,'" our letter-writer's term for one who practiced law without any formal legal training. Griffin's son, DeWitt, was a trained lawyer who practiced his profession out of an office in today's Valkyrian Motel on Fleischmanns' Main Street.

Basil Todd's granddaughter remembers him as a highly social and gregarious man, well-liked in his community, who was always interested in politics and current events. His extroverted nature is perhaps suggested by his own memory of a suit of clothes he bought one Easter season in Halpern's Department Store on the main drag in Fleischmanns. That store "carried a very complete line of merchandise, such as Hart, Schaffner & Marx men's suits, Crosset patent leather shoes and other popular brands of the times and a complete line of women's wear."

That particular Easter, Basil Todd walked out of the store in "a green suit of clothes, green shoes and a green derby hat with a red feather in it, all purchased from Halpern's." An extrovert's outfit if I ever heard of one!

Basil Todd left his father's Redkill Ridge farm at the age of 17 to go to college to learn to be a telegraph operator and bookkeeper. He operated the telegraph at the Fleischmanns Railroad station where the aforementioned Charles Vermilyea was the station agent. Basil also worked during his long life as a carpenter, tax assessor, door-to-door vegetable salesman, and caretaker of the Emery Estate up in Highmount.

It is fitting that a road is named after him. He operated a steam-roller one summer when the Redkill Road was first built for automobile traffic.

Basil Todd died in 1973 just before his 83rd birthday. The historical letters he wrote two years earlier left some of what he remembered to the rest of us. We can all learn from that example.

Poets in the Catskills

ThE 48TH POET LAUREATE OF THE UNITED STATES visited the Catskills. Charles Simic was the guest of Ulster County Community College where he appeared in the annual Ellen Robbins Poetry Forum, an event held every April to bring "well known and award winning poets to SUNY Ulster for intimate question and answer sessions, as well as a special evening reading of their poetry."

Simic, a Professor Emeritus at the University of New Hampshire, served as the United States Poet Laureate in 2007-08. Originally the position was called *Consultant in Poetry to the Library of Congress*. In 1985, Congress changed the name to match the 370-year-old title of the state poet of Great Britain, member of the Royal Household, official poet of the realm.

"The Poet Laureate Consultant in Poetry to the Library of Congress serves as the nation's official lightning rod for the poetic impulse of Americans. During his or her term, the Poet Laureate seeks to raise the national consciousness to a greater appreciation of the reading and writing of poetry," the Library of Congress web-site tells us. Kay Ryan of California is the present US Poet Laureate.

Simic is certainly an award winning poet. He won the Pulitzer Prize for Poetry in 1990, and from 1984 to 1989, got one of those MacArthur Foundation "genius" grants, where the recipient gets something like a half million dollars over five years to free them up to create. Not bad.

As for well-known, he certainly is—at least in the increasingly shrinking poetry world. When I was growing up, poets like Robert Frost and Carl Sandburg were celebrities, appearing, I recall, on the Sunday night variety-hour *Ed Sullivan Show*. Today, it is hard for most folks to name a famous living poet.

Part of the problem is the high-falutin' atmosphere that the poetry world seems to seek. It's almost as if reaching out to write for "the masses" is considered low-brow. Most "award-winning poets" are college professors who act as judges on the panels that pick the poets who win awards. It all gets a tad incestuous.

The poet Sparrow—that's his name—has been a long-time resident of Phoenicia. A student of the late New York School poet Ted Berrigan, Sparrow has forged a pretty successful career taking himself a lot less seriously than most of the poetry world likes to take itself. He has been widely published in periodicals like *The Sun*, *The New York Observer*, and *Chronogram*, and has published several books, including *America: A Prophesy*, *The Sparrow Reader* (Soft Skull Press, 2005).

Before he came to the Catskills, Sparrow and his compatriot poets, called The Unbearables, led a protest at *The New Yorker*, the magazine that, more than any other, sets the tone and taste for contemporary American poetry, one that rarely strays from the rarified standards of the professor-poets.

At the protest, Sparrow and his friends carried this message on their protest signs: "Publish our poems! They're just as bad as the ones you do publish!" Eventually, *The New Yorker* did publish one of Sparrow's poems.

Charles Simic seemed a bit bloodless for my taste. In the morning question-and-answer session, he called a poem "a very deliberate and clever contrivance", suggesting, to me, that a poem is a kind of carefully cut jewel, a word-design, a puzzle, rather than an expressive composition, a sometimes messy work of art. Academics seem to prefer these craftsman-poets, members of a guild open only to the few.

Edward Sanders of Woodstock is an accomplished poet of Simic's generation, yet one who represents an entirely different view of poetry. He and his wife, Miriam, a painter, have been Catskill Mountain residents for many years. Sanders is the author of large, expansive poems, imaginative projections, often book-length, that encompass history and biography, the polar opposite of the deliberate and clever contrivances of the academics.

And the award-winning Sanders is well known, originally as a musician and lyricist in the 1960s folk-rock-poetry-satire band, The Fugs. The Woodstock resident has won a Guggenheim Fellowship in poetry, A National Endowment for the Arts Fellowship in poetry, and a National Book Award. He has written biographies-in-verse of the Russian writer, Anton Chekhov, and the American poet Allen Ginsberg. His *America: A History in Verse* (Black Sparrow Press, 2000) is a

2000-page tour de force! It is also available on CD (americahistoryinverse.com).

The late Allen Ginsberg had a few Catskill Mountain connections, himself. He was, I understand, a regular visitor to the Zen Monastery in Mount Tremper. For a number of years, Ginsberg owned a farm just north of the Catskills in Cherry Valley. I hear folks would sometimes bump into him on the Pine Hill Trailways bus.

A poet on the bus. There's something in that concept I like.

Catskill Mountain Quilters

"DAD, WE'RE GOING TO WANDA'S." I was one of many 1980s-era New Kingston parents who heard that call from the kids nearly every summer day. Soon, the late Lois Squires' big station wagon would sway out of her driveway, filled with a gaggle of children, towels and a toy or two, heading up the New Kingston Valley to the village swimming hole.

Seems like every Catskill Mountain hamlet had one: Big Rocks on the Margaretville stretch of the Delaware River's East Branch, Red Falls on the Schoharie up towards Jewett, the old swimming hole is one country cliché that was real. Probably still is.

"Wanda's" was a wide, deep spot in the Plattekill on the downstream side of the culvert-under-the-road that led into the farmstead of Wanda Lanzi, a Catskill Mountain native who's lived on that farm since 1935. Wanda graciously and joyfully opened her property, welcoming the local kids to enjoy the cool of the stream on a hot summer day.

Wanda Lanzi is also a member of the Catskill Mountain Quilters Hall of Fame, inducted in 1986. The Quilters Hall of Fame was organized about the same time as the kids were swimming, its first meeting held on July 14, 1982, at the Erpf Catskill Cultural Center in Arkville, now the headquarters of the Catskill Center for Conservation and Development.

Quilting has been a Catskill Mountain art form since settlers first came to the mountains, an art form born of the marriage of necessity and creativity. In a cold, often inhospitable climate, warm bedding is needed. To weave a blanket one needs spinning wheel and loom. To buy a blanket one needs cash. A quilt can be had with little more than hard work.

Essentially, a quilt is two pieces of cloth sewn together with an insulating filler in between. "Quilting is a simple concept," writes Steve Hoare in *The Unbroken Thread, A History of Quiltmaking in the Catskills* (Black Dome Press, 1996). "Three separate layers closely stitched together create a warmer and more durable garment or bedcover."

Traditionally the top and bottom layers are cotton fabric, the middle insulating layer, unspun wool or cotton. Today, most quilters fill with polyester. Some old quilts contain unusually inexpensive and readily available filling: newspapers, rags, old socks, tree bark, animal skins, bird feathers, political circulars, love letters, diary pages, and tree leaves.

The outside layers of a quilt can be pieced together from whatever varied pieces of fabric are available, pieced together in patches. Hence, the patchwork quilt.

Creativity and artistic design set in early in the history of quilt making, as quilters composed repetitive patterns over the face of the quilt, and turned the stitches required to bind the fabric-layers into embellished designs: "wreaths, ferns, flowers, leaves and vines, even entire representational scenes," Hoare writes.

The Catskill Mountain Quilters Hall of Fame grew out of a Pine Hill quilting circle that used to meet in Charlie's Gun Shop, owned by the husband of Nancy Smith who first came up with the idea. "I just thought there was a Baseball Hall of Fame, and every kind of Hall of Fame you can think of, why not a Quilters' Hall of Fame?" Nancy and her friends Bertha Mayes and Lena Johnson decided to make it happen.

The Hall of Fame honors quilters from five Catskill Mountain counties: Ulster. Greene, Delaware, Sullivan, and Schoharie. It draws from a variety of quilters' guilds and societies, including The Patchworkers of East Jewett, Liberty's Calico Geese, Kingston's Wiltwyck, Delhi's Town and Country Quilt Guild, Vega's Sunbonnet Quilters, the Piecemakers Quilt Guild of the Schoharie Valley, and Arkville's Catskill Mountain Quilters.

And lots of folks simply quilt on their own.

Quilting is a labor-intensive art form. "You prick your finger going down and going up," Hall of Fame quilter Peg Barnes is fond of saying. It is also a gregarious and social art form that brings circles of people together to talk and laugh while they work.

Wanda Lanzi made her first quilt when she was a teenager and continues, now in her nineties, to quilt with her friends every week. The late Eleanor Faulkner, elected to the Hall of Fame in 1984, didn't start quilting till she was 76. In the four years between taking up the art and being recognized as a Hall of Famer, Eleanor made, or assisted in making, over 50 quilts.

There is something beautiful about an art form that opens its doors to the new practitioner at the time in life when so many other doors close. There is something beautiful about an art form that encourages creativity in the manufacture of such a useful artifact as bedding.

And there is something beautiful about discovering the Hall of Fame credentials of a neighbor who welcomed the children to the swimming hole back in the day.

Civil War!

ON NOVEMBER 6, 1860, Abraham Lincoln of Illinois was elected President of the United States. Lincoln, a one-term Congressman and former Illinois state legislator, had made a name for himself two years previous, when, as a candidate for the United States Senate, he had argued persuasively against the extension of slavery into any new territories in westward-expanding America.

Lincoln was the presidential candidate of the newly established Republican Party, founded in 1854 as a union of anti-slavery activists, free-market entrepreneurs, and progressive modernizers, who sought to move America beyond the debates that had dominated the country for decades toward a more prosperous middle-class future. The new party was organized under the slogan "Free Soil, Free Labor, Free Men."

Lincoln was actually something of a moderate on the slavery question, clearly opposed to its extension, but always careful to avoid suggesting any federal action that would disturb slavery in the states where it existed. He was criticized by more activist Republicans for this moderate stance.

But states rights Democrats and southern apologists for slavery were downright frightened by Lincoln's election. Six weeks after the election, South Carolina seceded from the United States, repealing, on the 20th of December, its 1788 ratification of the Constitution. A week later, the U.S. Army garrison at Fort Moultrie in South Carolina relocated to the more defensible island-base at Fort Sumter.

Lincoln was three months away from taking office, and already political division was breaking up the country. The newspapers were full of talk of war. Mississippi, Florida, Alabama, and Georgia were preparing Articles of Succession of their own. Hostility was rampant.

It was against this backdrop that fourteen officers of the New York State Militia – what we would today call the National Guard – met on January 7, 1861, in the parlor of an elegant home in Rondout, NY, now Kingston's waterfront district. Colonel George W. Pratt, commander of the 20th Regiment of the State Militia, addressed the group. His topic: preparation for the war that Pratt thought was inevitable.

Pratt was a Greene County native, born in Prattsville, where his father, Zadock Pratt, ran the Catskills' largest tannery. George Pratt was highly educated, both in the United States and abroad. He spoke several languages, had a large personal library, and had long been active in the state militia and in state politics.

A Democrat, Pratt had represented several Catskills counties in the State Senate in the 1857-58 term. We can't know how he voted in the 1860 presidential election. We do know that, for George Pratt and hundreds of thousands of others, patriotism trumped party loyalty.

Late that night, after much heated discussion, these volunteer part-time citizen-officers authorized Colonel Pratt to "tender the services of the regiment to the Federal Government if and when needed."

It was needed on April 12, 1861, when artillery units under orders from the governor of South Carolina bombarded their fellow soldiers garrisoned in Fort Sumter. The next day, the United States Army at Fort Sumter surrendered the fort to South Carolina.

Two days later, President Lincoln issued a call for 75,000 volunteers to enlist for 90 days to help put down the rebellion. The governor of New York quickly echoed the call for volunteers.

Colonel Pratt and his officers immediately resolved to answer the call. They established recruiting offices in Kingston, Rondout, Ellenville, Shokan and Samsonville. A surge of patriotism brought hundreds of volunteers.

Dubbed the "Ulster Guard," the 20th New York Militia sought volunteers from 18 to 45 years of age, men in "physical strength and vigor" who would rally "to defend the National Capitol and to maintain the Constitution and the Union."

Since Greene County had no regiment of its own, recruitment offices for the Ulster Guard were set up in Hunter, Windham, and Prattsville.

The Ulster Guard left the Catskills to serve their country on Sunday, April 28th, sailing down the Hudson to New York City. From there they later embarked to Annapolis, Maryland, entering the fight in June, suffering their first active duty death on June 15th.

Meanwhile, in Delaware County, volunteers answered the call of Governor Edwin D. Morgan to join the 72nd New York Volunteers, a state-wide regiment established under the authority of the War Department at Camp Scott on Staten Island. Company I was recruited and organized in Delhi under the command of Captain Robert T. Johnson.

The Delaware County company left Delhi on June 4, 1861, marching downriver to Walton and Hancock before leaving the county to make their way to Staten Island. There, Company I, along with the rest of the 72nd Regiment, was incorporated into the Brigade commanded by General Dan Sickles, later a hero at Gettysburg.

The Ulster Guard also went on to play their part in the pivotal Battle of Gettysburg in July 1863. Today, a monument stands to their memory on that battle-field. Another stands in memory of George W. Pratt, who died in September 1862 as a result of wounds suffered in the Second Battle of Bull Run.

That Catskill Mountain native was one of over 618,000 Americans killed in the Civil War.

Mountain Culture

I HAVE BEEN THINKING A LOT ABOUT CULTURE LATELY. Not culture like opera and poetry and art museums—the high culture that we think of when we use the word to describe refined taste, as in "Jacqueline Onassis was a cultured woman."

No, I've been thinking about culture in the way sociologists use the word: the way of life of a people. Maybe, what got me thinking about culture was the column I wrote a couple weeks ago about quilting. After all, the patchwork quilt has been, for the past thirty years or so, the operative metaphor for America's cultural mosaic (another metaphor!).

When I was in school, America was described by my social studies teachers as a melting pot. Immigrants came to this country immersed in the culture of the Old World, the culture of southern Italy, or the Yiddish-speaking Pale, or Ireland, or China, or any one of a hundred other regions. Soon, they were meld-ed into Americans in the melting pot of America, dripping-off their Old World ways to emerge "culturally American."

The turmoil of the 1960s destroyed that metaphor. The melting pot failed as a symbol because it failed to recognize that people became Americans while holding on to their own heritage. The Civil Rights movement morphed into Black Power and Black Pride. Cultural identity became important. We needed a new symbol for the variety of American life, the diversity of American commu-nities.

The patchwork quilt was perfect. Quilting is a quintessentially American art form. The quilt itself is a single, unified thing, a unity that could stand for our national unity. But the patches! Each diverse and different piece of fabric that makes a patchwork quilt has its own identity, just as each cultural community in America maintains its own identity. The symbol works.

Here in the Catskills, the patchwork quilt of American communities and cul-tures is alive and celebrated. The Borscht Belt of Sullivan County, while not as vibrant as it once was, continues to be a center of American Jewish culture. East Durham, in Greene County, known locally as Little Ireland, boasts the Michael J. Quill Irish Culture and Sports Center. The German-American Club of the North-ern Catskills meets monthly in Arkville and sponsors an annual Oktoberfest.

Sometimes cultures and communities that were once unrecognized and uncelebrated emerge with a new sense of pride and confidence. A new documentary video celebrates the Catskills' Mexican-American community, a community which stepped out recently to sponsor its own *Cinco de Mayo* festival.

A vibrant Gay, Lesbian, Bisexual, and Transgendered Community makes our mountains a more interesting place to live. Diversity is good.

Yet, with all this cultural diversity and recognition, it is ironic, and sad, that one American culture seems often invisible, even on its home turf. That is the Mountain Culture that is indigenous to the Catskills. It is time we paid attention.

When I came to the Catskills, thirty-eight years ago, I was part of a substantial migration of young people, who, in the midst of the cultural upheaval of the sixties and early seventies, were looking for a new way of life in the mountains, a way of life that would be more authentic and rooted and genuine than—it seemed to us—the empty and phony suburban ethos from which we fled. We found that way of life, that culture, here, among rural people, mountain people whose sense of place and family and community seemed more real to us than the materialism and consumerism that seemed to mar urbane life.

Recently, the *New York Post* listed Andes as number 38 in its series of 100 destinations within six hours of New York City. The *Post* describes Andes as "funky" and "shabby chic." It says "gentrification has begun making inroads here" and notes that "there's a strikingly cosmopolitan air to some of the businesses here."

Now, I love the little shops and galleries that have opened in the last few years in Andes and many of our other mountain towns. Our area needs the economic development that new businesses represent. And new residents, both full and part-time, enrich our communities. But, I fear that "gentrification" submerges Mountain Culture, makes marginal the very way of life that makes the Catskills special, authentic, genuine, and real.

After all, gentrification means "to renovate and improve (especially a house or district) so that it conforms to middle-class tastes; to make more refined or dignified" (*Oxford Dictionary*).

The Mountain Culture that was here before we got here has all the dignity that it needs. That Mountain Culture requires no further refinement, and, certainly, won't be improved by conformity to middle-class taste. Whenever we may have arrived in the mountains, we came, not just for the pristine natural surroundings, but for a little more sanity than the fast-paced, rat-race metropolitan world allows.

That sanity is right here, an integral part of Mountain Culture. It is the hallmark of a people who feel a sense of place, who live connected to the land, who value community and family above ideas and things, who live in the present guided by a living past, who combine faith and work and honesty and openness into a way of life with feet firmly planted on the ground, this ground.

All we have to do is look, listen, recognize, and respect.

Mountain Academies

IN 1847, William Stoddard established the Andes Collegiate Institute, an academy. In them-there days, an eighth-grade education was the norm for rural and urban New Yorkers. In the Catskills, literally hundreds of local Common School Districts provided that elementary education to thousands of local students.

A handful of private academies charged tuition to provide secondary education, often preparing older students for college. Delaware Academy in Delhi was established in 1820 and the Delaware Literary Institute in Franklin was founded in 1835. Both continue today as public schools.

The Delaware Literary Institute was incorporated by the state legislature on the traditional birthday of William Shakespeare, April 23, a fact, perhaps, not lost on the 24 men named as the first trustees of the Literary Institute. Its county-wide support and appeal is evidenced by Daniel Waterbury's inclusion on that founding board.

A Town of Middletown minister, Rev. Waterbury was the son of an Andes pioneer—the first of three prominent Daniel Waterburys—who came to Andes from Connecticut around the time of that town's founding. The second Daniel, the Reverend and academy co-founder, married Mary Lewis Grant, heir to the original Grant homestead, one of the first places in the Town of Middletown. It was there they settled.

A glimpse at the academic offerings of the Delaware Literary Institute gives us an idea of what secondary education meant in the nineteenth-century. There were separate male and female departments. The English education program included surveying and the mathematics of measuring geometric lengths, magnitudes, areas, and volumes. The "English" program was designed for the practical secondary education of students who would not go on to college.

Latin, Greek, algebra, and geometry were the core subjects for those preparing for higher education. The school charged extra for French, a frill. The female department offered young women physics, geometry, and algebra, along with evidences of Christianity, and moral and intellectual philosophy.

William Stoddard operated the Andes Collegiate Institute for ten years before selling it to Henry Davie, who enlarged the school and reincorporated it

The mountaintop lake above Allaben was once home to a private school, exclusive enough to be covered by *The New York Times*. Camp Timberland thrives there now.

as a stock company. By 1863, six teachers taught 121 students in the academy. That year, the school sent John Taylor to Monmouth College, J. J. Dean to Union College, and R. T. Doig to Westminster College. W. R. Gladstone also graduated the academy and went on to higher education.

Sometime after the Civil War, the Andes Collegiate Institute died. Perhaps, the death, in an academy building, of the principal, Rev. Peter Smeallie, hastened the school's demise. Its buildings stood vacant for years, perhaps decades.

Meanwhile, under the authority of the state's Union Free School Act, several common school districts united to form larger districts which established graded schools with an academic department, the beginning of today's high schools. By 1891, graded schools had been established in Roxbury, Griffin's Corners, Margaretville, Andes, Downsville, Delhi, Hobart, and Walton.

In 1906, Manetha Hilton of St. Louis, owner of the vacant academy property, presented the buildings and grounds to the Andes Union Free Board of Education for the establishment of a high school. Hilton required that the high school be a continuing memorial to his father, so it was called The Hilton Memorial School from its establishment until centralization in 1934.

Manetha Hilton was, no doubt, a descendent of Silas Hilton, a prominent leader in the 1840s Anti-Rent movement, active in politics as an anti-rent candidate for the state assembly and as a two-year Andes Town Supervisor, and seven-year Justice of the Peace. His grandfather had settled in Bovina, trekking to the Catskills from Connecticut in the years after the Revolutionary War.

Catskill Mountain youth might, alternately, seek further education through appointment to one of the two normal schools located just outside the mountains. In 1891, the State Normal & Training School at Oneonta had 501 students and a faculty of 13. The State Normal & Training School at New Paltz educated 417 students that same year.

The purpose of the Normal Schools was to train teachers for the common schools, the vast majority of which were still one-room schools in the late nineteenth and early twentieth-centuries. Appointment was made by the State Superintendent of Public Instruction, upon recommendation of the local school commissioner.

The appointee must be at least 16, and present evidence of ability to "read readily and intelligently, spell correctly, write legibly and neatly." He or she must express a willingness "to enter honorable obligation" to teach in the public schools of the state. I believe tuition was free. Appointment was to the Normal School closest to one's home.

The Normal Course was for two terms. First term, a student took philosophy of education, school economy, drawing, methods of teaching common branch subjects, and a course of reading connected to a teacher's professional work.

The second term included history of education, school law, kindergarten methods (very progressive, for the day), methods of teaching yet other common branch subjects, a course of reading connected to professional work, and discussion of educational themes.

Upon successful completion, graduates received a diploma, but no college degree. Today, all New York State public school teachers must hold both a bachelor's and a master's degree to remain certified.

Yoo-hoo, Gertrude Berg!

"YOO-HOO, MRS. BLOOM!" Those of a certain age will immediately recognize the catchphrase of the character Molly Goldberg, leaning out of her Bronx brownstone kitchen window calling to her neighbor across the air shaft. Molly was played by pioneering comedian Gertrude Berg.

I remember well the television show *The Goldbergs*, one of my favorite early childhood TV watching experiences. My neighbor Bud remembers the show from the radio. Either way, Gertrude Berg was a fixture in American popular culture from the thirties through the fifties. She learned her craft in the Catskills.

Gertrude Edelstein was born October 3, 1899, in Harlem, the only child of Jacob and Diana Edelstein. Young Gertrude divided her childhood years between New York and Fleischmanns, where her parents operated a resort hotel in the hilltop houses vacated by the Fleischmanns family just a few years earlier.

Gertrude started writing and performing early, creating skits and entertainments for her parents' hotel guests. It was there that she learned her craft: how to appeal to an audience and generate laughs in short character-driven, story-based performances. Later, she honed that craft by taking playwriting classes offered by Columbia University.

Gertrude met Lewis Berg while working her parents Catskills resort. In 1919 they were married. The couple had a son and a daughter.

Several of Gertrude and Lewis Berg's grandchildren were in attendance the other day at a special preview screening of a new documentary by filmmaker Aviva Kempner called *Yoo-hoo, Mrs. Goldberg*, at the Center for Jewish History on West 16th Street in New York City. The film premiered at the High Falls Film Festival in Rochester last month, and will have its theatrical release in July.

Gertrude Berg was a pioneer, as a comedian, as a creative artist, and as a woman. She is credited with paving the way for female comedic stars like Lucille Ball. Some even credit her with inventing the sit-com format. She was one of the first performers who also wrote and produced their shows. And she was one of the first female voices on the radio. "Yoo-hoo! Mrs. Berg."

Gertrude Berg's radio career began as a writer, selling several dramatic scripts to the networks. In 1929, she convinced NBC executives to buy her series *The Rise of the Goldbergs*, by reading her script aloud to them. Her clever writing was animated by her dialect-accented characterization, and the executives were sold.

The radio show, its title later shortened to *The Goldbergs*, premiered that year on the NBC Blue radio network as a 15-minute comedy, Monday through Friday. This was an era of ethnic stereotypes, and The Goldbergs played to mainstream America's stereotype of Jewish life just as NBC's Amos 'n' Andy played to stereotypes of African-Americans.

As a daily 15-minute show, The Goldbergs was like a comedic soap opera, with story lines extending from one show to the next. It was one of the first programs to focus on the family and domestic life as a source for comedy, a staple of the situation comedies that came after. Molly was the archetypal Jewish mother. She, her husband Jake, and live-in in-law, Uncle David, spoke with sing-songy stage-Yiddish accents, their speech littered with malapropisms and inversions: "Answer the door already."

The children, however, Rosalie and Sammy, spoke in mainstream English, thus symbolizing the Goldberg family's "rise" into the assimilated American middle-class.

Gertrude Berg wrote over 5000 episodes of the radio show, which ran on NBC from 1929 to 1934 and on CBS from 1938 to 1949. In 1935, *The Goldbergs* temporarily off the air, Gertrude produced and starred in a short-lived program *The House of Glass*, set in a fictional summer resort, based on the Edelstein's Catskill Mountain hotel.

The Goldbergs premiered on CBS television in 1949 and was featured on several networks each season until 1955, one of TV's first situation comedies. In it, Molly would often lean out her fictional Bronx window and talk directly to the camera, creating a personal intimacy with her audience.

Gertrude Berg also wrote and starred in movies, toured the country with a Goldberg-themed vaudeville act, and appeared as a guest star on numerous 1950s and 60s television variety and dramatic shows. She wrote several books including *The Molly Goldberg Cookbook* and her autobiography, *Molly and Me*.

She won both the Emmy for her TV work and the Tony Award for her 1959 performance in *A Majority of One*.

And she was a woman of conscience. In 1951, Gertrude refused to fire series co-star Phillip Loeb after he was blacklisted in a McCarthy era political witch hunt. Loeb resigned anyway to save the show from cancellation, taking a generous severance package from his generous producer-writer-star. Sadly, unable to work, he later committed suicide, a victim of those sorry times.

On September 14, 1966, Gertrude Berg died while in rehearsal as the lead in a new play written from an idea she had conceived. She is buried in Clovesville, in her beloved Catskills.

Master of Mountain Writing

MY ARRIVAL IN THE MOUNTAINS and the publication of Alf Evers' monumental history *The Catskills: From Wilderness to Woodstock* (Doubleday, 1972) occurred at about the same time, so I have always felt a bond with the author. Alf Evers died in 2004, a month short of his 100th birthday. He was a Catskill Mountain institution.

I never met Alf. Wish I had. These mountains had been much written about before him, but the Catskills lacked a comprehensive regional history until his 800-page book filled the void. His book was thoroughly researched, full of historical detail, infused with the ear of a folklorist whose sympathies were with the people of whom he wrote. Alf Evers was a great storyteller.

Once, while researching the spoken dialect of the Catskills, I listened to a series of local history tapes, listening for specific features of spoken language identified with mountain speakers from the southern portion of the Appalachian chain. Alf was on one of the tapes. I well remember my surprise when, after hearing just a few words and sentences, I realized that this lover of all things Catskill was not native to the region.

Alf's spoken language gave away his Bronx roots. He was born in that borough in 1905. When he was nine, his architect father moved the family to a small farm in Tillson, just outside the Catskills in Ulster County. There, Alf met Charley Woods, a local farmer, whose stories and rural turn-of-speech captivated the youngster and began his lifelong interest in folklore.

Later, the family moved to New Paltz, where his father worked on the restoration of an historic stone house in the old Huguenot Street part of town, a project that drew Alf into history and the connections between the artifacts of today and yesterday's people. Arrowhead collecting with one of his New Paltz High School teachers further inspired that interest.

In 1925, Alf attended Hamilton College where his roommate was B. F. Skinner. Legend has it that Alf turned the future behaviorist toward psychology as a career field. Skinner was interested in art, but supposedly, young Alf Evers told him "Science is the art of the future." Skinner went on to become a groundbreaking behavioral scientist.

Ironic, then, that Alf Evers left college the following year to study painting and drawing at the Art Students League in New York City. It was there that he met his wife, illustrator Helen Baker, with whom he had three children.

Alf and Helen Evers wrote and illustrated over 50 children's books. They lived first in Trumbell, Connecticut, moving in 1931 to Woodstock. Alf supplemented his writing with work as a Fuller Brush salesman and insurance investigator. He and his wife divorced in 1950.

In 1955, Alf published his classic children's book *The Treasure of Watchdog Mountain*, an early "attempt to teach children what ecology was, about the relationship of man to the land. It was a pioneer book of its kind," Alf later wrote. "I based it on Overlook Mountain, which I saw through my studio window," he went on to say.

That writing experience kindled his interest in the history of the mountains, and he began the long process of research that resulted in his 1972 Catskills regional history. He dedicated the book to Barbara Moncure, his longtime companion, a folksinger whose 1963 recording *Folksongs of the Catskills* was itself a significant contribution to the documentation of Catskill Mountain history.

Alf Evers followed his 1972 regional history with an equally comprehensive history of his home town. *Woodstock: History of an American Town* (Overlook Press) was published in 1987. His *In Catskill Country: Collected Essays on Mountain History, Life and Lore* (Overlook Press) was published in 1995.

Alf next turned his attention to Kingston. He was working on his history of Kingston when he died. *Kingston: City on the Hudson* (Overlook Press, 2005) was published the year after his death.

No collection of Catskill Mountain books can be complete without Alf Evers' work. He was the master, the collector and teller of tales who set the standard for all writing about these mountains that follows.

Interestingly, Alf, so intimately connected to Woodstock, almost moved to Roxbury in 1959. He had sold his house in Woodstock and was living in rented quarters when he contracted to buy a Roxbury home. The new house burned down before Alf could make the move. There was some drilling for gas and oil going on in Roxbury at the time, and Alf, always a bit suspicious of corporate America, suspected that the house had been deliberately set aflame.

Researching this column, I discovered that Alf's first children's book was a little illustrated story called *This Little Pig*, about a pig with a curly tail who wanted a straight tail. I remember that book! Seems like I've been reading Alf Evers longer than I'd realized.

Yankees and Yorkers

TODAY, the term *Yankee* refers to the baseball team in the Bronx or, perhaps, to any American abroad, but once the term clearly identified New Englanders.

The Red Sox Nation of the six states of New England (can you name them?) must swallow hard and recognize that they were once, eek, *Yankees*!

At the time of the American Revolution, settled New York was pretty much limited to the lands of the Hudson Valley from New York City to Albany. *Yorkers*, as they were called, were a mixed lot, often termed Dutch, although settlers who traced their ancestry to Holland were merely one part of a polyglot mix of French Huguenots, Flemish Walloons, Palatine Germans and others who spoke any of the eighteen languages common to New York at the time of independence.

America's first internationally acclaimed writer was Washington Irving, a New Yorker who invented for his state a colorful mythic history rooted in Dutch-ness.

Rip Van Winkle, the literary character, was that exceedingly rare lazy Dutch farmer who'd rather drink than work, and found himself among Hendrik Hudson's Dutch mariners playing a game of nine-pins. Henry Hudson was an Englishman, but for the readers of "Rip Van Winkle," the Dutch *Hendrik* captured more colorfully the exotic history of New York.

Dietrich Knickerbocker was Irving's invented historian of New York, a literate and amiable old Dutchman who symbolized the city and state's difference from the Yankees of New England. Ironic it is that Manhattan's basketball team and the baseball team from the Bronx share the city as icons of New York-ness.

How did Yorkers become Yankees? As one might guess, the Catskills had something to do with it. Cheap land in the Catskills, that is.

Rip was from the Village of Catskill, but his was the old Dutch Catskill, today the hamlet of Leeds. The Village of Catskill we know today was an English invention, an extension of the old Dutch landing called *Het Strand*. The Strand—many still refer to the Rondout waterfront section of Kingston by that name—was a place to load and unload supplies, not a place to live. The fertile flatlands up-hill and inland were more attractive home-sites to the Dutch.

Not so the New England Yankees, who transformed *Het Strand* into Catskill, a port and commercial center developed by New England business and professional men shortly after independence. Yankees were moving west.

The Hudson River had long been the actual, authentic boundary between New England and New York. Border disputes were common among New York, Massachusetts, and Connecticut right into the 1800s, the lands east of the river claimed by each. Drive east from the Hudson and you pass into Massachusetts and Connecticut without any natural border marking the change. You've already crossed the natural border: the Hudson!

The city of Hudson, on the east bank of the river, was always a Yankee town, settled by whalers from Nantucket and Martha's Vineyard. In the first half of the nineteenth century, Hudson was home to a whaling fleet second only to the New England whalers of New Bedford and those Massachusetts islands.

The plentiful empty lands west of the river in the old Hardenbergh Patent were mighty tempting to those east-bank Yankees, and, soon after independence, sawmills and iron foundries, barrel-stave mills and bell factories sprang-up in the northern Catskills, the products of Yankee ingenuity and Yankee pluck.

The incursion from Hudson was just the beginning. New York State historians refer to the years between 1790 and 1820 as "The Yankee Invasion of New York," and nowhere was that invasion more transformative than in the Catskills.

Settlements like Durham, Windham, and Westkill were like model New England hamlets, complete with Presbyterian Church, library, meeting house, and whipping stocks.

The population of New York State bloomed from 340,120 in 1790 to 1,372,812 in 1820. A huge birth rate—most families had more than seven children—was partially responsible, as was a tremendous influx of settlers who migrated from New England.

Englishman William Cobbett met an emigrant from New England in 1818. "He has migrated," Cobbett wrote. "His reasons are these; he has five sons, the eldest 19 years of age, and several daughters. Connecticut is thickly settled. He has not the means to buy farms for all the sons there." Cheap land was the answer.

The Catskills abounded in cheap land, and Yankees flocked into the mountains. Today, the Catskills still boast our share of Van Luevens and Van Benschotens and Dutchers, but we have many more Sanfords and Fairbairns and Millers. Woodstock and Roxbury, Shandaken and Shokan still have Reformed Churches, descended from the Dutch Reformed, but many more Presbyterian and Methodist churches grace our towns.

Many Catskill Mountain towns, such as Stamford and Colchester and Andes, were founded by Connecticut migrants, even, in the case of Stamford, named after the town back home.

And while the New York Yankees are world famous, no one speaks of Yorkers any more. Perhaps, we should bring back the term.

Catskills on the Web

EVERY ORGANIZATION I am associated with is obsessed with having a web site. Well, maybe obsessed is too strong, but every meeting I attend seems to include at least one discussion about developing, maintaining, and improving people's ability to gain, through the internet, information deemed important by that organization.

So, since the Catskills is the subject of this organization—this column, anyway—I thought it might be instructive to see what Catskill Mountain information is readily available to any information-seeking browser on the internet.

I googled "Catskills."

First up on the responding page is the link to the *Wikipedia* article entitled "Catskill Mountains." Depending on your point of view, *Wikipedia* is either the end of authoritative information as we have known it since the Enlightenment of the eighteenth-century, or it's the democratization of knowledge. I tend toward the latter view, although *Wikipedia*, open to any self-appointed editor, can sometimes be a tad sketchy.

The Catskill Mountain Wikipedia article begins with a disclaimer and a plea: "This article includes a list of references or external links, but its sources remain

Web designers might be impressed by the multi-focal layout on the cover of the 1879 *Catskill Mountain Guide*, put out by Walton Van Loan.

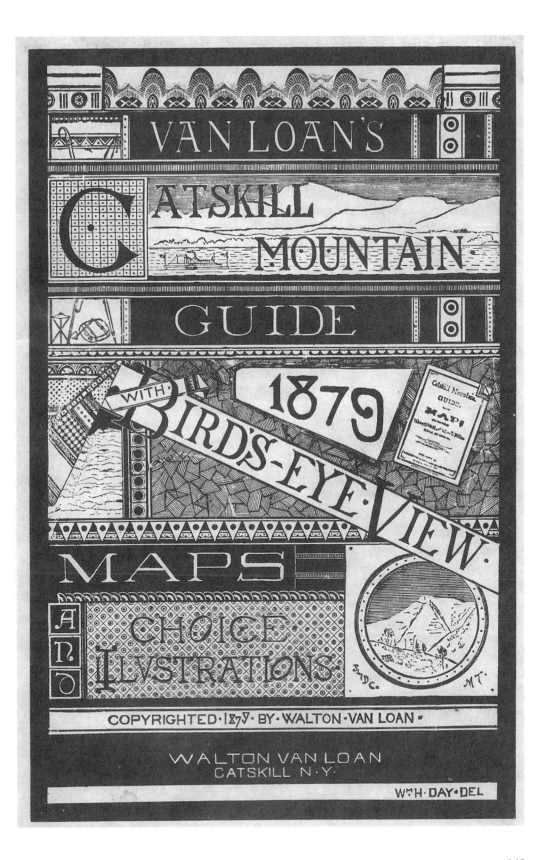

VAN LOAN'S

CATSKILL MOUNTAIN

GUIDE

WITH BIRD'S-EYE-VIEW

1879

MAPS AND CHOICE ILLVSTRATIONS

COPYRIGHTED ·1879· BY ·WALTON·VAN LOAN·

WALTON VAN LOAN
CATSKILL N·Y·

WM·H·DAY·DEL

169

unclear because it has insufficient inline citations. Please help to improve this article by introducing more precise citations where appropriate. (*April 2009*)." Suddenly, I felt too busy.

The article includes brief summaries of the geography, history, and geology of the mountains. Then, there follows a discussion of the name, Catskills, with several theories about its origins. Finally, a few Catskill Mountain connections to American culture are mentioned, and appearances in the movies listed. Strange, but the most famous Catskills movie, *Dirty Dancing*, was actually made in Virginia and North Carolina.

Back to the Google page. The first specifically *Catskills* website listed reads "Visit New York's Catskill Mountains/ Official Tourism Site. . . ." The website provides information and links to varied and extensive lists of mountain businesses and organizations. It is copyrighted by the Catskill Association for Tourism Services. Extensive listings abound: hotels, bed and breakfasts, campsites, activities and attractions, community organizations, calendar listings, and promotional tourism packages in Greene, Ulster, Delaware, and Sullivan Counties. One-stop webbing for the prospective tourist!

"Welcome to the Catskills Guide!" declares the next website title on our Google page. The *Online Guide to the Catskill Mountains* is copyrighted 1996-2009 by Timothy J. Mallery. Numerous ads surround the home page. This site contains an online Catskill Mountain bookstore, all books listed available from Amazon.

There is also a pretty good set of links to mountain history sites, including the fascinating Camp Ta-Ri-Go summer camp memories site.

Camp Ta-Ri-Go, located on Little Red Kill Road in Fleischmanns, was a "summer camp for several hundred boys and girls from before World War II to 1977." Its memories' web site is worth a visit. Here, we find out that, at Ta-Ri-Go, the boys' bunks were named after Indian tribes – Seminole, Seneca, Shawnee—and the girls' bunks after prestigious woman's colleges: Barnard, Bryn Mawr, Skidmore, Vassar. An annually created totem pole listed the name of every camper.

Several general travel websites present Catskill Mountain tourism pages. Fodors.com, iloveny.com and bedandbreakfast.com all present Catskill information. Catskillpark.com, presented by LOOKSEEK.com, provides a series of activity-based and town-based links.

One of the most interesting mountain websites is that of the Catskills Institute, "promoting research and education on the significance of the Catskill Mountains in American Jewish life." This site presents a cornucopia of internet links focused on the Borscht Belt of Sullivan and southwestern Ulster Counties. I particularly like the photo galleries.

Classiccatskills.com similarly focuses on the memories of the Borscht Belt in its 1940s and '50s heyday. The web site presents stories that have been published in the Middletown *Times Herald-Record*.

The *Catskill Mountain News*, of course, has its own web site, with all the content of the paper available on-line to subscribers. I buy the paper every Wednesday morning at Sam's, so I can only call up the first paragraph or so of each of the columns that have comprised, so far, *A Catskill Catalog*.

Every issue of the *Catskill Mountain News* from July 13, 1902 to December 31, 1937 is available on-line at history.catskills.net It is a great resource and it's actually fun just to read a very old newspaper. The ads are great!

www. catskillarchive.com is produced by the same Timothy J. Mallery who produces the Online Guide. A number of nineteenth-century and early twentieth-century articles on the mountains are presented in this excellent web site. I googled Mallery's name, but was unable to learn much about this accomplished Catskill Mountain web master.

And there are lots of other regional words one can search under. I wonder what will show up when I google "Esopus" or "Pakataken?"

The First Fourth of July

ON JULY 4, 1776, several farms sat along the banks of the upper Pepacton, as the East Branch of the Delaware was then called. Farmers named DuMond and Von Waggoner, Hendricks and Kittle, Slyter, Green, Yaple and Carpenter made-up a little outpost of settlement on the frontier. Similar groupings of farms sat in the Shandaken Mountains along the upper Esopus Creek.

Most of the land along those streams belonged to Robert Livingston, who himself lived across the Hudson at his Clermont Estate, but, that July, had been, all summer, at the Continental Congress in Philadelphia. In fact, on the previous June 11th, Mr. Livingston had been appointed to a five-member committee to draw up a statement asserting American separation from the British Empire, clearly a bold and radical Congressional step.

The 13 colonies had been in open insurrection—a civil war, to that point— since the spring of the year before. A Declaration of Independence would change the terms of the conflict.

Livingston and his fellow committee-members, John Adams of Massachusetts, Roger Sherman of Connecticut, and Benjamin Franklin of Pennsylvania, agreed to work from a draft prepared by fifth member, Thomas Jefferson of Virginia. On June 28th, the committee submitted its proposed Declaration to Congress. Congress, as Congresses often do, voted to table the motion.

The farmers on the Pepacton and along the Esopus must have known very little of these goings-on. I don't think there was any regular mail service up into the mountains until after the Revolution and the establishment of the new United States. Colonel John Grant is generally credited with being the first postmaster in these parts, but he was closer to 1800 than to 1776. And what newspaper would have regularly penetrated the mountain wilderness to carry the Congressional news to the pioneers?

The proposed declaration was debated extensively among the representatives of the 13 separate and distinct colonial governments, assembled in what is today called Independence Hall in Philadelphia. John Hancock of Massachusetts presided. Declaring independence would change the very definition of the struggle of General Washington's vastly outnumbered Continental Army, presently camped, that hot July, warily, in and around Manhattan. The fight would be transformed from a dispute among countrymen over taxes to the defense, from foreign conquest, of home and freedom.

On July 2nd and 3rd, Congress debated. On July 4th, Congress adopted. "We hold these truths to be self-evident, that all men are created equal, that they are endowed by their Creator with certain unalienable Rights, that among these are Life, Liberty and the pursuit of Happiness.—That to secure these rights, Governments are instituted among Men, deriving their just powers from the consent of the governed. . . ."

How those words resound today in places like Tehran, Pyongyang, and Darfur.

As soon as Congress adopted the declaration, a hand-written copy was sent down the street to the print shop of John Dunlap, who had previously secured a lucrative printing contract with Congress. Dunlop printed 150 to 200 single-page broadsides, the *Dunlop Broadside*, distributed by presiding officer Hancock to publicize the action of Congress.

On July 8, John Nixon read one of those broadsides aloud to the crowd outside Independence Hall. The next day, General Washington had his officers assemble their units in New York to hear a reading of the Declaration of Independence. On the same day, the New York Provincial Congress, pretty much hiding-out from the Brits in White Plains, endorsed the declaration.

The farmers along the rivers of the Catskills were, I'll bet, ignorant of these occurrences. When did the Declaration come to them?

The Declaration of Independence began to get some circulation in the weeks after July 4th. It had been published almost immediately in *The Pennsylvania Evening Post*, a four-times-a-week Philadelphia newspaper, and in the *New York Packet*, a waterfront weekly.

John Holt, a former Mayor of Williamsburg, Virginia, who had moved to Manhattan, published in New York a widely-circulated broadside-printing of the Declaration. Copies passed throughout the colony. Later, Holt fled the city, continuing to publish a revolutionary newspaper as he moved, in Fishkill Poughkeepsie, Esopus, and Kingston.

At some point, perhaps up-river on the Delaware from Philadelphia, and up-river form Kingston on the Esopus, the Declaration of Independence came to our Catskill Mountain pioneers.

But the past is never simple when it is the present. The farmers on the upper Delaware and on the Esopus had to be concerned with what their Indian neighbors would do in relation to the idea of American independence. While many patriots emerged from these parts, others remained loyal to the British, often in response to the military power of the English-allied Iroquois nations to their immediate west.

Similarly, the identification with the Declaration of the fabulously wealthy landlord, Robert Livingston, must have made it a bit hard to swallow for some living on the vast land-patent that the Livingston dynasty had, for too long, considered the family manor. One can understand Tories.

But, by the end of following year, the struggle to turn that Declaration of Independence into a fact on the ground, had affected every settler, every family, every farm on the banks of our Catskill Mountain rivers, no matter where their sympathies lay.

Up From Revolutionary Ashes: NK, NY, USA

MENTION NEW KINGSTON to residents of Kingston, New York, and receive blank stares, with mutterings of "where's that?" But shortly after the Revolution, New Kingston offered recovery and opportunity to the people of that battered Hudson River town.

The Hudson River marked the clear dividing line between the ardent revolutionists of New England and the seemingly more temperate Middle Atlantic colonists. The British could cut-off New York and Pennsylvania from New England by gaining control of the Hudson. Divide and conquer. In addition, the Middle Atlantic was the breadbasket of the colonies, a wheat-growing region whose control could both feed the British and starve the rebels. Take the Hudson and quash the revolution.

So the officers of the British fleet, sent to put down the insurrection, anchored at New York harbor with a clear strategy in mind: conquer the Hudson Valley, control that waterway, divide the colonies, isolate New England, win a quick victory, and hang the revolutionaries. Simple.

General Washington was a Virginian, but he stationed the Continental Army he commanded in New York City right from the start. He knew where this war would be fought, and he knew the quickest way to lose the war was to lose the Hudson. While he fortified the harbor, he commissioned General George Clinton, of Ulster County, to fortify and protect the Hudson Highlands, up-river, mid-valley.

The British plan was a beautifully simple military strategy. Forces from New York City would move up-river in mass. Barry St. Leger's troops would march in force from Fort Niagara, in the west, down the Mohawk Valley to the Hudson. General John Burgoyne's army would use Lake Champlain to invade south from Canada. They'd all meet around Albany. Home by Christmas. Nice.

To protect the valley, general Clinton had Fort Montgomery and Fort Clinton built on the highlands. A huge iron chain was forged in Sterling Forest and stretched across the river just below the river-surface to try to block British ships.

Meanwhile, the overwhelming British force at New York forced Washington out of the city and sent the infant revolutionary assembly running. First, the rebels set up shop in White Plains, then in Fishkill and Poughkeepsie, until an official state government was established and constituted in Kingston, the new state capital. As an important settlement on the river, Kingston would have been a target of British attack anyway, but as the state capital it was particularly attractive.

In October 1777, a British force of over 1100 British soldiers and mercenaries from the German state of Hesse-Hanau – Hessians, as they were called – set sail in flatboats up the Hudson, burning and looting whatever they could find. General John Vaughn was their commander. On October 16, they reached Kingston.

The Brits landed at Ponckhockie, just north of the place where the Rondout Creek empties into the river. Forewarned by patriots fleeing the British from the south, Kingston's settlers took refuge in Woodstock, Hurley, Marbletown and other inland settlements. The British overcame the vastly outnumbered defenders of the place, marched up-hill to the stockaded village, and set it aflame.

The day after the burning of Kingston, Burgoyne surrendered his army to the Americans at Saratoga. The British Hudson Valley strategy was not going to succeed. Too late, however, for Kingston.

About Kingston, the British-sympathizing New York *Gazette* reported the burning of "three hundred and twenty-six houses, with a barn to almost everyone of them." Even if the Tory paper exaggerated the British success, that's a lot of destruction.

And that is where New Kingston comes in. The newly named Chancellor of the New York State Courts was Robert Livingston, whose own home, Clermont, across the river, was likewise burned. Chancellor Livingston owned pretty much the entire Catskills, the old Hardenbergh Patent.

The Chancellor offered any 5000 acres of unsettled land in the Patent to the burned-out citizens of Kingston. Kingston's trustees were required to cover the cost of a survey and to select the site—not Woodstock or Shandaken or any other settled place—within three months. It was an act of enormous generosity, or an act of shrewd economic and political self-interest, or, likely, both. It also took seven years to consummate.

After all, there was a revolution to wage. Kingston's trustees didn't manage to send out a surveyor until 1784. Samuel Cockburn, who often worked for the Chancellor, was accompanied by a young Revolutionary war veteran, Jacob Van Benschoten, who was looking for land.

Anyone who has driven up the Margaretville Mountain Road, north from Walnut Street in Margaretville, up over the mountain to just beyond the summit, where the road turns on the hill's shoulder, anyone who has seen that view of the New Kingston Valley will understand why Jacob Van Benschoten chose the valley he chose for the 5000 acre settlement. Inspiring.

Used to be, that Mountain Road was called by some "Uncle Jacob's Trail."

Cockburn's survey divided the valley into 50-acre lots, deeded to those Kingstonians who suffered at the hands of the British. Most sold. Some, like Jacob Van Benschoten, stayed to clear the land and make a life: build farms, stores and shops, a church or two, a community. Jacob's descendents reside today on lands he opened 215-odd years ago.

And the stone walls that marked many of those 50-acre "settling-lots" still run through the woods and fields of New Kingston.

The Remarkable Scudder Family

A T THE HIGH POINT of Delhi's Woodland Cemetery, a memorial obelisk to Osman Steele rises. Along the stone wall of the Halcott Cemetery, a blue sign indicates the burial place of Warren Scudder. Steele was the county lawman killed in the line of duty, on August 7, 1845, while conducting a forced sale to raise rent-due on Moses Earle's Dingle Hill farm. Scudder was the leader of the men who shot him.

The Catskill Mountaineers' dual allegiance: the up-rent respect for law, for good order, for established authority, and the down-rent sympathy with the underdog, resentment of elitism, rebellion against class division. Steele and Scudder, names intertwined in history's deep echoes.

These days, I'm not sure if there are any Steeles left in the mountains, but there sure are a lot of Scudders. When I first taught in the public school, I had a kid named Scudder in 4 out of 5 classes. Turns out, they are part of a distinguished American family whose Anti-Rent War action was a mere moment in a much larger story.

David Scudder, formerly of Roxbury, moved out of the mountains, seeking the public transportation and convenient services that seem to thrive closer to sea level. He had lots of Scudder family papers to deal with before he left.

David discovered his own Scudder family heritage when he inherited the home of Mary Katherine Scudder, teacher, farmer and David's great-aunt. She had had the Roxbury house built in 1930, after her husband ran away from their Lew Beach farm with the school-teacher boarder. Mary Katherine became a schoolteacher herself, a very good one, who conducted school over in Wolf Hollow and up Dingle Hill.

When David got the house, back in the late 70s, he discovered trunks full of family papers. It was in those trunks that he discovered the Scudder Association, a non-profit, worldwide, family association. It is a testament to the work David has done in family genealogy and research, in the intervening years, that he was, in 2007, named "Scudder of the Year" by the Scudder Association. Annual association dues fund educational grants and scholarships for medical outreach, social work and Christian ministry.

The Scudder Family traces its history back to Kent, England. Two brothers emigrated from there to the Massachusetts Bay Colony in the early 1600s. One, Thomas, settled in Salem, and, then, a whale man by trade, relocated to Huntington, Long Island. His descendent, William Smith Scudder, lost two fingers and the use of his hands in Revolutionary War service, receiving a disability pension in 1778. William Smith Scudder followed his son, Jotham, to Roxbury in the 1790s. His son had cleared a farm in 1794 on the hill above Roxbury, where the Shepherd Hills Golf Course is now.

Warren, the anti-rent agitator, was the youngest son of Jotham. He was elected chief of the Roxbury tribe of calico Indians, as the anti-rent forces were known. At the Moses Earle farm sale that August morning, Warren was in command of the combined force of Anti-Rent calicos, better than 200 men. Who shot the under-sheriff? We'll never really know, but we do know that Warren Scudder was in command.

At the Delaware County Courthouse, David Scudder has read the testimony of Jotham Scudder during the investigation of his rebellious son. Much as he may have sympathized with the tenants' plight, it must have been painful for the Old School Baptist Church Deacon to have his son a wanted fugitive. There is, after all, a bit of Steele in all of us.

It has been in medicine and ministry that the Scudders have been particularly fruitful. Six generations of Scudders have been overseas missionaries, through the Reformed Church of America, focusing on medical and social work in India. John and Harriett Scudder went to India in 1819 and worked there for thirty years. Thus began a 188 year history of Scudder ministry to the people of India, over 1000 person-years of service to the poor.

Dr. Ida Scudder's story is, perhaps, the most compelling. She is the subject of several books, including *Dr. Ida* by Dorothy Clark Wilson (New York, McGraw-Hill, 1959) now out of print. As the daughter of missionaries, Ida witnessed the death, in childbirth, of three Indian women who would not consult western doctors simply because they were men. She vowed to gain the training that would allow her to help. She became a doctor.

Ida Scudder first made local news 110 years ago. "A large and attentive audience was in attendance at the Gould Church Tuesday evening, July 18," *The Roxbury Times* reported in 1899, "incident to listening to the lecture delivered by Miss Ida Scudder, M.D., who gave an informal talk on her successful work in India." Notice how Dr. Scudder is referred to as Miss Scudder, M.D., the announcement of her marital status evidently trumping medical school.

Dr. Ida's successful work in India was bringing modern gynecological medicine to patients whose husbands would only consent to the examination of their wives by a woman. Her clinic grew into a major hospital and training center, Vellore Christian Medical College & Hospital, which still thrives in Vellore, India.

Summer Camps

SOMEWHERE IN UPSTATE NEW YORK, the word *camp* changes meaning. As a college freshman from the metropolitan area, I was confused by an upstate classmate who spoke of a family camp in the woods, a rustic retreat used to get away from it all. What he called a camp, I called a cottage. To me, *camp* meant something entirely different.

What I had in mind was a rustic campus in the country, a place to which my suburban elementary schoolmates seemed to go every July and August. I never went to camp, but grew up 45 minutes from Broadway in a train-line suburb where spending six or eight weeks in an upstate or New England summer camp was considered essential for most of my schoolmates.

"Summer camps—overnight camps attended by children without their parents—were first established in the 1880s in North America, fueled by Victorian convictions about nature's moral and physical benefits," the *Encyclopedia of Children and Childhood in History and Society* tells us. The first summer camps were established in northern New England, far from the temptations and complications of city life.

It didn't take long for summer camps to reach the Catskills. Harry W. Little ran the region's first summer camp, up in Woodland Valley. In 1904, Little, a graduate of Weslyan University, was hired by Edward Miller to set-up and manage a children's camp as an adjunct to Miller's hotel business, The Roxmor Inn. Little operated Camp Wake Robin on the Roxmor grounds in Woodland Valley for the next 25 years.

Roxmor Inn, Woodland in Ulster County, birthplace of kids' summer camps.

Camp Wake Robin, of course, was named after John Burroughs' first book, *Wake-Robin*, published in 1871. Summer camps took their inspiration from conservationists and naturalists like Burroughs, who reminded late nineteenth-century Americans of the importance of the natural world, a natural world threatened by urbanization and industrialization. Most camps also offered their young male charges a good dollop of military-style order and discipline, a kind of muscular masculinity thought needed by boys some worried were in danger of being "over-civilized."

The horror of the First World War made a military model less appealing, and in the 1920s, summer camps began to structure themselves around Native American lore as the model and inspiration for childhood interaction with nature. At the same time, camping for girls became more common.

In 1930, Camp Oquago was established on Perch Lake in Andes as a girls' camp. Louis Mirsky and Ben Steinberger, founding partners, also established Lake Tunis as a boys' camp on the small lake of that name between Andes and Delhi. For the next 19 years, Lake Tunis-Camp Oquago, Inc. operated the two camps, with 170 or so girls at Oquago and about 150 boys at Tunis.

In August 1937, Camp Oquago made news as the first summer camp to produce and perform a modern opera. The German composer, Paul Hindemith, had visited the United States the previous Spring. Inspired by theatrical visionary Bertolt Brecht, Hindemith, wrote a number of compositions intended to be played by amateurs. One, "Let's Build a Town," was designed to be played entirely by children, which the Camp Oquago girls did.

Dr. Paul A. Pisk, a Viennese composer who had immigrated to the United States in 1936 to escape Nazi persecution, was the Music Director of Camp Oquago that summer of '37. He directed the production. Pisk was already a celebrated composer, having written 36 musical opuses in Europe. He went on to become a professor at the University of Texas, an important twentieth-century composer and musicologist. The American Musicological Society awards an annual Paul A. Pisk Prize for an outstanding scholarly paper by a grad student.

In 1948, Henry and Fromma Wellman bought Camp Oquago and made it co-educational. David Stern, Commissioner of the National Basketball Association, was one of their many campers who went on to successful careers. The Wellmans, in 1977, turned operation of the camp over to Laura and Stuart Chase, who ran it until Camp Oquago closed in 1993.

Camp Ta-Ri-Go was founded by Louis Wilder on the grounds of his New Orchard Hotel in Fleischmanns in 1935. The co-ed camp featured a man-made lake, recreation hall, infirmary, and campers' cottages "equipped with baths and showers," that made it, in the words of the *Catskill Mountain News*, "one of the most complete and up to date recreational centers in the mountains."

Pary Salzman, Executive Director of the Union, New Jersey YMHA, brought his professional expertise to the direction of camp activities, making Ta-Ri-Go, in the words of its owners, "a model of discipline and refinement."

Camp Ta-Ri-Go operated on Red Kill Road until 1977. A housing development now occupies the site.

Ta-Ri-Go opened its doors in July 1935 only to endure one of the wettest Julys on record, with flash-flooding and lightening-strikes causing problems all month. Fortunately, the campers remained safe, although, over in New Kingston, lightening struck and killed a cow.

Catskill Mountain Cauliflower

HERE'S HOW a bit of the local mountain economy worked in 1937. On July 26th of that year, a cauliflower auction block was opened on the G.L.F. grounds in Margaretville. Cauliflower was once a major cash crop on the west slope of the Catskills where the Delaware River drains.

The G.L.F. was the Grange League Federation, created in 1920 through a combination of three farmers' organizations: the New York State Grange, the Dairymen's League, and the State Farm Bureau. The G.L.F. had a Margaretville operation just west of Bridge Street on land that is now paved over.

Cauliflower was a natural, a cash crop that was popular with consumers and a perfect agricultural fit for mountain growing. The cool nights that made the Catskills a great summer retreat from city heat were also perfect for cauliflower, which thrives in moderate temperatures—the heads get grainy in excessive heat or drought—and seems to do best at elevations over 2000 feet above sea level.

Diane Galusha, our talented local historian, is the author of several important regional books, including *When Cauliflower Was King* (Purple Mountain Press, 2004). It's a 48-page booklet that tells the story of cauliflower's first-half-of-the-twentieth-century run as the local cash cow, or, at least, the local cash producer to supplement the income from the cow.

For this was dairy country, and was right up into the 1970s and early 1980s. The dairy business provides a regular income—I believe the milk check came to the farmer once a month or so—but the check went in the bank account, and the heavy expenses of farming came out and there was seldom much left. Cauliflower provided cash that hadn't already been spent.

So here's how it worked—at least once that auction block was built down on Fair Street in Margaretville that summer of 1937. The producer picks and crates his cauliflower, starting the harvest in late July. A crate packed a dozen heads. He'd truck his crates of cauliflower to the auction block in the morning, offering to sell whatever number of crates he chose. Buyers arrive. Most buyers were local truckers who would bid the produce at auction, hauling what they buy to New York or Philadelphia or even Boston, and selling it at, what the truckers hoped would be, a profit.

The auction block was established by the producers, farmers who felt that they could get a greater return than the price they had been getting from commission houses that handled the sale of the harvest, every August and September, for a percentage.

The first day's handle at the auction block was $580.55, with a top price of two dollars 37 and a half cents per crate, about 20 cents a head. Interestingly, the next day, 483 crates of cauliflower were offered for sale, but only 264 sold. The farmer could refuse any bid he deemed too low. Tuesday must have been a low-bid day.

Buyers had to pay for their purchase before they carried it away. Producers received a check every Friday.

Cauliflower producers were a well-organized lot, and the auction block came about through the efforts of the Catskill Mountain Cauliflower Co-opera-

Grown in the
CATSKILL MOUNTAINS

RIP VAN WINKLE BRAND
Grown and Packed by
The Margaretville Cauliflower Growers Cooperative Inc.
Margaretville, N.Y.

tive which represented farmers from around the region. William and Thankful Van Benschoten were the first farmers to grow cauliflower, back in the 1890s, on their Margaretville Mountain farm, where the Inn is today. William was a leader in organizing producers to work together.

An Advisory Committee of the Co-operative represented the producers' interests in the operation of the auction block. Among them were Harold Garrison of Arkville, Leslie Stahl and Casper Bellows of Margaretville, Andrew Van Benschoten of New Kingston, Floyd Davis of Shavertown and John Burns of Bovina, as well as farmers from Stamford, Walton, Meridale, and Harpersfield.

The Co-operative marketed Catskill Mountain cauliflower with three different labels pasted on the crates: *Rip Van Winkle*, *Pride of the Catskills*, and *Mountain Brand*. *The Catskill Mountain News* reported, in its July 30, 1937, issue, that Basil Todd offered a load "whose crates bore a brand new label, *Sunset Brand*." Perhaps, Mr. Todd was marketing outside of the co-operative. That's fine. The auction block was open to all, buyers and sellers both.

The Round Barn in Kelly Corners is, perhaps, the early twenty-first-century equivalent of the auction block, a place where producers and buyers can meet directly to transact business. The retail market is, of course, a contrast with the wholesale selling producers could do at the auction block, which operated for 15 years or so, closing down around 1950.

Cauliflower continued to be an important mountain product into the 1990s. Ruff Farms, in New Kingston, trucked as many as 30,000 crates of cauliflower a year to markets throughout the East, ceasing operations in the mid-nineties.

I can't help thinking that a cash crop, produced here in the Catskills, couldn't once again put some of our now-fallow agricultural land back into production, and some much-needed cash in our local economy. Our proximity to New York City, America's love affair with fine food, widespread concern with healthful eating: all the factors seem to be in place to find a market for a locally-produced crop. But what?

I asked a friend, a talented local horticulturalist and green-house gardener. Kale, she said.

Kale is healthful, extremely popular, easy to grow. Could kale one day be king?

A Tourist in the Home Turf

EVERYWHERE I GO IN THE CATSKILLS, I pick up brochures, pamphlets, and those shiny rack-cards that seem to be everywhere promoting tourism in our mountains. I picked up a bunch just the other day, on a jeep-ride tour of nearby mountain attractions: new construction, old houses, some ruins, the Hunter bookstore, with lunch at Brio's.

I picked-up "August at the Catskill Mountain Foundation," "The Catskill Mountain Region Guide," "Hunter, NY Visitors' Guide," "Mountaintop Map and Guide," and "Eateries: A Food Reference Guide—Greene County 2009."

A good friend, now gone, used to say, "Someday that stuff will be worth a lot of money," and, of course, he was right. Keep travel brochures and other printed material long enough and they become collectors' items, valuable relics from another time. If, in their useful life as travel brochures, they are well-written and interesting, attractively illustrated and laid-out, they can, when they pass into collectibles, become windows into another era.

Such a window is R. Lionel De Lisser's *Picturesque Ulster*, printed in six parts in 1894 as pioneering travel promotion material, a series of beautifully illustrated books, with scores of terrific photographs accompanied by text aimed at attracting the dollars of middle-class vacationers. Recently, I bought a battered copy of Picturesque Ulster, Part 6 Township of Shandaken from another friend, a dealer in postcards and ephemera—the term for miscellaneous collectible printed material.

"The Township of Shandaken: The Artist's Rambles in Ulster County," is the title of De Lisser's opening essay in the 11 by 14-inch book, with another author providing text on "The Passing of the Hemlock," followed by a long, rambling, fake Native tale "The Legend of Blossom Falls, with notes by the editor." All three texts are designed to provide the mountain township a romantic, misty atmosphere, a primitive, natural, and simple world to wash the ravished cares of late-nineteenth-century living.

It's the photographs that are worth the price of admission—and, by the way, Hope Farm Press advertises, on its web site, a $35 reprint of the full-length, 300-page, more-than-just Shandaken *Picturesque Ulster*. De Lisser was a talented photographer and had a great eye for what photographs to take.

The first photo you see in the Shandaken book is the narrow, high-sided bridge over the small stream that separates Shandaken from the Town of Olive on the one-lane dirt road that is, today, Route 28. You might recognize the old Winnie house, just below present-day Winnie Road, then the Beechford Post Office. First time I ever heard of Beechford!

Turns out, place names are a kind of crap-shoot in the late 1800s, with post offices, railroad stops, and bends-in-the-road all likely to adopt their own. So, the rail stop, Cold Spring, served the post office, Beechford, and Mount Pleasant rail depot served the hamlet, The Corner, which I guess would be Mount Tremper today.

Encouragingly, De Lisser's bank-level photos of the Esopus look very much like the same views today. The rocks and rapids are palpable. The mountains seem forested to about the same degree. The many small hotels and boarding houses pictured are pleasantly shaded in Victorian groves, as inviting today as they were intended to be then. 1890s Shandaken looks really nice.

But then, today's Shandaken is still a beautiful part of the earth. Not so many hotels, certainly, but lots of second homes, and a great state recreation center open to anyone with the price of a lift ticket, and a little public lake and picnic ground, and The Shandaken Wild Forest, not to mention the Big Indian Wilderness Area. Open to us all.

The town was struggling economically back in the 1890s, just as it is today. Pretty much all Catskill Mountain towns and villages struggle economically today.

De Lisser's book had an economic motive. It was an entrepreneurial attempt to sell books that would, in turn, sell more hotel stays, more week-long residences in boarding houses.

Lionel De Lisser himself was an American artist, an easel painter who worked his representational subjects—he was best known for his figures and interiors—in oil paint. His Herd Crossing, a sentiment-filled print idealizing rural life, is presently for sale on the web with a starting bid of $150. *Tea Time*, oil on canvas, will sell for much more, its warm interior inviting the viewer to join the two well-dressed women pictured at tea.

An accomplished painter, De Lisser's photographs of the Catskills are also among his best work. His high altitude, panoramic shots must have been pioneering in the history of photography, still in its infancy in 1894. His book has a great photograph of the Big Indian Valley from on high, and another of the Pine Hill Valley from Monka Hill. Both pretty awe-inspiring in the comfort of your parlor chair!

I'll continue to collect travel brochures from mountain tourist towns, as season turns to season, striving, each day, to let mountain living offer its everyday adventures, a Catskill Catalog of home-turf discoveries.

Index

20th Amendment 122
20th Congressional District 44, 45
21st Congressional District 45
22nd Congressional District 44

Aaron, Henry 50
Abrahao, Dr. Humberto100
Actors Equity 53
Adams, Abigail 62
Adams, John 14, 30, 31, 61, 171
Adams, John Quincy 14
Adirondacks 11, 45, 87, 95, 132
Adirondack Forty-Sixers 79
Adirondack Mountain Club 79
Africa 36
Age of Innocence, The 91
Alabama 156
Albany Academy 81
Albany Argus 31
Albany County 58, 59, 76, 95, 96, 96, 133
Albany, NY 19, 20, 25, 31, 32, 34, 45, 47, 51, 54, 65, 77,
    81, 85, 92, 106, 117, 131, 132, 135, 166, 174
Albany Post Road 85
Albany Regency 31
Algonquin 40, 41
Allaben, Dr. Orson 82, 83, 84, 104
Alleghany River 55
Alleghany River Valley 25
Allen, John 98
America: A History in Verse 153
America: A Prophecy 153
American Centennial Exhibition, 1876 92, 124
American Colonies 24, 25, 59, 171, 172, 173
American Frontier 23, 24, 25, 29
American Journal of Science 112
American Legion 65
American Musicology Society 179
Amos 'n' Andy 163
Amsterdam, NY 45
Andes, NY 49, 65, 82, 97, 98, 106, 120, 141, 144, 145,
    146, 159, 160, 161, 162, 168, 178
    Andes Central School 106, 141, 161
    Andes Collegiate Institute 160, 161
    Hunting Tavern 98
    Men's Community Club 107
    School District Number 21 140
Andover, NY 53
Andre, Major13
Andrews, Mary 129
Annals of Onteora 92
Annapolis, MD 157
*Another Day, Another Dollar: The Civilian Conservation
    Corps in the Catskills* 110, 111
Anti-Rent War 93, 94, 95, 96, 97, 98, 99, 107, 162, 176

Anti-Semitism 47, 125
Appalachian Mountains 119,165
Archaeology 36, 37
Archaic Period 37
Archibald, Sinclare 100
Architecture 11, 25
    Bluestone 50
    Bridges 142,
    Dutch-style 25
    Nineteenth century 11
    Post Civil War 11
    Tudor 53
    Victorian 138
Arena, NY 106
Arkville, NY 12, 17, 18, 19, 21, 25, 28, 40, 43, 74, 77,
    83, 86, 87, 88, 104, 119, 143, 150, 154, 155, 158, 182
    Ooga Booga 74
    Oral History Project 22, 119
Arkville-Erpf Fund 18
Armstrong, General 11, 12, 13
Armstrong, John 11, 12
Armstrong Tract 76
Arnold, Benedict 13
Art Awareness 53
Art Students League 165
Arts and Crafts Movement 127
Artisan-Republicanism 30, 45
Asher, Joanie 100
Ashland Collegiate Institute 33, 66
Ashokan Reservoir 93
Associated Artists 92
Auburn, NY 95
Austria 39

Babylon, NY 46
Bainbridge 117
Baker, Helen 165
Ball, Lucille 163
Ballantine, David 144
Ballantine, Lillie 144
Banker, Dr. John M 151
"Bark Study, The" 90
Barnes, Peg 155
Bartram, John 25
Baseball 46, 50
    A. Bartlett Giamatti Baseball Research Center
        and Library 50
    American League 47
        Baltimore Orioles 47
        Boston Red Sox 47, 166
        Brooklyn Dodgers 47, 48
        Chicago White Sox 47
        Cincinnati League Park 18-3
        Cincinnati Reds 47
        Cleveland Indians 19-2

Baseball Hall of Fame 13, 46, 47, 50, 126, 155
  Downsville Town Team 50
  Mountain Tourists 47
  National Baseball Association 179
  National League 47
  Naponach Chevvies 49
  Negro Leagues 48
  New York State League 47
  New York Yankees 47, 85, 126, 167
  Philadelphia Phillies 47
  Phoenicia Town team 49
  Reds 47
  Semi-Pro Baseball Congress 47
  Shamrocks 47
  Woodstock AC 49
Batavia, NY 28
Bates, Peg Leg 147
Beach, Charles L. 112
Beachwood Seminary 81
Beaverkill 42, 65
Bedandbreakfast.com 170
Beekman, Margaret 62
Beinvenidos a Fleischmanns: An Immigrant
  Community in Rural America 148
Belgium 25
Belleayre Mountain 86, 110
Bellows, Casper 182
Benedict, Homer 13, 14, 15
Bennett, Reginald 135, 136
Bennett, Rupert 136
Berg, Gertrude 162, 163, 164
Berg, Lewis 163
Berkshire Mountains 91
Berle, Milton 17
Bernard, Eugene 132
Berne, NY 95, 131
Berra, Yogi 48
Berrigan, Ted 153
Beth, Karen 17
Beverly Hillbillies, The 119
Big Indian NY 111, 113, 132, 133, 184
Big Indian- Oliveria Valley 128
Big Indian Wilderness Area 184
Big Rocks 37, 154
Binghamton, NY 45, 46, 51
  Veteran's Arena 51
Binnekill 83
Black Power Movement 158
Blenheim- Gilboa Power Project Visitors Center 77
Blenheim, NY 35
Blenheim Patent 77
Blish, John 124
Blood, Sweat, and Tears 69
Bloomville Mirror 33
Bloomville, NY 70
Blue Mountains see Catskill Mountains
Bohlinger's Fruit Farm 35

Boiceville, NY 73, 110, 111
  Bread Alone 73
  Boiceville Inn, The 73,
  Fabulous Furniture 111
Bonanza 23
Borscht Belt 111, 158, 170
Boston, MA 7-2
Boston University 53
Bouchard, Bruce 53
Bouck, William C. "Dutch Governor" 34
Bouck's Island, NY 34
Bouton, Donald W. 72, 74, 138
Bouton, Marshall 72
Bovina, NY 65, 76, 88, 141, 162, 182
Brant, Joseph 28
Breakabeen, NY 110
Breezy Hill Road 38
Brecht, Bertolt 179
Bretz, John 145
Broad Street Hollow, NY 22
Broadlands 86
Browere, J.H.I.13
Bryan, William Jennings 113, 114
Burgoyne, General John 174
Burns, John 182
Burr 85
Burr, Aaron 30, 31, 85
Burr, John 59
Burrell, Anson 98
Burroughs, Curtis 90
Burroughs, John 31, 32, 33, 63, 65, 66, 68, 81, 82, 89,
  90, 91, 97, 127, 178
Burroughs, Julian 33, 89, 90
Burroughs, Ursula 33, 89, 90
Burrows, James 29
Bush, George 122
Bush, Henry 20, 28
Bushkill Creek 29, 117, 130
Bussy, Ethel 103
Bussy, Stanley 123
Butler, John 28
Butler, Walter 28
Butler's Ranger's 28, 29
By The Light of the Kerosene Lantern 72, 138

Cabin Hill, NY 117, 118, 145
Cadosia, NY 143
Calico Indians 176
California 53, 121, 137
Callicoon, NY 147
Camp Burroughs 63
Camp Furusato 37, 38
Camp Oquago 63, 178, 179
Camp Ta-Ri-Go 170, 179
Camp Wake Robin 64, 178
Camp Woodland 64, 65
Campbell, Bill 17

Campbell Brook 143
Canada 174
Candace Wheeler: The Art and Enterprise of American Design 1875-1900 92
Cannonsville Reservoir 70
Cantine, Colonel 29
Cantine, Moses 117
Cape Cod, MA 24
Capitol Repertory 53, 54
Caribbean 39
Carlyle, PA 11
Carnegie, Andrew 81
Carter, Jimmy 85
Catskill Association for Tourism Services 170
Catskill Catalog, A 171
Catskill Center for Conservation and Development 17, 18, 19, 22, 119, 154
Catskill Creek 56
Catskill Folk Festival 64
Catskill Institute 170
Catskill Mountain Agricultural Society 84
Catskill Mountain Cauliflower Co-operative 180, 182
Catskill Mountain Crafts 111
Catskill Mountain Foundation, The 52
Catskill Mountain News, The 39, 84, 101, 102, 103, 104, 121, 123, 131, 150, 171, 179 182
Catskill Mountain Quilters Hall of Fame 154, 155
Catskill, NY 22, 23, 26, 27, 28, 43, 56, 73, 93, 167
Catskill Park 108
Catskill Rivers: Birthplace of American Fly Fishing 43
Catskill Songbook, A 64
Catskill Turnpike 54, 56
Catskill Watershed Corporation 33
Catskill 3500 Club 78, 80
Catskillarchive.com 171
Catskillpark.com 170
Catskills
    Region 12, 13, 18, 19, 20, 21, 22, 24, 25, 26, 31, 32, 33, 34, 38, 41, 42, 44, 45, 46, 48, 49, 50, 51, 52, 53, 54, 56, 63, 64, 65, 66, 67, 68, 69, 71, 72, 73, 74, 76, 81, 84, 85, 86, 87, 89, 92, 100, 101, 104, 110, 116, 118, 119, 120, 121, 122, 122, 124, 126, 127, 128, 130, 131, 132, 133, 134, 135, 137, 139, 140, 141, 142, 143, 145, 146, 147, 149, 150, 153, 154, 155, 156, 157, 158, 159, 160, 162, 164, 165, 166, 167, 168, 170, 171, 172, 173, 175, 178, 179, 180, 182, 183, 184
    Mountains 18, 20, 25, 35, 36, 41, 51, 54, 58, 59, 61, 68, 70, 74, 75, 78, 79, 80, 93, 111, 112, 113, 115, 124, 128, 165, 167
        Balsam Mountain 78, 80
        Big Indian Mountain 80
        Black Dome 80
        Blackhead 78, 80
        Bovina Mountain 56
        Cornell Mountain 80

        Doubletop 79, 80
        Durham Mountain 56
        Giant Ledge 128, 129
        Graham Mountain 80
        Halcott Mountain 41, 80
        Hunter Mountain 80
        Monka Hill 184
        Mount Utsayantha 41
        North Dome Mountain 41
        Panther 78, 80
        Peekamoose Mountain 80
        Plateau Mountain 41
        Round Top 112
        Slide 78, 80, 112, 128, 129
        Southwest Hunter Mountain 79
        Table Mountain 80
        Thomas Cole 80
        Warren Mountain 56
        West Kill Mountain 41
        Wittenberg Mountain 80
        Winnisook 129
Catskills, From Wilderness to Woodstock, The 21, 22 67, 68, 68, 164
Cauliflower 179, 180, 180, 182, 182
Cazden, Norman 64, 65
CBS 144
Cedar Grove 26 27
Census Bureau 24
Central America 148
Center for Jewish History 163
Chapters in the History of Delaware County New York 60, 117
Charleston, SC 92
Chase, Laura 179
Chase, Stuart 179
Cheever, John 53
Chekhov, Anton 153
Cherry Hill, NY 154
Chesecock's Patent 93
Chicago 92, 150
Chichester, Frank 136
Chichester, Lemuel 136
Chichester, NY 132, 135, 136, 137
China 158
Chivaree 69
Christianity 62
Christman, Henry 107
Christmas 114, 115
Christmas Carol, A 114
Chronogram 153
Church, Frederick 27
Chute, Rastus 71
Ciccone, Nat 89
Cincinnati 47, 118, 124
Cincinnati Enquirer 47
Cinco de Mayo 159
Civil Rights Movement 158

Civil War 33, 51, 57, 76, 89, 92, 122, 128
    Camp Scott 157
    Fort Moultrie 156
    Fort Sumter 156, 157
    Gettysburg 157
    New York State Militia 156
    Second Battle of Bull Run 158
Ulster Guard 157
    72nd New York Volunteers 157
Civilian Conservation Corps 110
Clark, Edward Cabot 14
Clark, Steven13
Clarke, John D. 46
Clarke, Marian Williams 46
Clarksville, NY 132, 133
Classiccatskills.com 170
Clay, Henry 2-3
Clermont 20, 171, 174
Cleveland 3-2
Clinton, Bill 84, 85
Clinton, DeWitt 31
Clinton, Gov. George 29, 30, 31, 174
Clinton, Hillary 84, 85
Clovis point 36
Cobbett, William 168
Cockburn, Samuel 62, 175
Colchester, NY 142, 144, 168
Cold Spring, NY 43
Cold War 3-2
Cole, Thomas 26 27 68
Columbia College 115
Columbia County 20 31, 45, 59, 96
Columbia University 64, 163
Commemorative Biographical Record of Ulster County
    128
Common Schools 141
Complete Angler, The 42
Concord, MA 33
Condon, Barbara 149
Conesville, NY 164
Congress 44, 44, 45, 45
Connecticut 45, 64, 69, 88, 160, 162, 167, 168, 168, 171
    Hartford Stage 53
    Long Warf Theater, The 53
Connecticut River 24,
Connell, Marion 58, 66, 67,
Continental Congress 61, 171, 172
Contraband 26
"Conversion as Process: Catherine Livingston
    Garretson's Search for Sanctification" 62
Cooks Falls, NY 143,
Cooper, James Fenimore 13, 32, 59, 112
Cooper, Judge William13, 59
Cooperstown, NY 13, 45, 46, 50, 126, 127
Cooperstown Seminary 33, 66
Cope, Rachel 62
Corbett Acid Factory 142, 143, 144

Corbett and Stuart 142
Corbett Bridge 142
Corbett, Julius 143
Corbett, Merrit 143
Corbett, NY 71, 142, 143, 144
Corn Mountain see Vroman's Nose
Cornell Steamboat Company 78
Cosmopolitan 111
Country Journal and Poughkeepsie Advertiser 115
Cowles, Dr 83,
Cox, George B. 47
Crane, Ichabod 65
Crockett, Davey 23
Cropsey, Jasper 27
Crossroad, The 4-1
Cuban Giants 46
Cumberland County, PA 11
Czechoslovakia 143

Dairymen's League 180
Darfur 172
Dark Genius of Wall Street: The Misunderstood Life of
    Jay Gould, King of the Robber Barons, The 81
Davenport, NY 145
Davy, Sir Humphrey 74, 75
Davie, Henry 160
Davis, Floyd 182
Davis, Howard 134
Davis, Parthena 98
De Lisser, R. Lionel 183, 184
Dean, J. J. 161
Declaration of Independence 61, 171, 172, 173
Decoration Day 57
Decoration of Homes, The 91
Democratic National Convention 84, 86
Democratic Party 30 95, 96, 107, 113, 122, 123, 156
Democratic-Republicans 30, 31
DeLancey, NY 83, 117, 145
Delaware 71
Delaware Academy 66, 83, 141, 160
Delaware and Eastern Railroad 144
Delaware and Hudson Canal 142
Delaware and Northern Railroad 143
Delaware and Ulster Rail Ride 41
Delaware Bay 71
Delaware County 14, 17, 33, 45, 51, 58, 59, 60, 65, 81,
    82, 86, 87, 91, 93, 97, 100, 103, 104, 107, 134, 141,
    155, 157, 170
Delaware County Courthouse 176
Delaware County Historical Association 60
Delaware County New York 60
Delaware County Schoolmaster's Dinner 65
Delaware Indians see Lenni Lenape
Delaware Literacy Institute 66, 142, 160
Delaware National Bank 86
Delaware River 20, 25, 28, 29, 32, 41, 42 59, 61, 70, 71,
    83, 117, 131, 142, 173, 179

East Branch 18, 20, 25, 28, 29, 41, 42, 58, 61, 70, 71, 83, 97, 107, 117, 142, 154 171
    West Branch 61, 70, 76, 93, 97
Delaware River Valley 18, 35, 42, 106
Delaware Turnpike *see* Route 443
Delaware Water Gap National Recreation Area 18, 117
Delhi, NY 43, 45, 46, 49, 54, 59, 60, 66, 70, 76, 83, 83, 84, 91, 92, 93, 97, 99, 108, 109, 118, 141, 145, 146, 155, 157, 160, 161, 175, 178
Denman, Ann 113
Denman, William 113
Denver-Vega Valley 41, 116, 130
Department of Environmental Conservation 52
DeSilva, Chan 49
Dewey, John 64
Dick and Jane 32
DiMaggio, Joe 126, 127
Dimmick Building 18
Dimmick, Noah 17, 18, 83, 104
Dimmick, Thankful 83, 104
Dimmick's Tavern 18 83
Dingle Hill 88, 97, 98, 99, 107, 119, 121, 175, 176
DiNicola, Dan 54
Dirty Dancing 170
Disney, Walt 23, 44
Doig, R.T. 161
Donahue, Father Ray 80
Dooin, Charley "Red" 47
Doolittle, Eliza 118
Doubleday 67
Downhill River 53
Downsville, NY 28, 33, 49, 134, 142
    Downsville Central School 39, 106, 120, 141, 161
    Episcopal Church 80
    Fireman's Park 50
Downtown Community School 64
Dr. Ida 177
Draper, Andrew S. 140
Drew University 63,
Dry Brook, NY 18, 44 68
    Dry Brook Community Hall 53
Duchess County 59, 85
Duerden, Tim 60
DuMond, Harmonus 25, 28, 29
DuMond, Peter 25
Dunlap Broadside 172
Dunlap, John 172
Dunraven, NY 37, 102, 117
Durand, Asher B. 27
Durham, NY 167
Dutcher, Hooper 129
Dutcher, Jim 113, 128, 129

Earle, Moses 98, 99, 107, 175, 176
Early Show, The 114
East Branch Valley 100, 104

East Durham, NY 148, 158
East Jewett, NY 155
Ed Sullivan Show 153
Edgarton, Constable Erastus 98, 99
Edelstein, Diana 163, 164
Edelstein, Gertrude *see* Gertrude Berg
Edelstein, Jacob 163, 164
Edwards, Colonel William 75
Edwardsville, NY *see* Hunter, NY
Egypt 40
Erie Canal 51
Eire Railroad 80, 81
Emerson, Ralph Waldo 33, 89
Emery Estate 152
Encyclopedia of Children and Childhood in History and Society 177
English Royal School of Art Needlework 92
Environmental history 67
El Salvador 148
Elk Creek Road 54
Ellenville, NY 49, 157
Erpf, Armand G. 17, 18
Erpf-Catskill Cultural Center 17, 18, 19, 22, 119, 154
Esopus Creek12, 20, 29, 41, 42 110, 112, 113, 117, 129, 171, 172, 173, 184
Esopus Indians 41
Esopus, NY 173
Esopus Valley 62, 113
Essex County 45
Europe 27, 39, 58, 92, 179
Evers, Alf 21, 22 67, 68, 112, 164, 165, 166
Exorcist, The 52

Fairbairn, Niles 44
Farleigh, Joe 33
Fashion of the Times 111
Faulkner, Doug 148, 149, 150
Faulkner, Eleanor 155
Faulkner, Fran 88
Faulkner, Guy "Sharky" 150
Faulkner, M. J. 149
Faulkner, June 149
Federalists 30
Fenimore Art Museum 13, 14
Finger Lakes 23-2
Fishkill, NY 173, 174
Fishs Eddy, NY 143
Fisk, Jim 80
Fitch, Judge Fitz-James 43
Fleischmann, Charles 47, 124, 125, 126
Fleischmann, Josephine 124
Fleischmann, Julius 47, 48
Fleischmann, Max 47, 48, 124
Fleischmanns Flyer 130, 131
Fleischmanns, NY 11,13, 37, 38, 39, 40, 52, 60, 63, 66, 76, 103, 120, 121, 124, 125, 126 129, 130, 131, 148, 150, 151, 163, 179

Armstrong Park 11, 19, 125
Fleischmann's High School 39
Fleischmanns Park 125
Halpern's Department Store 151
Main Street 38, 39, 40, 151
Museum of Memories 46
Railroad Station 151
Wagner Avenue 126
Fleischmann's Yeast 124
Florida 156
Fodors.com 170
Folk Songs of the Catskills 64, 165
Foote, Ebenezer 59
Fort Amsterdam 19
Fort Duquesne 11
Fort Orange 19
Fort Shandaken 29
Foster, Don 115
France 13, 25, 36, 62, 142
Francis, Austin M. 43
Frankel, Martha 111
Frankenstein 54
Franklin, Benjamin 61
Franklin, NY 54, 60, 66, 97, 142, 160, 171
Free Soil Party 31
French and Indian War 11
Frisbee House Museum 60
Frisbee, Howard 107
Frisbee, J. D. 107
Frontier Thesis 24
Frost, Robert 146, 153
Frost Valley YMCA 63
Fugs, The 153
Full Moon Resort 129
Fultonham, NY 34

Gallo, Dr. William 22
Gallupville, NY 131
Galusha, Diane 91, 110, 180
Garcia, Arturo 148
Garretson, Catherine Livingston 62
Garretson, Freeborn 62
Garrison, Harold 182
Gates, Bill 47, 124
Gates, Dr. 145
Gates, General Horatio 12
Gazette 174
Genesee River 25
George, Bucky 100
Georgetown 47
Georgia 156
German- American Club of the Northern Catskills
158
Germany 39, 92, 142, 146, 147
Gerry, Commodore Elbridge T. 145, 146
Gerry Estate *see Broadlands*
Gifford, Sanford 43

Gilbert Lake State Park 110
Gilboa, NY 33, 34
Gilboa Dam 56
Gilboa School 56, 120
Gillibrand, Kirsten 45
Ginsberg, Allen 154
Glaciers 35
Gladstone, Dr 144, 145, 146
Gladstone, Wayland 107
Gladstone, W.R. 161
Goldbergs, The 162, 164
Google 28
Gordon, Phil 135
Gould, Anna 82
Gould, Edwin 82
Gould, Frank 82
Gould, George 82
Gould, Helen 82,
Gould, Jay 32, 33, 42, 60, 65, 70, 80, 81, 82
Gould, John Burr 81
Gould, Mary More 81
Gouldsboro, PA 82
Grand Gorge, NY 34, 56, 70, 81, 120, 131
Grant, Colonel John 172
Grant, Mary Lewis 160
Graham, Frank 144, 145, 146
Grand Army of the Republic 57
Grange League Federation 180
Gray, Olive 146
Great Depression 101, 102, 103, 110, 122
Great Lot Number 7, 25
Green Mountains 132
Greene County 43, 45, 58, 59, 72, 75, 93, 137, 141, 155,
157, 158, 170
Griffin, Betty 100
Griffon, DeWitt 151
Griffon, Matthew 151
Griffin's Corners, NY 11, 124, 126, 141, 151, 161
Grinder's Stand 54
Grocholl, Jackie 130, 150
Grocholl, Lewis 130
Grossinger, Jennie 146
Grossinger, Melke 146, 147
Grossinger, Selig 146
Guggenheim Fellowship 153
Gunsmoke 23
Guyot, Arnold Henry 112

Haines Falls, NY 75, 112
Hamilton, Alexander 30, 31
Halcott Center, N 57, 72
Halcott, NY 45, 130, 137, 138, 141, 175
Halcott Valley, NY 22, 41, 72
Hale Eddy, NY 143
Half Moon 40
Halim, Dr. Magdi 100
Hall, George Henry 92

Hall, Oakley III 21-3
Hamden, NY 49, 83, 117, 145, 148
Hamilton College 165
Hamptons 126
Hancock Hospital 100
Hancock, John 172
Hancock, NY 71, 157
Hanukah 114
Hardenbergh, Johannes 20, 25, 76,
Hardenbergh Patent 12, 20, 21 25 61, 76, 93, 115, 117,
    167, 174, 175
Hardenburgh, NY 141
Hardscrabble Rd. 32
Harpersfield, NY 56, 59, 182
    Bloomfield-West Harpersfield Road 56
Harpersfield Seminary 33
Harriman, Averill 86
Harter, Linda 17
Harter, Rev. Bill 17
Hartford, CT 27 92
Hathorn, John 45
*Hats and Eyeglasses: A Family Love Affair With
    Gambling* 111
Haufrecht, Herbert 64
Havana, Cuba 51
Have Gun Will Travel 23
Haynes, Glentworth 67
Haynes Hollow, NY 68, 119
Health Alliance Planning 101
Heart of the Catskills, The 112, 129
Hebrews 74
Helderberg Mountain 95, 96, 131
Heller, Steve 111
Hemingway, Ernest 139
Hemlock 74, 75
Hendricks, Peter 7-3
Herd Crossing 184
Herkimer, General Nicholas 28
Herrick, Everett 103
Hessian 60, 174
Het Strand 167
Hewitt, Joe 35, 36
Hewitt, John 116
Hewitt, Martha 116
High Falls Film Festival 163
Highland, NY 58
Highmount, NY 20, 62, 67, 135, 152
Hilton, Manetha 161
Hilton, Silas 161
Hinchey, Maurice 45
Hindemith, Paul 179
Hirsch, Baron Maurice de 146
*History and Stories of Margaretville and Surrounding
    Areas* 103
History of Delaware County 60
History of Delaware County and Boarder Wars 60
History of Delaware County, N.Y. 11, 42

*History of Delaware County, NY: A Catskill Land and
    Its People 1797-2007* 60
History.catskills.net 171
Hoare, Steve 154
Hobart, NY 46, 70, 81, 87, 141, 161
Hoeko, John 39, 40
Holland 166
Holland Land Company 95
Holt, John 172, 173
Holy Cross Monastery 91
Hoover, Herbert 85, 122
Hope Farm Press 183
Hosier, Marvin "Hap" 150
Hospital of Sidney, The 100
Hotaling, George 145
Hotels 11, 38
    The Alpine 11
    The Andes Hotel 85, 123
    The Argyle Hotel 46
    Blackthorne Resort 148
    The Breezy Hill Hotel 38
    Brown's Hotel 147
    The Catskill Mountain House 110, 112
    The Concord 147
    Friendship Manor 147
    Funcrest Hotel 147
    The Grand Union Hotel 47, 125
    Grossingers 147
    The Hendrick Hudson House 43
    Kutsher's Country Club 147
    The Locust Grove Hotel 77
    The Mathes 11
    The Mountain Star House 137, 138
    Mullen's Irish Spring Hotel 148
    The New Lorraine 11
    The New Orchard Hotel 179
    The Otsego Hotel 14
    The Panther Mountain House 129
    Peg Leg Bates Country Club 147
    The Phoenicia Hotel 85
    The Raleigh 147
    The Regis Hotel 151
    The Roxmor Inn 64, 178
    Slide Mountain Forest House 147
    Valkyrian Motel 151
    Villa Roma 147
    Villa Vosilla 147
Housatonic River 69
House of Glass, The 164
House of Mirth, The 91
Howdy Davis's Flat 41
Howe, General 28
Howe, Sheriff's Deputy James 99
Hubbard, Elbert 127
Hubbell Corners 34
Hubbell, Fanny 123
Huckleberry Finn 139

Hudson, Henry 37, 40, 75, 166
Hudson Highlands 174
Hudson, NY 20, 23, 75, 167
   Warren St. 23
Hudson River 19, 20, 24, 26, 28, 32, 36, 45, 51, 56, 59,
   60, 62, 75, 89, 93, 112, 115, 117 132, 134, 157, 167,
   171, 173, 174
Hudson River School 26, 27, 43, 68, 117
Hudson River Valley 60, 69, 73, 89, 93, 119, 173, 174
Huggans, Dr. C. Ray 101
Huggins, Miller 47
Huguenot 25, 166
Hunter, NY 49, 52, 75, 157, 183
Hunting, Ephraim 99
Huntington, Long Island 176
Hurley Flats 41
Hurley, NY 25, 28, 45, 174
Hurley Patent 93
Hurley Woods 51
Hurleyites 25
Hyde Park, NY 20, 85

Illinois 156
Iloveny.com 170
*In Catskill Country: Collected Essays on Mountain
   History, Life and Lore* 165
Independent Coalition of American Women 123
India 176, 177
Indiana 55
Indiana Repertory 53
Institute of Man and Science 144
Iowa 55
Iraq 58
Ireland 11, 148, 158
Iroquois 28, 29, 36, 41, 173
Iroquois Confederation 41
Irving, Washington 32, 166
Israel 137
Italy 143, 158
Ithaca, NY 45
Ives, Ralph 37

Jackson, Andrew 31
Jacksonian Democrats 95
Jake Moon Restaurant and Café 132, 133
James, Dr. Robert C. 145
James, Duke of York 19, 94
Japan 37, 58, 142
Jasper 26
Jefferson, NY 70
Jefferson, Thomas 13, 30, 31, 61, 115, 171
Jericho, NY 117
Jewett, NY 154
Jewish Agricultural Society 146
Jim Crow 46
John Boyd Thatcher State Park 132
John of the Cross 62

Johnson, Captain Robert T. 157
Johnson, Lena 155
Johnson, Lyndon Baines 57
Johnson, Sir William 28
Judd, Harold "Jimmy" 130

Kaaterskill Creek 75
Kaaterskill Falls 26
Kakiate Patent 93
Kale 182
Kapitko, Barb 100
Kasanof, Mr. 57
Keller, Helen 44
Kelley, Ezekiel 98
Kelly Corners, NY 123, 182
Kempner, Aviva 163
Kennedy, John F. 23
Kent, England 176
Kentucky 46
Kerhonkson, NY 147
Kittatinny 117
Kinderhook, NY 31, 85
King Charles 94
King George III 28, 77
Kings Road 36
Kingston: City on the Hudson 166
Kingston, NY 22, 25, 28, 29, 31, 41, 45, 49, 62, 67, 73,
   88, 91, 108, 116, 117, 118, 119 133, 135, 155, 156,
   157, 166, 167, 173, 174, 175
   Broadway 88
Kingston City Hospital 100, 101
Kingston Old Dutch Church 31
Kingston Point 61
Kingston Patent 93
Kirkside 70
Kittle, Frederick 25
Kittle, widow 25
Knapp, Lewis 98
Knickerbocker, Dietrich 167
Kryptonites, The 26
Kubik, Dorothy 56
Kudish, Michael 128
Kuralt, Charles 144
Kwanzaa 114

La Bergerie *see* Rokeby Farm
La Varenne School of Cuisine 132
Lackawaxen, PA 142
Lake Albany 134
Lake Champlain 174
Lake Delaware, NY 53, 76, 86, 145
   St James Church 53
Lake George 112
Lake Schoharie 35
Lake Switzerland 151
Lake Tunis-Camp Oquago, Inc. 178

Lake Winnisook 113
Lambert, Dr. Adrian V.S. 145
Lamoka 37
Lamoka Lake 37
Landfield, Bryan 143
Landon, Alf 123
Lanesville, NY 135
Lansing, Frances 77
Lansing, John 77
Lansing Manor 35, 77, 78
Lanzi, Wanda 154, 155
Last of the Homemade Dams: The Story of the Ashokan Reservoir, The 113
League of Resident Theatres 53
Leatherstocking District 32, 59
Leatherstocking Tales 13, 32
Leaves of Grass 33, 89
Leeds, NY 56, 167
Lenni Lenape 24, 36, 41
Lenox, MA 91
"Let's Build a Town" 179
Lew Beach, NY 176
Lewis, Gertrude 21
Lewis, Margaret 21
Lewis, Meriwether 54
Lewis, Morgan 21 117
Lexington, NY 53, 54, 75, 141
     Lexington Conservatory Theater 53, 54
Liberty, NY 111, 155
Lincoln, Abraham 122, 156, 157
Lindenwold 31, 85
Liquid Assets: A History of New York's City Water System 110
Little Delaware River 65, 108
Little, Harry W. 64, 178
Livingston, Alida 12, 13
Livingston, Catherine *see* Garretson, Catherine Livingston
Livingston, Edward 21 62, 77
Livingston, Gertrude 5-4
Livingston, Henry Jr. 115
Livingston, Janet *see* Montgomery, Janet
Livingston, Judge Robert R. 12, 13, 19, 20, 62
Livingston Manor 19
Livingston, Margaret 21
Livingston, Phillip 20
Livingston, Robert 'Of Claremont'12, 20 25
Livingston, Robert 'The Chancellor'12, 20, 21, 25, 60, 61, 62, 115, 171, 173, 174
Livingston, Robert 'The Founder' 20, 25, 59
Locust Grove 115
Loeb, Phillip 164
Logan, John A. 57
London 92, 118
Long Island 46, 116
Long Island Sound 24
LOOKSEEK.com 170

Louis C. Tiffany and Company Associated Artists 92
Louisiana 30, 62
Lunn, Dot 65
Luray, Virginia 110
Lutz, Bill 49
Lynch, Dr. and Mrs. 38
Lyndhurst 70, 82

MacArthur Foundation 152
Madison, James 13, 29, 31
Maine 24
Majority of One, A 164
Making Mountains: New York City and the Catskills 67, 68
Mallery, Timothy J. 170, 171
Manorkill, NY 56
     Durham Rd. 56
Manumission Society 30
"Map of the Catskills" 112
Maplecrest, NY 52
Marbletown, NY 28, 174
Marbletown Patent 93
Marc Black Band, The 26
Marcy, Governor William 95, 96
Margaretville Messenger 102
Margaretville, NY 18, 19, 20, 21, 25, 26, 28, 34, 37, 43, 48, 51, 52, 65, 66, 70, 82, 83, 84, 86, 100, 102, 104, 107, 108, 110, 120, 123, 134, 149, 154, 161, 175, 179, 180, 182
     American Legion Hall 58
     Bussy's Store 48, 123
     Dugan Hall 103, 123
     Episcopal Church 80
     Fairview Library 42, 66
     Granary Building 103, 123
     High School 58, 66, 134
     Main Street 83, 102, 103, 123
     Margaretville Cemetery 84, 101, 103, 104
     Margaretville Central School 39, 65, 81, 85, 106, 120, 139, 150
     Margaretville Fair 84
     Margaretville Family Health Center 88
     Margaretville Memorial Hospital 66, 88, 100, 101, 103, 104
     Margaretville Mountain Rd 175
     Margaretville/ New Kingston Presbyterian Church 17, 18
     Old Stone School House 65
     Open Eye Theater 52
     People's National Bank 102
     Presbyterian Church 66
     Republican Woman's Club 103
     Sacred Heart Church 18, 19
     Walnut Street 83
Marks, Ray 104
Martha's Vineyard, MA 167
Mason-Dixon Line 118

Masonville, NY 110
Massachusetts 20, 167, 171, 172
Massachusetts Bay Colony 176
Mastodon 36
Matamoras, PA 51
Mattice, Floyd 78
Maurer, Dr. Gordon Bostwick 100, 101, 103, 104, 105
Mayes, Bertha 155
Mayes, Melvin 129, 130, 131
McCarthy Era 65, 164
McEntee, Jervis 43
McFadden, Barney 47
McGraw- Hill Encyclopedia of Science and Technology
    143
McKinley Hollow, NY 128
Meadows Golf Center 86
Meeker Hollow, NY 121
Meeker Hollow School 81
Memorial Day 57
"Memories of Fleischmanns" 131
Mercer, General 12
Meredith Hill 54
Meredith, NY 54, 56
Meridale, NY 182
Merritt, Dutch 49
Mesopotamia 40
Metropolitan Museum of Art 92
Mexico 30, 118, 148
Mia Steiner Childhood Awards 139
Mia Steiner Prizes 139
Michael J. Quill Irish Cultural and Sports Center 158
Middle Atlantic 173
Middle East 27
Middleburgh, NY 34, 35, 41, 131
Middletown, NY (Township) 12, 18, 45, 65, 83, 84, 97,
    98, 141, 160, 171
    Dean's Corners 18, 83
    Galli-Curci Theater 100
    Historical Society 101
    Utilitarian, The 84, 102
Milford, PA 18, 51
Millbrook Stream 42, 43
Millbrook, NY 41
Millen, Lenny 44
Miller, Daniel S. 82
Miller, Edward 63, 64, 178
Miller, Helen Day 82
Miller, Ivan 106, 107
Miller, Kenny 48
Miller, Steve 107
Milwaukee 51
Minekill Falls 34, 56
Minekill Sate Park 35, 77
Mining 52
Minisink Ford, NY 142
Minisink Road 117
Minneapolis 53
    Guthrie Theater 53

Mirsky, Louis 178
Mississippi 156
Mississippi River 71
Missouri Pacific Railroad 81
Mitchell, Fred 47
Mohawk River 41
Mohawk Valley 132, 174
Mohawks 41
Mohicans 13, 36
Mohonk Mountain House 78
Molly and Me 164
Molly Goldberg Cookbook, The 164
Moncure, Barbara 165
Monet, Claude 137
Monmouth College 161
Monroe, John D. 60, 107, 117
Montgomery Hollow, NY 19, 121
Montgomery, General Richard 62, 115
Montgomery, Janet 21, 115
Monticello, NY 76, 93, 111
Montrose, PA 51
Moon, Jake 132
Moore, Clement 115
Moore, Sheriff Green 98, 99
Moresville, NY *see* Grand Gorge, NY
Morgan, Governor Edwin D. 157
Morrison, Bill 151
Morse, Dan 42
Morse, Myron 138
Morse, Samuel F.B. 27, 115
Moshe Y'oel Yeshiva 63, 76
Mount, The 91
Mount Tremper, NY 12, 117, 154, 183
    Beechford Post Office 183
    Cold Springs 183
    Mt. Pleasant 183
    The Corner 183
    Winnie Rd. 183
Mountain Athletic Club 46, 47
Mountain Speech 119
Mountaineer, The 104
Mountains Look Down: A History of Chichester,
    A Company Town in the Catskills, The 136
Munsee Indians 40, 41, 42
Munsell, W. W. 11, 60
Murray, David 60
My Fair Lady 118

Nassau County 116
National Academy of Design 27
National Book Award 153
National Endowment for the Arts 153
National Park Service 31
Nazis 179
NBC 163, 164
Nestledown 92
Neversink River 143
Neversink Valley 113

New Amsterdam 19, 20
New Bedford 167
New Deal 39, 110, 120 123
New England 19, 24, 30, 53, 54, 94, 166, 167, 168, 173, 177
New Jersey 25, 40, 69, 71, 137
New Kingston, NY 16, 17, 22, 38, 50, 56, 60, 61, 62, 74, 88, 133, 135, 149, 154, 173 174, 175, 179, 182
   New Kingston Association 17
   New Kingston General Store 149, 150
   Old Smith Farm 74
   Ruff Farms 182
   Wanda's 154
   Whoop De Doo16, 17, 134
   Winter Hollow 88
New Netherlands 19, 59
New Orleans 77
New Paltz, NY 78, 162, 165
New Paltz Patent 93
New York
   City 19, 20, 22, 27, 31, 34, 37, 38, 47, 51, 53, 56, 60, 63, 67, 70, 74, 77, 79, 81, 82 85, 92, 92, 113, 115, 124, 126, 136, 145, 148, 149, 157, 159, 160, 163, 165, 166 167, 172, 173, 177, 182
      Brooklyn 46
      Borough Park 11
         Williamsburg 11
      Brooklyn Bridge 142
      Jamaica, Queens 92
      Roundabout Theater Company 53
      Studio 54, 53
      Swamp 74, 75
   State 13,13, 28, 29, 30, 34, 38, 44, 52, 54, 55, 57, 58, 59, 60, 66, 69, 71, 89, 91 92, 94, 95, 96, 110, 112, 18, 120, 137, 140, 142, 151, 157, 166, 167, 173
      Department of Public Instruction 141
      Department Register of 1891-92 140
      New York Provincial Congress 172
      New York State Fourth Supervisory District of Schools 120
      New York State Historical Society 13
      New York State Power Authority 77, 78
      New York State Regional Books 60
      State Education Department 106
      State Normal School and Training Schools 162
      State Supreme Court 77
      State Teachers College 135
      Union Free School Act 161
New York 126
New York District 4, 45
New York District 14, 45
New York Observer, The 153
New York Packet, The 172
New York Post 159
New York School 153
New York State Grange 180

New York State Historical Association 14
"New York State Re-Vegetation Procedures Manual" 52
New York Times, The 39, 143
New Yorker, The 111, 153
Newburgh, NY 148
Newman, Hazel 144
Niagara Falls 27 112
Nicaragua 148
"Night Before Christmas, The" 115
Nixon, John 172
North Blenheim, 131
North Carolina 41, 170
North Carolina State University 119
North Lake 110, 112
North, Ursula *see* Burroughs, Ursula
Norton (Druggist) 145

O'Conner, Edward 99
O'Connor Hospital 100
Ohio 47, 55, 118
Ohio River Valley 25, 54, 124
Oklahoma 41
Olana 27
Olana Preservation 27
Old Ironsides see USS Constitution
Old John Burroughs 127
Old Mine Road *see* Minisink Road
Old Post Road 31
Olive, NY 135, 141, 183
Olivebridge, NY 33, 65
Oliver, James 32, 33, 65, 66, 67, 81
Oliverea, NY 135
Oliverea Valley 41, 113, 128, 147
Onassis, Jackie 158
Oneonta, NY 49, 54, 100
Oneonta Normal School 121, 135, 162
Oneonta Star 102, 123
Onistagrawa *see Vroman's Nose*
Online Guide to the Catskill Mountains, The 170
Onteora High-Middle School 135
Onteora Park, NY 92, 93
Onteora School District 135
Orange County 36, 45, 59
Otsego County 59
Otsego Lake 13
Our Town 53
Overlook Press 67
Owen, Reginald 114

Paige, Satchel 48, 50
Pakatakan settlement 28, 29 15-2
Palatine Germans 34, 166
Palen, Dr. Gilbert 88, 101
Palen, Jeanne 88
Palen, Jonathan 75
Palenville, NY 75

Paleolithic era 36
Paleontology 36, 37
Palmer Hill, NY 117
Pam Window and the Shades 26
Panic of 1837 95
Pantherkill Creek 64
Pardini, Earle 17
Park, Nathanial 28
Parker, Alton B. 113
Party Platform 31
Pasteur, Louis 124
Paul A. Pisk Prize 179
Peck, Bus 17
Peekamoose Restaurant 132
Pennsylvania 19 40, 49, 52, 54, 55, 69, 71, 82, 110, 143,
    171, 173
Pennsylvania Evening Post, The 172
Pepacton, NY 106
Pepacton Reservoir 28, 37, 41, 70, 106, 142, 172
Perch Lake 63, 178
Philadelphia 70, 71, 92, 101, 124, 172, 173
    Independence Hall 172
Phillips, Ike 84
Phoenicia, NY 26, 49, 51, 52, 63, 117, 135, 153, 183
    Phoenicia Theater 52
    Simpson's Hill 110
Picturesque Ulster 183
Pike County, PA 51
Pine Hill Lake 147
Pine Hill, NY 20, 29, 88, 117, 155, 184
Pine Hill Tavern 26
Pine Hill Trailways 154
Pine Orchard, NY 112
Pine Plains, NY 117
Pisk, Paul A. 179
Pittsburgh, PA 11
Platte Clove 26
Plattekill Creek 44, 60, 61, 117, 133, 154
Plymouth Valiant, '65 38
Poland 143
Ponckhockie, NY 174
Port Jarvis, NY 117
Portertown Creek 130
Portland, OR 111
Poughkeepsie 14, 45, 88, 115, 173, 174
Pratt, Colonel George W. 156, 157, 158
Pratt, Zadock 75, 82, 128, 156
Prattsville, NY 75, 128, 141, 156, 157
Pre-Raphaelite school 92
Princeton University 12, 112
Protestants 25
Pulitzer Prize 152
Pultz, Min 49
Purple Mountain Press 60, 130, 136
Pyongyang 172

Quarryville, NY 51

Queen Anne 20, 76, 93
Quillen, Boney 71
Quilting 154, 155

Radcliff, John 117
Railroads 71
Reagan, Ronald 86
Red Falls 154
Red Kill Valley 41
    Camp Ta-Ri-Go 63
Redding, Otis 15
Redkill, NY 121, 151
Redkill Ridge 152
Reed, Bob 49
Reese, Pee Wee 46
Reginald Bennett Elementary School 135
Renehan, Edward 80
Rensselaer and Saratoga Railway 82
Rensselaer County 45, 59, 94, 96
Rensselaerwyck Manor 94, 95, 96
Republican Party 45, 102, 103, 106, 107, 122, 123, 129,
    156
Republican Women's Club 123
Revolutionary War 12,13, 20, 25, 28, 29, 35, 60, 61, 77,
    81, 161, 166, 171, 172, 173, 174 175, 176
    Battle of Saratoga 12, 28, 174
    Burning of Kingston 60, 61, 62, 173, 174, 175
    Continental Army 172, 174
    Fort Clinton 174
    Fort Montgomery 174
    Fort Niagara 174
    Middle Fort 35
    Siege of Quebec 62, 115
Rhine River Valley 34
Rhinebeck, NY 84
    Beekman Arms Tavern 84
Rhinecliff, NY 117
Rhode Island 24
Rider Hallow, NY 128
"Rip Van Winkle" 32
Rip Van Winkle Bridge 27
Rise of the Goldbergs, The 163
Riverby 89
Robertson, Lillian 88
Robertson, Ruthvan "Robbie" 50
Robertson, Ruthven 88
Robinson, Jackie 46
Roebling, John Augustus 142
Rochester, NY 163
Rochester Patent 93
Rock 'n' Roll Hall of Fame 15
Rockefeller, John D. 81
Rockefeller, Nelson 27
Rohe, George "Whitey" 47
Rokeby Farm 13,
Roman Republic 55
Rominger, Loni 130

Rominger, Wray 130, 131
Rondout Creek 76, 167, 174
Rondout, NY 156, 157
Roosevelt Democratic Club 123
Roosevelt, Franklin D. 39, 85, 103, 110, 120, 122, 123
Roosevelt, Theodore 85, 113, 127
Root, Erastus 45
Rosendale, NY 49
Rotkov, Dr. Abe 100
Route 9H 31, 85
Route 9W 91
Route 10 49
Route 14 56
Route 23 23, 41, 56
Route 23A 26
Route 23 B 56
Route 23C 93
Route 28 13, 17, 34, 41, 54, 65, , 77, 86, 100, 108, 110,
    111, 116, 117, 135, 183
Route 30 34, 37, 41, 56, 77, 131, 133, 142
Route 33 56
Route 42 53
Route 97 142
Route 145 56
Route 209 117
Route 214 75
Route 443 132, 133
Route 990V 56
Rowland, Len 71
Roxbury, NY 21, 22, 32, 33, 34, 37, 41, 42, 43, 49, 51,
    65, 70, 81, 82, 83, 89, 90, 91, 97 98, 116, 120, 121,
    127, 130, 141, 150, 161, 166, 168, 176
    Jay Gould Memorial Reformed Church 82
    Roxbury School 120
Rudi: In His Own Words 111
Rudi's Big Indian 132
Ruff, Fred 107
Russell, Bob 44, 150
Russell, Frank 133, 134, 135, 150
Russia 143, 146
Ruth, Babe 47, 85
Rutland and Washington Railway 82
Ryan, Kay 152

Samsonville, NY 157
San Francisco 51
    American Conservatory Theater 53
Sanford, Kenny 150
Salem, MA 176
Salisbury, CT 117
Salzman, Pary 179
San Quentin 130
Sandburg, Carl 153
Sanders, Edward 153, 154
Sanders, Miriam 153
Sanford, Clarke 102, 103, 104, 105
Sanford, Courtney 102

Santos, Alfredo 130
Saratoga County 45, 45
Saratoga, NY 47, 125
Saratoga Springs, NY 62
Saugerties, NY 41, 51
Savetman, Abe 137, 138, 139
Sawkill Creek 51
Schenectady, NY 45, 106
Schuyler Van Rensselaer, Alida 5-2
Schoharie County 58, 70, 77, 96, 155
Schoharie Creek 41, 53, 54, 75, 128, 154
Schoharie Guards 29
Schoharie, NY 29 29, 35, 41, 131, 133
Schoharie Reservoir 56
Schoharie Valley 34, 35, 155
Schoonmaker, Cornelius 45
Schrage, Gerte (New Lorraine) 11
Schwarzwaelder, W. O. 136
Scorsese, Martin 91
Scotland 5-2
Scott, George C. 114
Scudder Association 176
Scudder, David 176
Scudder, Dr. Ida 177
Scudder, Harriet 176
Scudder, John 176
Scudder, Jotham 176, 177
Scudder, Mary Katherine 176
Scudder, Thomas 176
Scudder, Warren 175, 176
Scudder, William Smith 176
Seager, NY 44
Seligman, Joseph 47, 125
Sentinel, The 115
Severo, Richard 39
Seward, William 95, 96
Shady, NY 117
Shakespeare, William 160
Shandaken Mountains 112, 171
Shandaken, NY 12, 21, 28, 29, 41, 43, 45, 84, 117, 128,
    129, 141, 168, 175, 183, 184
    Emerson Spa 84, 111
    Shandaken Theatrical Society 52
    Shandaken Wild Forest 184
    Timber Lake Camp 63
Shaver Hollow, NY 106
    Shaver Hollow School 106
Shavertown, NY 106, 107, 143, 182
Shelly, Mary 54
Shepherd, Finley 70
Shepherd, Helen Gould 70
Sherman, Roger 171
Shinhopple, NY 143
Shokan, NY 20, 157, 168
Shultis, Ray 123
Sickles, General Dan 157
Sife, Bud 130

Silk Stockings District 44
Simic, Charles 152, 153
Sing Sing Prison 98
Singer Sewing machine 14
Six Nations 28
Skimmelton 68, 70
Skinner, B.F. 165
Skinner, David 71
Slabsides 89, 90, 91
Slabsides, the Movie 89
Slavery 30 31, 78, 122
Sloan, Rebecca 19
Slover, Harold 130
Slover, Ray 130
Smeallie, Reverend Peter 161
Smiley, Dan 78, 79
Smith, Dan 132, 133
Smith, Harriet 70
Smith, Nancy 155
Society of Decorative Art of New York 92
Soliloquy of a Careless Philosopher, The 115
Somelofski, Sonny 140
Soules Hill, NY 143
South America 27, 75
South Cairo, NY 56
South Carolina 92, 148, 156, 157
South Gilboa Road 56
South Lake 26, 112
Southern Tier 45
Spangenberger, Bill 78
Spangenberger, Kay 78
Spangler, Lynn C. 33
Sparrow 153
Sparrow Reader, The 153
Spector, Dr 100
Spink, Erwin S. 64
Sprague, Walter 107
Spring, Edmund 77, 78
Squires, Lois 154
Stahl, Leslie 182
St. Augustine, FL 46
St. Leger, Barry 174
St. Louis 51, 92, 161
Stamford, NY 41, 56, 70, 85, 87, 120 182
    Delaware Inn 85
    Stamford Hospital 100
Stamford School 120
State Farm Bureau 180
State Highway 212, 117
State Normal School 32, 65
Staten Island, NY 114
Steele, Sheriff Osman 97, 98, 99, 107, 175, 176
Steinberger, Ben 178
Steiner, Mia 137, 138, 139
Sterling Forest 174
Stern, David 179
Steuding, Bob 112, 113, 114, 129

Stoddard, William 160
Stone
    Bluestone Expo 51, 52
    Catskill Mountain Bluestone 50, 51, 70
    New York and Pennsylvania Bluestone
        Association 51
    Normanskill Flint 37
    North River Bluestone 51
    Pennsylvania Bluestone 51
    Pennsylvania Jasper 37
Stony Clove 75, 116, 136
Stony Clove Notch, NY 132
Stradling, David 67, 68
Stradling, Jodie 67
Streetcar Named Desire 54
Stroudsburg, PA 82
Stuart, Bula 144
Stuart, John 142, 143, 144
Stuart, Leonard 143
Stuart, Merrit 143
Studer, Norman 64, 65
Stuyvesant, Peter 20
Sullivan County 45, 58, 93, 111, 155, 158, 170
Sun, The 153
Sunday Morning 144
Sunset View Farm 151
SUNY Cobleskill 33
SUNY Delhi 17, 108, 109
SUNY Oneonta 102, 121
SUNY Ulster 152
    Ellen Robbins Poetry Forum 152
Susquehanna River 55, 117
Susquehanna River Valley 25, 59
Susquehanna Turnpike *see Catskill Turnpike*
Susquehanna Turnpike Association 55
Sutherland, Jacob Livingston 77, 78
Swami Rudrananda 111
Sweeney, John 45
Syracuse University 66

Tammany Hall 81
Tannersville, NY 26, 92, 93, 110, 112 147
Tannersville School 120
Tanning 74, 75, 128, 136
Tarrytown, NY 13
Taylor, John 161
Tea Time 184
Tehran 172
Tennessee 137
Teresa of Avila 62
Theodore Roosevelt Elementary School 63
Thirty Years War 34
This Little Pig 166
Tompkins, Silas 98
Thompson, Frank P. 46
Thompson, James 56
Thurber 91

Tiffany, Louis Comfort 92
Times Herald-Record 171
Tilden, Samuel 84
Tillson, NY 165
Tin Horns and Calico 107
Tiskilwa Park 136
Todd, Basil 150, 151, 152, 182
Tom Pacheco's Band 26
Tomb of the Unknown Soldier 57
Tongore, NY 33, 65
Tonko, Paul 45
Transcendentalism 33
Travis, Zena R. 120, 121
Treadwell, NY 14
Treasure of Watchdog Mountain, The 165
Tremperskill, NY 98, 106
Tremperskill County Store 140
Trenton, NJ 70
Trout Creek, NY 52
Trout fishing 42, 43, 44
Trout Fishing in the Catskills 43
Troy, NY 45, 92, 115
Truman, Harry 86
Trumbell, CT 165
Tubbs, Harry 130
Tunis 29
Turner, Frederick Jackson 24
Tuscarora 41, 42
Tuscarora Club, The 41
Twain, Mark 32, 138
Tweed, Boss 81
Two Stones for Every Dirt: The Story of Delaware County, New York 60

Ulster and Delaware Railroad 51, 84, 87, 124
Ulster and Delaware Turnpike 117
Ulster County 30, 33, 45, 50, 51, 58, 59, 81, 84, 89, 93, 113, 135, 141, 155, 165, 170, 174
Ulster Patriot Militia 29
Un-American Activities Committee 65
Unadilla, NY 55
    Wattles Ferry 55
Unadilla River 41
Unbearables, The 153
Unbroken Thread, A History of Quiltmaking in the Catskills, The 154
Union College 106, 161
Union Grove, NY 106
Union, NJ 179
Union Pacific Railroad 81
University of Albany 106
University of California at Irvine 53
University of Cincinnati 67
University of New Hampshire 152
University of Texas 179
University of Washington Press 68
U.S. Constitution 30, 31, 122

USS Constitution 71

Van Benschoten, Andrew 182
Van Benschoten, Jacob 62, 175
Van Benschoten, Thankful 182
Van Benschoten, William 182
Van Buren, Martin 13, 31, 85, 95
Van Damme, Roger 19
Van Gaasbeck, Peter 45
Van Keuren, E.A. 107
Van Landingham, Michael 54
Van Put, Ed 43
Van Put, Judy 42, 43
Van Rensselaer, Killiaen 94
Van Rensselaer, Stephen III 94, 96
Van Steenbergh, John 99
Van Winkle, Rip 166
Vassar College 119, 127
Vaughn, General John 60, 174
Vaux, Calvert 27
Vecchione, Jessica 148
Vega, NY 155
Veile, Aernout Cornelius 25
Vellore Christian Medical Center 177
Vermilyea, Charles 151
Vermilyea, Glen 86
Verplanck, Charlotte 98
Victorian Age 91, 177
Vidal, Gore 85
Vienna 179
Vietnam War 57
Villanova 47
Virginia 29, 30, 40, 170, 171, 174
"Visit From St. Nicholas, A" 115
Vly Creek 130, 151
Von Waggoner, Johannes 25
Vroman, Colonel 29
Vroman's Nose 34, 35

Wake Robin 178
Walloon 25, 166
Walton, Isaak 42
Walton, NY 49, 70, 71, 97, 145, 157, 161, 182
    Delaware Valley Hospital 100
War of 1812 13, 71
Warner Creek 136
Warren County 45, 117
Washington 129
Washington County 45
Washington, DC 13, 33, 46, 83, 89, 122
Washington, George 11, 31, 61, 172
Waterbury, Reverend Daniel 160
Waterloo, NY 57
Waterville, ME 83
Waterville Medical College 83
Weatherhead, John 77
Weehawken, NJ 30

Welles, Henry 57
Wellman, Fromma 179
Wellman, Henry 179
Wesleyan College, 64, 178
West Athens Hills 36
West Conesville, NY 56
West Hurley, NY 135
West Kortright Center 56
West Park, NY 89, 91
West Settlement 32 81
West, Thomas 40
West Through the Catskills: The Story of the Susquehanna Turnpike 56
Westchester County 59, 70, 82
Western Union telegraph company 81
Westkill, NY 167
Westminster College 161
Weyerhaeuser Corporation 131
Weyerhaeuser Environmental Books 67
Wharton, Edith 91
Wheeler, Candace 91, 92, 93
Wheeler, Thomas 92
When Cauliflower was King 110, 180
Whig Party 95, 96, 99
White, Harry 47
White Plains, NY 172, 174
Whitewater Depot 26
Whiting, Brad 79
Whitman, Walt 33, 89, 127
Whittredge, Worthington 43
Wikipedia 168, 170
Wild West *see American Frontier*
Wilder, Louis 179
Wilder, Thornton 53
Wiles, Tim 50
William Schwarzwaelder and Sons 136
Williams, Tennessee 54
Williamsburg, VA 172
Williamson Veneer Plant 131
Willowemac 42
Wilson, Dorothy Clark 177
Windham, NY 28, 33, 52, 112, 157, 167
Windham School 120

Winnisook Club 113, 114
Winter, Frank 88
Winter, Jimmy 87, 88
Winter, Rob 88
Wolf Hollow 176
Wolfram, Wolf 119
Woodchuck Lodge 33, 90, 91
Woodland Cemetery 46
Woodland School, The 64
Woodland Stage 37
Woodland Valley 41, 63, 64, 132, 178
    Campground 110
    Irondale Road 64
Woods, Charley 165
Woodstock Festival 67
Woodstock: History of an American Town 165
Woodstock, NY 22, 26, 49, 52, 61, 117, 141, 153, 165, 168, 174, 175
    Corner Cupboard 84
    Tinker Street 84
    Tinker Street Theater 52
    WDST 84
Works Project Administration 39, 120
    Writers' Program 39
World War I 57, 110, 142, 143, 178
World War II 15, 15, 19, 49, 53, 57, 58, 142, 149, 170
    Pearl Harbor 58
Wright, Dr. 145
Wright, Peter 98
Wright, Reverend R. V. 107
Wright, Silas 97
Wynette, Tammy 69

Yale Drama School 53
Yale Medical School 104, 105
Yankees 166, 167, 168
Yeltsin, Boris 85
Yeshiva 11, 63
Yoo-hoo, Mrs. Goldberg 163
Yorkers 166, 167, 168
Young, Governor John 99
Zen Mountain Monastery 154